Social Psychology

The PsychologyExpress series

UNDERSTAND QUICKLY
REVISE EFFECTIVELY
TAKE EXAMS WITH CONFIDENCE

'All of the revision material I need in one place – a must for psychology undergrads.'

Andrea Franklin, Psychology student at Anglia Ruskin University

'Very useful, straight to the point and provides guidance to the student, while helping them to develop independent learning.'

Lindsay Pitcher, Psychology student at Anglia Ruskin University

'Engaging, interesting, comprehensive ... it helps to guide understanding and boosts confidence.'

Megan Munro, Forensic Psychology student at Leeds Trinity University College

'Very useful ... bridges the gap between Statistics textbooks and Statist8icxs workbooks.'

Chris Lynch, Psychology student at University of Chester

'The answer guidelines are brilliant. I wish I had had it last year.'

Tony Whalley, Psychology student at the University of Chester

'I definitely would (buy a revision guide) as I like the structure, the assessment advice and practice questions and would feel more confident knowing exactly what to revise and having something to refer to.'

Steff Copestake, Psychology student at the University of Chester

'The clarity is first rate ... These chapters will be an excellent revision guide for students as well as providing a good opportunity for novel forms of assessment in and out of class.'

Dr Deaglan Page, Queen's University, Belfast

'Do you think they will help students when revising/working towards assessment? Unreservedly, yes.'

Dr Mike Cox, Newcastle University

'The revision guide should be very helpful to students preparing for their exams.'

Dr Kun Guo, University of Lincoln

'A brilliant revision guide, very helpful for all students of all levels.'

Svetoslav Georgiev, Psychology student at Anglia Ruskin University

Social Psychology

Jenny Mercer
University of Wales Institute, Cardiff

Debbie Clayton
University of Wales Institute, Cardiff

Series editor:
Dominic Upton
University of Worcester

Psychology Express

Prentice Hall
is an imprint of

Harlow, England • London • New York • Boston • San Francisco • Toronto
Sydney • Tokyo • Singapore • Hong Kong • Seoul • Taipei • New Delhi
Cape Town • Madrid • Mexico City • Amsterdam • Munich • Paris • Milan

Pearson Education Limited
Edinburgh Gate
Harlow
Essex CM20 2JE
England

and Associated Companies throughout the world

Visit us on the World Wide Web at:
www.pearson.com/uk

First published 2012

ISBN: 978-0-273-73719-3

British Library Cataloguing-in-Publication Data
A catalogue record for this book is available from the British Library

Library of Congress Cataloging-in-Publication Data
Clayton, Debbie.
  Psychology express : social psychology / Debbie Clayton, Jenny Mercer.
    p. cm.
  Includes bibliographical references and index.
  ISBN 978-0-273-73719-3 (pbk.)
1. Social psychology. I. Mercer, Jenny. II. Title. III. Title: Social psychology.
  HM1033.C5977 2011
  302—dc23
                          2011026908

ARP impression 98

Typeset in 9.5/12.5 Avenir Book by 3
Printed and bound in Great Britain by Ashford Colour Press Ltd

Contents

Supporting resources

Visit www.pearsoned.co.uk/psychologyexpress to find valuable online resources.

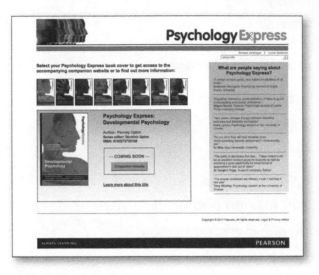

Companion website for students

→ **Get help in organising your revision:** download and print topic maps and revision checklists for each area.

→ **Ensure you know the key concepts in each area:** test yourself with flashcards. You can use them online, print them out or download to an iPod.

→ **Improve the quality of your essays in assignments and exams:** use the sample exam questions, referring to the answer guidelines for extra help.

→ **Practise for exams:** check the answers to the Test your knowledge sections in this book and take additional tests for each chapter.

→ **Go into exams with confidence:** use the You be the marker exercises to consider sample answers through the eyes of the examiner.

Also: The companion website provides the following features:

● Search tool to help locate specific items of content.

● E-mail results and profile tools to send results of quizzes to instructors.

● Online help and support to assist with website usage and troubleshooting.

For more information please contact your local Pearson Education sales representative or visit www.pearsoned.co.uk/psychologyexpress.

Acknowledgements

Authors' acknowledgements

We would especially like to thank the series editor Dominic Upton for all his advice and guidance on the format of this book and helpful comments and feedback throughout. The reviewers for their insightful comments on draft chapters and all at Pearson Education for making the book happen.

This text is aimed at a student population and we would like thank our own students for giving us the inspiration and ideas behind some of the tips and exercises. We hope that you have helped us to help others like you!

Finally, we wish to thank our families.

Jenny Mercer would like to thank Jim for his support and putting up with me while writing; and Pat and Peter Mercer for always being there and keeping me grounded.

Debbie Clayton would like to thank Tony for taking over at home, looking after Maisie and providing never-ending encouragement, without which this book would never have been completed.

Series editor's acknowlededgments

I am grateful to Janey Webb and Jane Lawes at Pearson Education for their assistance with this series. I would also like to thank Penney, Francesca, Rosie and Gabriel for their dedication to psychology.

Dominic Upton

Publisher's acknowledgements

Our thanks go to all the reviewers who contributed to the development of this text, including the students who participated in research and focus groups, which helped to shape the series' format:

Dr Sanjay Jobanputra, University of Westminster

Dr Catherine Lido, Thames Valley University

Drs Marijke Slotboom, Fontys Sporthogeschool, the Netherlands

Dr Lindsay St. Claire, University of Bristol

Dr Rachel Taylor, University of Glamorgan

Dr Belinda Winder, Nottingham Trent University

Dr Liz Winter, University of Leicester

Acknowledgements

Student reviewers:

Steff Copestake, Psychology student at the University of Chester

Svetoslav Georgiev, Psychology student at Anglia Ruskin University

Megan Munro, Forensic Psychology student at Leeds Trinity University College

Introduction

Not only is psychology one of the fastest-growing subjects to study at university worldwide, it is also one of the most exciting and relevant subjects. Over the past decade the scope, breadth and importance of psychology have developed considerably. Important research work from as far afield as the UK, Europe, USA and Australia has demonstrated the exacting research base of the topic and how this can be applied to all manner of everyday issues and concerns. Being a student of psychology is an exciting experience – the study of mind and behaviour is a fascinating journey of discovery. Studying psychology at degree level brings with it new experiences, new skills and knowledge. As the Quality Assurance Agency (QAA) has stressed:

> psychology is distinctive in the rich and diverse range of attributes it develops – skills which are associated with the humanities (e.g., critical thinking and essay writing) and the sciences (hypotheses-testing and numeracy). (QAA, 2010, p. 5)

Recent evidence suggests that employers appreciate these skills and knowledge of psychology graduates but, in order to reach this pinnacle, you need to develop your skills, further your knowledge and, most of all, successfully complete your degree to your maximum ability. Your skills, knowledge and opportunities that you gain during your psychology degree will give you an edge in the employment field. The QAA stresses the high level of employment skills developed during a psychology degree:

> due to the wide range of generic skills, and the rigour with which they are taught, training in psychology is widely accepted as providing an excellent preparation for many careers. In addition to subject skills and knowledge, graduates also develop skills in communication, numeracy, teamwork, critical thinking, computing, independent learning and many others, all of which are highly valued by employers. (QAA, 2010, p. 2)

This book, is part of a comprehensive new series, Psychology Express, that helps you achieve these aspirations. It is not a replacement for every single text, journal article, presentation and abstract you will read and review during the course of your degree programme. It is in no way a replacement for your lectures, seminars or additional reading. A top-rated assessment answer is likely to include considerable additional information and wider reading – and you are directed to some of these in this text. This revision guide is a conductor: directing you through the maze of your degree by providing an overview of your course, helping you formulate your ideas and directing your reading.

Each book within Psychology Express presents a summary coverage of the key concepts, theories and research in the field, within an explicit framework of revision. The focus throughout all of the books in the series will be on how you should approach and consider your topics in relation to assessment and exams. Various features have been included to help you build up your skills and knowledge ready for your assessments. More detail of these can be found in the Guided tour for this book on page xii.

By reading and engaging with this book, you will develop your skills and knowledge base and in this way you should excel in your studies and your associated assessments.

Psychology Express: Social Psychology is divided into 11 chapters and your course has probably been divided up into similar sections. However, we, the authors and series editor, must stress a key point: do not let the purchase, reading and engagement with the material in this text restrict your reading or your thinking. In psychology, you need to be aware of the wider literature and how it interrelates and how authors and thinkers have criticised and developed the arguments of others. So, even if an essay asks you about one particular topic, you need to draw on similar issues raised in other areas of psychology. There are, of course, some similar themes that run throughout the material covered in this text, but you can learn from the other areas of psychology covered in the other texts in this series as well as from material presented elsewhere.

We hope you enjoy this text, and the others in the Psychology Express series, which cover the complete knowledge base of psychology.

- *Biological Psychology* (Emma Preece): covering the biological basis of behaviour, hormones and behaviour, sleeping and dreaming and psychological abnormalities.

- *Cognitive Psychology* (Jonathan Ling and Jonathan Catling): including key material on perception, learning, memory, thinking and language.

- *Developmental Psychology* (Penney Upton): from prenatal development through to old age, the development of individuals is considered. Childhood, adolescence and lifespan development are all covered.

- *Personality and Individual Differences* (Terry Butler): normal and abnormal personality, psychological testing, intelligence, emotion and motivation are all covered in this book.

- *Social Psychology* (Jenny Mercer and Debbie Clayton): covering all the key topics in Social Psychology including attributions, attitudes, group relations, close relationships and critical social psychology.

- *Statistics in Psychology* (Catherine Steele, Holly Andrews and Dominic Upton): an overview of data analysis related to psychology is presented, along with why we need statistics in psychology. Descriptive and inferential statistics and both parametric and non-parametric analysis are also included.

- *Research Methods in Psychology* (Steve Jones and Mark Forshaw): research design, experimental methods, discussion of qualitative and quantitative methods and ethics are all presented in this text.

- *Conceptual and Historical Issues in Psychology* (Brian M. Hughes): the foundations of psychology and its development from a mere interest into a scientific discipline. The key conceptual issues of current-day psychology are also presented.

This book, and the other companion volumes in this series, should cover all your study needs (there will also be further guidance on the website). It will, obviously, need to be supplemented with further reading and this text directs you towards suitable sources. Hopefully, quite a bit of what you read here you will already have come across and the text will act as a jolt to set your mind at rest – you do know the material in depth. Overall, we hope that you find this book useful and informative as a guide for both your study now and in your future as a successful psychology graduate.

Revision note

- *Use evidence based on your reading, not on anecdotes or your 'common sense'.*
- *Show the examiner you know your material in depth – use your additional reading wisely.*
- *Remember to draw on a number of different sources: there is rarely one 'correct' answer to any psychological problem.*
- *Base your conclusions on research-based evidence.*

Go to the companion website at **www.pearsoned.co.uk/psychologyexpress** to access more revision support online, including interactive quizzes, sample questions with answer guidelines, 'you be the marker' exercises, flashcards and podcasts you can download.

Guided tour

→ ## Understand key concepts quickly

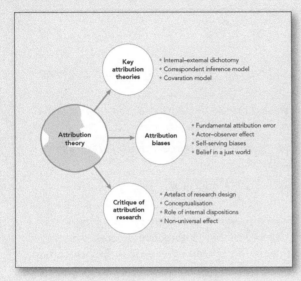

Start to plan your revision using the **Topic maps**.

Grasp **Key terms** quickly using the handy definitions in the glossary. Use the flashcards online to test yourself.

Glossary

acquiescent response set The tendency to agree to a statement regardless of the content of the statement or the person's actual opinion.

aggression Intentional behaviour aimed at doing harm or causing pain to another person.

→ ## Revise effectively

KEY STUDY

Sherif and Sherif (1953). The summer camp field experiments

A series of field experiments, each lasting three weeks, took place in actual summer camps (Sherif and Sherif, 1953; Sherif, White & Harvey, 1955). Participants (adolescent boys) were put into groups, unaware that they were part of a study. Experimenters (posing as camp workers) observed as the different stages took place: group formation, intergroup conflict and conflict reduction. Initially, as part of the group formation, participants were involved in various activities which encouraged them to bond.

In stage two, contests between the groups were staged (such as tug of war), for which prizes were awarded to the winning group. This introduced competition and with it came intergroup conflict.

Groups that had initially coexisted became two hostile factions. The out group was derided and, with meaningless tasks (such as picking up beans in a given time), in groups tended to overestimate their performance.

Negative intergroup dynamics evolved very quickly (illustrating the flaws in personality approaches to prejudice).

Stage three of the study involved reducing the hostility which had ensued. Both groups were forced to engage in tasks which required them to work together for a shared outcome (e.g., mending a water pipe). By jointly achieving a common goal, harmony was restored.

Quickly remind yourself of the **Key studies** using the special boxes in the text.

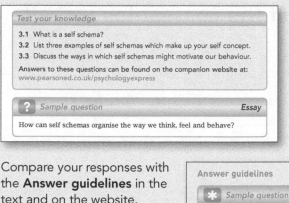

Prepare for upcoming exams and tests using the **Test your knowledge** and **Sample question** features.

Compare your responses with the **Answer guidelines** in the text and on the website.

Answer guidelines

❋ Sample question   Essay

Aggression is an innate response in humans. Discuss using evidence from social and biological accounts.

Approaching the question

In order to fully answer this question, you need to be able to discuss evidence for both social *and* biological accounts of aggression. Initially, though, you should make it clear that the statement 'aggression is an innate response in humans' relates to the *biological* approach. It would be sensible to focus on this part of the question by outlining and evaluating the types of theories which exemplify the biological perspective. The essay could then develop with a discussion of more social accounts.

→ Make your answers stand out

Use the **Critical focus** boxes to impress your examiner with your deep and critical understanding.

CRITICAL FOCUS

Bystander studies

As always, it is important that you maintain a critical edge when considering the research evidence provided for this topic. Here are some points you might wish to consider:

These studies are often based on students. How far can we generalise from such populations?

Look at the design of the Garcia et al. study in the Key Study above. One of the scenarios was to ask students about how much of their pay they would give to charity. This was a hypothetical question, the students did not have full-time jobs and were being asked to make a prediction about something in the future which had no consequences for them – they were not going to have to contribute any money to charity.

Make your answer stand out

Don't forget the methodological points made in the final section of this chapter. Including a few of these within your essay will indicate an awareness of the wider issues which are pertinent when applying social psychological knowledge to specific topic areas.

One way to bring the essay to an end could be the general aggression model. It is easy to see biological and social accounts as potentially competing views, but GAM illustrates how elements of both approaches interact (input variables include both biological and social factors). A brief acknowledgement of this model would also show your awareness of current thinking in the field of aggression research.

Answering the other three sample essays in this chapter will help you with both

Go into the exam with confidence using the handy tips to **make your answer stand out**.

Guided tour of the companion website

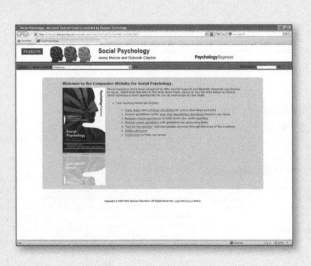

→ **Understand key concepts quickly**

Printable versions of the **Topic maps** give an overview of the subject and help you plan your revision.

Test yourself on key definitions with the online **Flashcards**.

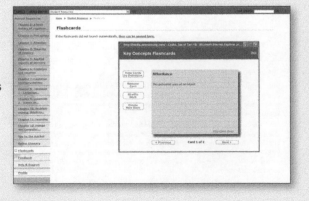

→ Revise effectively

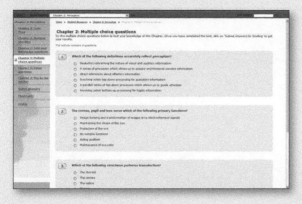

Check your understanding and practise for exams with the **Multiple choice questions**.

→ Make your answers stand out

Evaluate sample exam answers in the **You be the marker** exercises and understand how and why an examiner awards marks.

Put your skills into practice with the **Sample exam questions**, then check your answers with the guidelines.

All this and more can be found at
www.pearsoned.co.uk/psychologyexpress

1

Attitudes

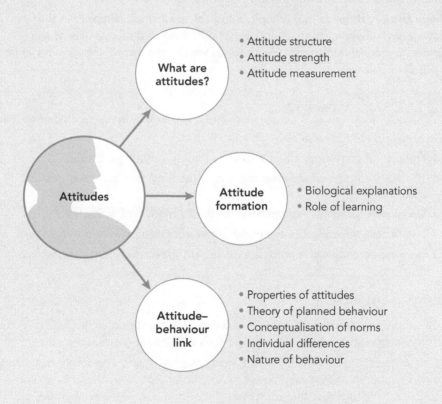

- **What are attitudes?**
  - Attitude structure
  - Attitude strength
  - Attitude measurement

- **Attitudes**

- **Attitude formation**
  - Biological explanations
  - Role of learning

- **Attitude–behaviour link**
  - Properties of attitudes
  - Theory of planned behaviour
  - Conceptualisation of norms
  - Individual differences
  - Nature of behaviour

A printable version of this topic map is available from:
www.pearsoned.co.uk/psychologyexpress

Introduction

The study of attitudes is a central part of any social psychology course. An understanding of this concept is vital to enable you to appropriately evaluate some of the key topics that follow in this chapter. For example, much of the research into stereotyping and prejudice is grounded in the concept of measuring attitudes.

This chapter cannot possibly cover the vast amount of research in the field of attitude research, so we will focus on the topics covered in the main social psychology texts. It is important that we first determine what is meant by the term attitude and that we establish how we form attitudes. The way we measure attitudes can be broadly divided into explicit and implicit techniques. The choice of methods is not simply a pragmatic decision but a reflection of the researchers' perspective concerning the definition of attitudes.

One of the key debates in this topic is the acknowledged disparity in the relationship between attitudes and behaviour. We will discuss some of the explanations for this disparity and theories which attempt to improve our ability to predict behaviour.

→ *Revision checklist*

Essential points to revise are:
- ❏ The role of cognition, affect and behaviour in defining attitudes
- ❏ The advantages and disadvantages of direct and indirect measures of attitudes
- ❏ Social psychological explanations for the formation of attitudes
- ❏ The factors affecting the relationship between attitudes and behaviour
- ❏ How expectancy-value models explain attitude–behaviour relationships

Assessment advice

- This topic is heavily theory-based and there are a number of unresolved debates. This should enable you to answer questions with a strong evaluative edge.
- One of the dangers when there are many opposing and seemingly contrasting views is that an answer can form a circular argument. You should be careful to put a case together that forms a strong argument. The best answers often come down on one side, whilst still acknowledging an opposing view.
- With a strongly theoretical topic such as this, it is often useful to include examples to illustrate the points you are making. Whilst reading the more applied chapters (such as Chapter 6, Prejudice and discrimination, and Chapter 9, Interpersonal attraction), you could try to apply the material from this chapter. Drawing on these applications will enhance an answer to a

theoretical question. The advice on answering the essay question given at the end of this chapter illustrates this.

Sample question

Could you answer this question? Below is a typical essay question that could arise on this topic.

> ✳ *Sample question*   *Essay*
>
> 'Our actions are determined by our attitudes.' Discuss with reference to psychological theory and research evidence.

Guidelines on answering this question are included at the end of this chapter, whilst further guidance on tackling other exam questions can be found on the companion website at: www.pearsoned.co.uk/psychologyexpress

What are attitudes?

Attitude structure

Maio and Haddock (2009, p. 4) define attitudes as 'an overall evaluation of an object based on cognitive, affective and behavioural information.' This definition is based on a consensus among attitude researchers that attitudes are multi-component evaluative judgements of objects (Eagly & Chaiken, 1993). Attitude objects can be concrete (e.g., a pair of shoes) or abstract (e.g., communism) and can comprise people (e.g., your mum, German people), including ourselves (e.g., self-esteem). Table 1.1 shows how attitudes are made up of the three components (cognitive, affective and behavioural) and how articles can vary in direction (or valence) from positive to negative.

Points to consider

- Attitudes are not always represented by all three components. For example, a favourable attitude towards a particular brand of computer may be based solely on cognitive beliefs about performance or battery life, whereas our attitude towards spiders may be based on an affective response ('Spiders make me anxious').
- One component may be more important than another in predicting attitudes. In a study of prejudice, cognitive beliefs were more likely to predict attitudes toward 'disliked groups' whereas feelings or emotions were more likely to predict attitudes towards liked groups (Esses, Haddock & Zanna 1993).

3

Table 1.1 **Tripartite model of attitudes**

Component	Definition	Positive valence	Neutral valence	Negative valence
Cognitive	Our beliefs about an object Based on perceptions of the facts	Maisie believes chocolate has high nutritional value	Maisie believes chocolate has some nutritional value	Maisie believes chocolate is an unhealthy food
Affective	Our feelings linked to an object Dependent on values	Maisie links chocolate with pleasurable feeling	Maisie has no emotional response related to chocolate	Maisie links chocolate with feelings of guilt
Behavioural	Our past behaviour towards an object Stems from our own observation of the way we behave	Maisie has eaten chocolate every day for the last year	Maisie occasionally eats chocolate if offered	Maisie has completed a diet plan which states she will not eat chocolate

Attitude strength

Our attitudes not only differ in valence but can also vary in strength. You may have completed questionnaires which ask you to indicate how strongly you agree or disagree with a statement. Psychologists have determined that strong versus weak attitudes are more persistent over time, more accurate predictors of behaviour and more resistant to persuasion (Krosnick & Petty, 1995). Many factors are likely to contribute to the strength of an attitude. Figure 1.1 identifies three of the most commonly cited factors that may affect attitude strength.

Accessibility

When asked for your opinion on a topic – for example, 'the state of the music industry' – how quickly can you respond? Evidence suggests affectively based attitudes may be more accessible than cognitive-based attitudes. See Chapter 4, Social influence, to understand how these findings have implications for designing persuasion campaigns.

Consistency

Researchers have studied consistency in two main areas

- evaluative–cognitive consistency (ECC)
- cognitive–affective consistency (CAC).

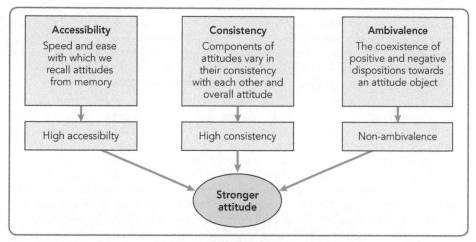

Figure 1.1 Three aspects of attitude indicative of attitude strength

We have low ECC if our overall evaluations ('I like chocolate') differ from our cognitive beliefs ('Chocolate is bad for me'). Low CAC would be demonstrated if Maisie held the views portrayed by the shaded squares in Table 1.1.

Ambivalence

Maisie may hold both positive *and* negative feelings of pleasure and guilt towards chocolate (affective ambivalence). Some researchers argue that, instead of treating ambivalence as a distinct aspect of attitude strength, the value of identifying ambivalence lies in the theoretical redefinition of attitudes as a bidimensional model (Wilson, Lindsey & Schooler 2000). The possibility of ambivalence certainly presents methodological challenges, as will be discussed later.

Cognitive dissonance

See the Key Study below for a discussion of how conflicts between attitude and behaviour may induce dissonance. The drive to reduce dissonance can result in behaviour shaping our attitudes rather than attitudes shaping behaviour.

KEY STUDY

Aronson and Mills (1959). Cognitive dissonance – when behaviour can shape attitudes

The term cognitive dissonance coined by Festinger (1957, 1964) describes the experience of our beliefs conflicting. We may believe it is important to exercise every day, but have just spent the evening sat in front of the television. Aronson and Mill's study was devised to test the hypothesis that the discomfort felt when our behaviour is in conflict with our attitudes may lead us to change our behaviour.

The study asked participants to join a discussion group where the topic would be sex. Before taking part in this part of the study, participants were told they needed to complete a screening test to determine their suitability for the task. There were two conditions. The severe initiation condition involved the participant reading a graphic description of sexual activity aloud. The mild initiation condition involved reading a list of polite sexual words aloud. Participants were then informed they could not participate in the discussion but could only listen to it. Furthermore, the recording was set up to be a boring discussion of the secondary sex characteristics of animals.

Participants in the severe initiation condition reported more positive attitudes to the discussion group than participants in the mild initiation group. The researchers contend their findings demonstrate the *effort justification effect*. That is, going through hardship (embarrassment of reading sexually explicit material aloud) can influence our subsequent attitudes. 'Why would I have gone through that embarrassment unless the discussion was interesting?' The application of effort justification has been shown in studies of weight loss. Completing complex monitoring tasks (hardship condition) led to greater engagement with exercise and weight loss regimes. Subsequently, participants in the 'hardship' group achieved greater weight loss compared with control groups (Axom & Cooper, 1985).

Attitude measurement

Techniques for measuring attitudes can be broadly divided into explicit (direct) and implicit (indirect) methods. Explicit measures ask participants to indicate their attitudes (usually via questionnaires) whilst implicit measures assess attitudes without asking the respondent directly (see Table 1.2).

Table 1.2 **Explicit and implicit measurement of attitudes**

	Assumptions	Some common techniques
Explicit	Attitudes are explicit, consciously endorsed and can be easily reported	The Thurstone scale (Thurstone, 1928)
		The Likert scale (Likert, 1932)
		The semantic differential (Osgood, Suci & Tannenbaum 1957)
Implicit	Attitudes are implicit, involuntary, and may be unconscious	Evaluative priming (e.g., Fazio, 1995)
		Implicit association test (Greenwald, McGhee & Schwartz, 1998)

Explicit measures of attitudes

Self-report attitude scales are widely adopted by researchers and tend to demonstrate high levels of internal and test–retest reliability. In other words, item scores are correlated with each other and similar attitude scores are produced when scales are administered at different time points. Self-report scales also have the advantage of being easily and quickly administered to large groups of participants at a relatively low cost. However, a number of concerns have been raised regarding the use of attitude scales:

- Social desirability biases can occur in the form of:
  - demand characteristics, where the design of the scale conveys the aim of the study, leading participants to give responses they think are desired
  - impression management where participants give a response that meets with social approval.
- Scales limit respondents to a set of standard options which are determined by the researcher and their underlying biases. Further, participants will not always interpret the meaning of the question and the response scale in the way intended by the researcher.
- The context can alter responses to attitude scales – for example, the order of questions can affect responses. Some argue simply asking questions may lead to the construction of an attitude or even a change in attitude, known as reactivity.
- As noted, attitudes may vary in accessibility and ambivalence. Psychologists have measured accessibility by recording the time taken to respond to attitude statements – known as response latencies (Fazio, 1995). Ambivalence cannot be captured using a standard one-dimensional scale because we would have no way of knowing whether a neutral response was in reality a neutral belief or represented a compromise between an individual's strong positive and strong negative beliefs. See Thompson, Zanna and Griffin (1995) for more on measuring ambivalence.

Implicit measures of attitudes

Implicit attitude measures were developed to overcome some of the limitations of attitude scales, particularly when there is potential for social desirability bias (e.g., people may not be willing to admit or may be unaware that they hold racist attitudes). These techniques include projective measurement techniques, priming, the lost-letter paradigm, behavioural measures and physiological measures. The implicit association test (IAT; Greenwald, Nosek & Banaji 2003) is one of the more popular techniques and has been widely used to measure racial attitudes. See Chapter 6, Prejudice and discrimination, for an explanation of this technique and its application in understanding prejudice.

CRITICAL FOCUS

What are attitudes?

Numerous studies have shown that social context can influence our attitudes. Our evaluations may vary depending upon our current goals, mood, bodily state, standard of comparison. Indeed, we may unwittingly change attitudes simply by conducting attitude research. Simply asking people to think about the reasons why they hold a certain attitude may be enough to cause change. This has led some researchers to conclude that attitudes are best understood as context-dependent, temporary

▶

constructions (Schwarz & Bohner, 2001) rather than stable representations stored in memory (Fazio, 2007). Even when stored attitudes exist, they may be deemed inappropriate in the current situation and new attitudes may be constructed on the spot – this is known as the construction hypothesis (Schwarz, 2007).

We have seen that weak attitudes are less likely to be stable and therefore may be more open to change or construction in context. Thus, we may need to adopt appropriate methodologies that allow for the role of context, particularly when studying topics where our attitudes are likely to be weak. For instance, comparisons between responses to attitude scales may reveal disappointing correlations in these situations.

Test your knowledge

1.1 Take a few minutes to write down your views on a) the current government, b) the nightlife in your local town and c) drinking alcohol and driving.

1.2 Which component(s) of the tripartite model of attitudes do your views fall into?

1.3 Do you hold any ambivalent attitudes? Explain your answer.

1.4 What would be the advantages and disadvantages of using self-report scales for measuring attitudes towards these objects?

Answers to these questions can be found on the companion website at: www.pearsoned.co.uk/psychologyexpress

? Sample question   Essay

How might our definition of attitudes affect the way we conduct attitude research and our subsequent conclusions?

Further reading The definition and measurement of attitudes

Topic	Key reading
Selected key papers on attitude structure	Fazio, R. H., & Petty, R. E. (Eds.) (2007). *Attitudes: Their Structure, Function and Consequences*. New York: Psychology Press.
Attitude ambivalence	Conner, M., & Armitage, C. (2009). Attitudinal ambivalence. In W. Crano & R. Prislin (Eds.), *Attitudes and Persuasion* (pp. 261–286). New York: Psychology Press.
Implicit measures of attitudes	Fazio, R. H., & Olson, M. A. (2003). Implicit measures in social cognition research: Their meaning and use. *Annual Review of Psychology, 54*, 297–327.

Construction hypothesis	Schwarz, N., & Bohner, G. (2001). The construction of attitudes. In A. Tesser & N. Schwarz (Eds.), *Blackwell Handbook of Social Psychology* (Vol. 1: Intraindividual processes, pp. 436–457). Oxford: Blackwell.

Attitude formation

There is no universal agreement whether explanations for formation of attitudes are distinct from explanations for attitude change (see Bohner & Wanke, 2002). For the purpose of this chapter we will discuss processes below awareness under the heading of attitude formation. See Chapter 4, Social influence, for a discussion of attitude change, where we discuss the Yale learning model of persuasion and cognitive dual processing models of persuasion.

Biological explanations

The role of genes in the formation of attitudes has received very little attention. Proponents for a genetic predisposition point to the observation that babies have a preference for facial patterns over other patterns from as early as one day old. Further, evidence from twin studies has shown a role for genes in political attitudes and vocational interests (see Tesser, 1993, for a review). However, it is unlikely that there are genes responsible for specific attitudes (such as enjoying studying statistics). It may be plausible that there is a genetic component for mediating factors, such as personality, taste preference, intelligence or, in this example, mathematical ability.

Role of learning

Much of the research into attitude formation has focused on the way attitudes are socially formed, investigating the role of mere exposure, conditioning and imitation. The evidence also seems to focus on the affective component of the attitude structure. Researchers tend to discuss our cognitive-based attitudes when discussing attitude change (see Chapter 4, Social influence).

Mere exposure

A plethora of experimental studies, building on the classic work of Zajonc (1968), have shown that repeated exposure increases liking for a stimulus, suggesting that familiarity with an object may lead to a positive attitude towards that object. The mere exposure effect has been shown to be stronger for unfamiliar stimuli, more complex stimuli and shorter exposure times (Bornstein, 1989). For a discussion of the theoretical explanations for the mere exposure effect, see Lee (2001). See further discussion of how mere exposure affects our attitudes towards people and may impact on our choice of friends in Chapter 9, Interpersonal attraction.

Evaluative conditioning

Our preference for attitude objects can also be influenced by simply pairing the object with stimuli that generate positive as opposed to negative emotions. For example, subliminal presentation of negative affective images (e.g., spiders) or positive affective images (e.g., flowers) has been shown to influence preference for unfamiliar faces (Krosnick, Betz, Jussim & Lynn, 1992). The empirical evidence supports the common marketing practice of pairing products with attractive or popular celebrities or taking a client out for a business lunch, therefore, transferring the pleasant feelings and emotions associated with a nice meal with the company hoping to secure a contract. Martin and Levey (1994) outline the subtle differences between evaluative and classical conditioning. The main points are that, in the case of evaluative conditioning:

- only a single pairing of conditioned stimulus (CS) and unconditioned stimulus (UCS) is required to instigate a long-lasting effect, which is thought to be resistant to extinction, suggesting we do not *learn* an if–then relationship between CS (e.g., business lunch) and UCS (e.g., company) but, instead, transfer our evaluation from the CS to the UCS
- association occurs *independently of the awareness* of pairings, therefore preference for an attitude object occurs even when participants are unaware of the link between the CS and the UCS.

Imitation

Attitudes can also be learned through observation, a child's values or prejudices can be influenced by observing their parents' interactions with others. In a similar way to Bandura's classic Bobo doll study (Bandura, Ross & Ross, 1961), research has demonstrated that children can acquire parents' emotional responses to objects through observation (vicarious learning). When mothers were asked to show a either a fearful or happy reaction to a toy when showing it to their child, the emotional response was subsequently expressed by the child when given the toy (Gerull & Rapee, 2002).

Test your knowledge

1.5 How do evaluative and classical conditioning differ?

1.6 How could parents influence their children's attitudes and what is the evidence for your position?

1.7 What is meant by the term vicarious learning?

Answers to these questions can be found on the companion website at:
www.pearsoned.co.uk/psychologyexpress

> **?** *Sample question*   *Essay*
>
> Critically evaluate social psychologists' explanations for the way we form our attitudes.

Further reading The formation of attitudes

Topic	Key reading
Distinction between attitude formation and attitude change	Bohner, G., & Wanke, M. (2002). *Attitudes and Attitude Change* (Part II, pp. 69–116). New York: Psychology Press.
Genetic influence on attitudes	Tesser, A. (1993). On the importance of heritability in psychological research: The case of attitudes. *Psychological Review, 100*, 129–142.
Mere exposure effect	Lee, A. Y. (2001). The mere exposure effect: An uncertainty reduction explanation revisited. *Personality and Social Psychology Bulletin, 28*, 129–137.
Evaluative conditioning	Martin, I., & Levey, A. B. (1994). The evaluative response: Primitive but necessary. *Behaviour, Research and Therapy, 32*, 301–305.
Subliminal conditioning	Dijksterhuis, A. (2004). I like myself but I don't know why: Enhancing implicit self-esteem by subliminal evaluative conditioning. *Journal of Personality and Social Psychology, 86*, 345–355.

Attitude–behaviour link

LaPiere's (1934) classic study demonstrated that hoteliers' attitudes towards serving a Chinese couple differed from their behaviour. Later, more methodologically sound studies added to the evidence that attitudes do not always predict behaviour (see Cook & Sheeran, 2004, for a review). We have already discussed how this discrepancy between attitudes and behaviour led to advances in methodology to enable measurement of implicit attitudes.

Properties of attitudes

We have also seen that attitude strength may have a role to play in the attitude–behaviour relationship. You will recall we have identified that low *accessibility*, low *affective–cognitive consistency* and high *ambivalence* may lead to *unstable*, weak attitudes. Behaviour will be difficult to predict when our attitudes are weak. As well as confirming these moderators, Cook and Sheeran's (2004) meta-analysis demonstrated *direct experience* with the attitude object and the degree to which we are *certain* about our attitude are also significant moderators of the attitude–behaviour relationship.

Theory of planned behaviour

The theory of planned behaviour (TPB; Ajzen, 1991) proposes that, to adequately predict behaviour, we need to consider further variables over and above attitudes. These are subjective norms (our beliefs about the views of 'important others', for example) and perceived behavioural control (our belief that we have control over our behaviour).

The TPB (see Figure 1.2) assumes that we perform cognitive algebra, weighing up the strength and value of our beliefs, which in turn influence our intention to act. The theory acknowledges that we may hold contradictory beliefs about attitude objects (e.g., cakes taste nice, but will also lead to weight gain).

The TPB has successfully predicted intentions, self-reported and objective behaviour for a range of behaviours, particularly in the health context (e.g., smoking, condom use, attendance at screening; Ajzen & Fishbein, 2005).

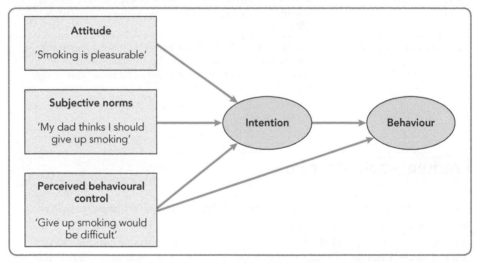

Figure 1.2 **Basic outline of the theory of planned behaviour**

Points to consider

- Although statistically significant regression models have been developed, the amount of variance in behaviour explained remains relatively small – between 20 and 30 per cent (Taylor et al., 2006).
- Attitudes are assumed to be rational (ignoring emotional and impulsive factors in decision making).
- Behaviour is considered to be a result of rational decision making based on a cost–benefit analysis of different behavioural options.

- The theory takes an individualistic view of behaviour which does not explicitly take into account the role of identity and remains undefined with regard to the functioning of norms.
- Many studies investigating the relationship between attitudes and behaviour have relied on correlational research which cannot make conclusions about cause and effect.

Extending the TPB

There is considerable debate in the social psychological literature as to whether or not additional variables should be added to the TPB to improve its ability to predict behaviour. For example, there is evidence that adding self-identity and moral norms to the TPB can lead to a more accurate explanation of behaviour (Conner & Sparks, 2005). However, Ajzen and Fishbein (2005) argue for caution in respect of adding other variables to the TPB and contend that the majority of suggested additions can be construed as part of the existing model.

Conceptualisation of norms

Despite the importance of norms in other areas of social psychology, subjective norms remain the weakest predictor in the TPB. This has led to a call for a theoretical reoperationalisation of norms in the TPB to take a more social psychological approach. Two main approaches have been suggested, drawing on social identity theory and the normative focus approach.

The social identity approach (see Chapter 3, Self) suggests that certain sources of normative influence will be more important depending on saliency of the group members for the individual. More specifically, groups that individuals belong to (in groups) will have more influence than groups that individuals do not belong to (out groups). Studies have supported this contention, showing stronger attitude–behaviour consistency in participants exposed to attitude-congruent in group norms, especially when participants strongly identify with the group (Smith & Terry, 2003).

The focus theory of normative conduct (Cialdini, Kallgren & Reno, 1991) purports that norms have two components, distinguishing between injunctive norms – perceptions of what other people approve or disapprove of (what people should do) and descriptive norms – what people actually do (see Chapter 4, Social influence). For evidence that descriptive and injunctive norms have independent effects on intentions and behaviours, across a wide range of behaviours see Smith and Louis (2008).

Individual differences

The TPB acknowledges that personality may influence behaviour but only indirectly, by moderating the variables of the TPB. For example, for high self-monitors, the role of subjective norms may be greater than the role of attitudes in predicting intention, so subjective norms should be weighted more strongly for this group in order to more accurately predict behaviour. However, a number of studies suggest personality traits, such as conscientiousness, impulsiveness and extraversion, may play a more direct role in influencing certain behaviours. For example, impulsivity may improve the prediction of snacking behaviour over and above key variables of the TPB model (Churchill, Jessop & Sparks, 2008).

Nature of behaviour

Many researchers have argued that the subjective expected-utility approach is not always a good descriptive model of the process people go through when they make decisions. Some of the variance left unexplained by the TPB could be due to the nature of some actions, in that we may act on impulse rather than through deliberative processing. For example, intentions may lose their predictive power once strong habits are formed.

The MODE model (motivation and opportunity as determinants of spontaneous versus thoughtful information processing; Fazio & Towles-Schwen, 1999) proposes that attitudes guide behaviour through *either* deliberate *or* spontaneous processes. When motivation and opportunity for deliberation are low, attitudes may activate behaviour directly in an automatic way. However, if a behavioural decision is important and we have the opportunity to deliberate, evidence about the possible alternatives is carefully evaluated, leading to a conscious intention to act. This model acknowledges that we do not always think through long-term consequences and for some behaviours we may be more disposed to make speedy, impulsive, non-reflective decisions.

Test your knowledge

1.8 List the key factors which may contribute to the attitude–behaviour discrepancy.

1.9 What role does attitude strength play in the attitude–behaviour relationship and what are the key moderators of attitude strength?

1.10 How does the TPB differ from the MODE model?

Answers to these questions can be found on the companion website at: www.pearsoned.co.uk/psychologyexpress

---

? Sample question   Essay

The theory of planned behaviour (TPB) leaves a large amount of variance in behaviour unexplained. Drawing on psychological evidence, explain why this might be the case.

Further reading The attitude–behaviour link

Topic	Key reading
Moderators of attitude–behaviour link	Cook, R., & Sheeran, P. (2004). Moderation of cognition–intention and cognition–behaviour relations: A meta-analysis of properties of variables from the theory of planned behaviour. *British Journal of Social Psychology, 43*, 159–186.
Extending the TPB	Ajzen, I., & Fishbein, M. (2005). The influence of attitudes on behaviour. In D. Albarracin, B. T. Johnson & M. P. Zanna (Eds.), *The Handbook of Attitudes* (pp. 173–221) Mahwah, NJ: Erlbaum.
Role of social identity	Smith, J. R., & Terry, D. J. (2003). Attitude–behaviour consistency: The role of group norms, attitude accessibility and mode of behavioural decision-making. *European Journal of Social Psychology, 33*, 591–608.
Normative focus theory	Cialdini, R. B., Kallgren, C. A., & Reno, R. R. (1991). A focus theory of normative conduct: A theoretical refinement and re-evaluation of the role of norms in human behaviour. In M. P. Zanna (Ed.), *Advances in Experimental Social Psychology* (Vol. 24, pp. 201–233). San Diego, CA: Academic Press.
Descriptive and injunctive norms	Smith, J. R., & Louis, W. (2008). Do as we say and as we do: The interplay of descriptive and injunctive group norms in the attitude–behaviour relationship. *British Journal of Social Psychology, 47*, 647–666.
Role of individual differences in TPB	Churchill, S., Jessop, D,. & Sparks, P. (2008). Impulsive and/or planned behaviour: Can impulsivity contribute to the predictive utility of the theory of planned behaviour? *British Journal of Social Psychology, 47*, 631–646.
The MODE model – predicting spontaneous behaviour	Fazio, R. H., & Towles-Schwen, T. (1999). The MODE model of attitude–behaviour processes. In S. Chaiken & Y. Trope (Eds.), *Dual Process Theories in Social Psychology* (pp. 97–116). New York: Guilford Press.

? *Sample question*   *Problem-based learning*

The local council wishes to implement a new scheme to encourage people to cycle to work. The scheme will involve distributing bicycles to hire around the town. The council wishes to ascertain attitudes towards the scheme. What are the key factors that you would consider when designing a study to measure attitudes towards the new scheme and what advice would you offer the council with respect to predicting behaviour?

Chapter summary – pulling it all together

→ Can you tick all the points from the revision checklist at the beginning of this chapter?

→ Attempt the sample question from the beginning of this chapter using the answer guidelines below.

→ Go to the companion website at www.pearsoned.co.uk/psychologyexpress to access more revision support online, including interactive quizzes, flashcards, You be the marker exercises as well as answer guidance for the Test your knowledge and Sample questions from this chapter.

Further reading for Chapter 1

Crano, W. D., & Prislin, R. (2006). Attitudes and persuasion. *Annual Review of Psychology*, *57*, 345–374.

Maio, G. R., & Haddock, G. (2009). *The Psychology of Attitudes and Attitude Change*. London: Sage.

Answer guidelines

✳ *Sample question*   Essay

'Our actions are determined by our attitudes.' Discuss with reference to psychological theory and research evidence.

Approaching the question

The question asks you to discuss the relationship between attitudes and behaviour. There are a number of key concerns which you should try to discuss in your essay. The way we define and measure attitudes and behaviour may affect the accuracy of our behavioural predictions. Attitudes differ in strength, which can affect attitude–behaviour consistency. Attitudes may only be one of many factors which are important in predicting behaviour. These factors may act as moderators or mediators and are likely to interact with each other. Attitudes may predict some behaviours more accurately than others.

Important points to include

You will need to define what is meant by the term 'attitudes'. There is significant debate about the definition and structure of attitudes. You will need to discuss the factors which have been proposed as moderating the relationship between attitudes and behaviour, such as attitude strength, individual differences and social norms.

It would also be important to acknowledge that the technique used to measure attitudes may affect the ability to predict behaviour and some techniques may be more appropriate for some behaviours.

The question also asks you to refer to relevant theory, so you could choose to evaluate the theory of planned behaviour (TPB). You should try to integrate this discussion with previous points. How does the TPB take into account the strength of attitudes, does it include some of the aforementioned moderators of attitude strength? Studies of the TPB tend to rely on self-report measures and focus on deliberative behaviour. Discussion of the MODE model could be linked in with the importance of measurement and to make the point that attitudes may predict some behaviours more adequately than others.

Make your answer stand out

There is a vast body of literature on this topic and you could be in danger of becoming overwhelmed by this. Sometimes this can lead to an essay which covers many issues but only at a shallow level. It is then difficult to demonstrate your evaluative skills. One technique for overcoming this and demonstrating originality is to focus the question on a particular topic. If you choose to do this, you should ensure that you make it clear that this is your intention at the beginning of your answer. In this case, you could apply the discussion to a topic, such as prejudice or health behaviours. In this way you would acknowledge the same overall debates but draw on specific research in your chosen topic. For example, a discussion of prejudice may benefit from relating the tripartite attitude structure to definitions of stereotypes, prejudice and discrimination (see Chapter 6, Prejudice and discrimination). A discussion of health behaviours may pick out the importance of considering the nature of behaviour. Some behaviours are one-off (e.g., attending screening), whilst others are ongoing and complex (e.g., healthy eating). This should bring your essay to life and allow you to explain complex theoretical discussions using examples from the empirical literature.

Explore the accompanying website at www.pearsoned.co.uk/psychologyexpress

→ Prepare more effectively for exams and assignments using the answer guidelines for questions from this chapter.

→ Test your knowledge using multiple choice questions and flashcards.

→ Improve your essay skills by exploring the You be the marker exercises.

Notes

2

Attribution theory

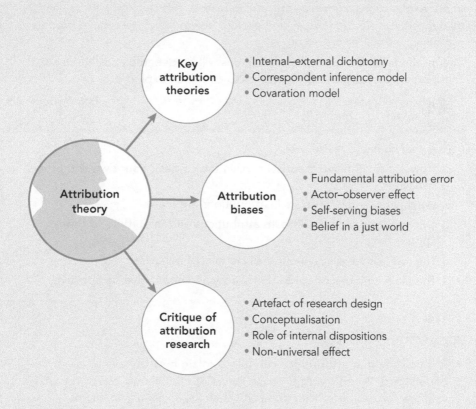

Key
attribution
theories

- Internal–external dichotomy
- Correspondent inference model
- Covariation model

Attribution
theory

Attribution
biases

- Fundamental attribution error
- Actor–observer effect
- Self-serving biases
- Belief in a just world

Critique of
attribution
research

- Artefact of research design
- Conceptualisation
- Role of internal dispositions
- Non-universal effect

A printable version of this topic map is available from:
www.pearsoned.co.uk/psychologyexpress

Introduction

Social psychologists have studied the processes by which people explain the causes of their own and other people's behaviour, under the domain of attribution research, for over half a century. Attribution theories try to explain the processes we go through when deciding why people behave in the way they do. For example, if a close friend turned up late for a meeting, how would you explain this behaviour?

Attribution theories suggest that both information about a person's character (internal disposition) and the situation (external influences) are used to make attributions about the cause of this lateness.

One of the key findings of attribution research is that shortcuts are taken when making attributions for our own and others' behaviour. This can lead to errors in our explanations, known as attribution biases. This chapter will evaluate the evidence for attribution biases and explore how psychologists have tried to explain why these errors occur.

The methods used to measure attributions will be debated and the idea that these errors apply universally across cultures will be explored.

> → **Revision checklist**
>
> *Essential points to revise are:*
> - ❏ How social cognitive theorists explain the causes of our own and others' behaviour
> - ❏ When, how and why errors in attributions are made
> - ❏ The methods used to measure attributions and the pitfalls of these approaches
> - ❏ The role culture plays in our explanations of behaviour
> - ❏ The main critiques of attribution theory and alternative perspectives

Assessment advice

- It is unlikely that attributions can fully explain how behaviour is understood. When trying to make sense of others' and our own behaviour we may, for example, also draw on schemas, social comparisons, stereotypes, prejudice and non-verbal communication. If you are asked to discuss how we infer causes of others' behaviour, it may be appropriate to refer to research from across social psychology as well as material on attribution theory.
- Your assessments may ask you to *apply* attribution to explain *our own* behaviour, in which case you may wish to consider our concept of self (see

Chapter 3, Self) or you may be asked to apply attribution to understand relationship satisfaction (see Chapter 9, Interpersonal attraction).

Sample question

Could you answer this question? Below is a typical essay that could arise on this topic.

✳ Sample question   *Essay*

The actor–observer effect is a widely accepted attribution bias in social psychology. Critically evaluate the evidence that this bias exists in reality.

Guidelines on answering this question are included at the end of this chapter, whilst further guidance on tackling other exam questions can be found on the companion website at: **www.pearsoned.co.uk/psychologyexpress**

Key attribution theories

Heider (1958) believed we are all naive scientists trying to make sense of other people's behaviour using commonsense psychology. Essentially, we want to understand why others behave in a certain way to help us predict their behaviour in the future.

Since mental states are not directly observable, people can only make attributions about a person's mental state based on observable features of the person (e.g., their behaviour) and the situational context that the person is in. Attribution theories adopt a social cognitive perspective to examine the way in which the causes of our own and others' behaviour are explained. Social cognition is, arguably, the dominant approach to studying phenomena in social psychology. This approach focuses on the way our cognitive processes are influenced by our interactions with the social environment and how our cognitions affect the world around us (e.g., Fiske & Taylor, 1991).

Internal–external dichotomy

One of the key aims of attribution theories is to outline the circumstances which lead us to make an *internal* as opposed to an *external* attribution for our own or others' behaviour. For example, if John is seen to drive into a lamp post, how is this behaviour explained? See Table 2.1.

Table 2.1 Internal versus external attributions for behaviour

	Internal	External
Definition	Behaving in a certain way because of something about the person (e.g., traits, motives, intentions)	Behaving in a certain way because of something about the situation (assumption that most people will behave in the same way in that situation)
Example	John drove his car into a lamp post because he is not a skilled driver and is easily distracted	John drove his car into a lamp post because there was a frost and the road was very slippery

Correspondent inference theory

Jones and Davis' (1965) theory of correspondent inference states that we are more likely to conclude others' behaviour reflects their internal stable dispositional traits if behaviour is:

● freely chosen

● yields distinctive, non-common effects

● is low in social desirability.

Non-common effects refer to effects produced by a particular cause that could not be produced by any other apparent cause. In other words, they are where we can eliminate other possible causes and more clearly identify that this one factor caused the behaviour. If an individual has a choice and if their actions differ in any way from expectations, then individuals are likely to make a correspondent attribution that ties their action to an internal disposition.

KEY STUDY

Jones and Harris (1967). Correspondent inference theory

Jones and Harris (1967) provide evidence for their correspondent inference theory in a series of experiments. The experimental paradigm involves asking participants to read a piece written by a student favouring a particular position on a topical issue (e.g., the legalisation of marijuana) and asking them to infer the position held by the author. Experimental conditions are created by informing participants that the author was assigned to defend a particular position or given free choice which position to take (no choice/choice condition).

Results confirmed correspondent inference theory in that:

● attitudes which were in line with behaviour were more decisively attributed to the target person in the choice than in the no choice condition

● however, degree of choice made a greater difference if the essay or speech ran counter to the expected or normative position.

However, counter to correspondent inference theory, even in the no choice condition, participants tended to attribute attitudes in line with the speech. Attributing too much

▶

importance to the person and not enough importance to the situation led to the hypothesis that a correspondence bias existed – this quickly became known as the fundamental attribution error (FAE).

Covariation model

Kelley (1967, 1972) argues that, when forming an attribution, information is gathered about how a person's behaviour changes (or covaries) over time, across situations and with different people. The theory proposes individuals draw on information regarding consensus, consistency and distinctiveness when deciding why someone acts in a specific way on a specific occasion. Using these three sources of information, it is possible to predict whether someone is likely to make an internal or an external attribution (see Table 2.2).

Table 2.2 **Outline of Kelley's covariation model**

	Consensus	Distinctiveness	Consistency
Definition	The extent to which other people act in the same way when in the same situation or with the same stimuli	The extent to which the person behaves in the same way in a different situation or with different stimuli	The extent to which the person acts in this way when in this situation/with this stimuli on different occasions
Example	High consensus	High distinctiveness	High consistency
	The majority of students fall asleep in statistics lectures	John only falls asleep in statistics lectures and not in other lectures	John always falls asleep in statistics lectures
Attribution made:			
Internal	Low	Low	High
External	High	High	High
Internal and External	Low	High	High
Unique situation	Low or high	Low or high	Low*

* Inconsistency information conveys a sense of uncertainty about future events – high consistency is needed to form an internal or external attribution

Focus on methods

Ployhart, Ehrhart & Hayes (2005) applied Kelley's covariation model when investigating the effects of explanations for decisions on students' applications to study at university. The paper describes an experimental and a field study.

In study one, participants imagined they had received a rejection or success letter following an application for a university place. The letters were designed to provide consensus, distinctiveness and consistency information explaining the reasons for the decision. Participants completed a standardised scale to determine whether they would make an internal or external attribution for the decision.

In study two, students reflected on acceptance or rejection letters they had actually received. Open-ended questions determined whether the students perceived covariation information from the letters received.

The findings suggested the way letters are worded may affect perceptions of the application process, the self and the organisation.

When reading this paper, you should evaluate the degree to which each of the two studies captures the process of making attributions. Consider the pros and cons of the two different methodologies – for example, what is the effect on recruitment and retention of participants, how do the recruitment methods affect applications of the findings and the extent to which variables can be controlled? In the field study, an actual letter is used whereas in the experimental study a letter is constructed and students are asked to imagine how they would react. What are the advantages and disadvantages of these approaches?

Points to consider

- **Assumptions and biases:** the correspondent inference theory and covariation model assume that people observe the clues and make attributions in a rational, logical way, but this is often not the case.
- **Extensions:** both these theories presented rely on the acceptance of the internal–external dichotomy in describing how causal attributions are made. Many studies support the idea that people make attributions in this way, but, others argue this dichotomy is overly simplistic. For example, Weiner (1995) argues that individuals make attributions based on:
  - stability of the causal factors over time – e.g., personality traits may be stable over time, whereas health or motives may be unstable
  - degree of control – e.g.,the amount of effort someone exerts is largely controllable whereas ability is uncontrollable.
- **Action identification:** research indicates that it isn't just what people do that is important but our interpretation of their action and whether the action is seen as having greater meaning. Low-level interpretations focus on the action itself, whilst higher-level interpretations focus on its ultimate goals. Our level of interpretation of others' actions may be crucial in influencing our explanations for an individual's behaviour (see Kozak, Marsh & Wegner, 2006).

Test your knowledge

2.1 Explain, using an example, what is meant by uncommon effects, as defined by the correspondent inference theory.

2.2 Compile a list of points to demonstrate how the correspondent inference theory and covariation theory are complimentary, contrasting and conflicting.

2.3 The majority of students arrive on time for social psychology lectures, with the exception of Rosie who is always late. Rosie does arrive on time when meeting for social events. How would the covariation model suggest we would explain Rosie's behaviour? What other factors do you think could be important in determining the attribution we make?

Answers to the questions can be found at: www.pearsoned.co.uk/psychologyexpress

---

? *Sample question* *Essay*

Compare and contrast theories of attribution, supporting your answer with empirical evidence.

Further reading Attribution theories

Topic	Key reading
Value of the internal–external dichotomy	White, P. A. (1991). Ambiguity in the internal/external distinction in causal attribution. *Journal of Experimental Social Psychology, 27*(3), 259–270.
Application of the covariation model	Ployhart, R. E., Ehrhart, K. H., & Hayes, S. C. (2005). Using attributions to understand the effects of explanations on applicant reactions: Are reactions consistent with the covariation principle? *Journal of Applied Social Psychology, 35*(2), 259–296.
Action identification and attribution	Kozak, M. N., Marsh, A. A., & Wegner, D. M. (2006). What do I think you're doing?: Action identification and mind attribution. *Journal of Personality and Social Psychology, 90,* 543–555.

Attribution biases

Although individuals are generally quite good at social perception and in many cases they reach accurate conclusions about others' traits and motives from observing their behaviour, we are not perfect. In an effort to understand ourselves and others a number of errors or biases in attribution are made. The most commonly cited of these are the fundamental attribution error, the actor–observer effect, self-serving bias and the just world hypothesis.

Fundamental attribution error

The fundamental attribution error, sometimes referred to as correspondence bias (Jones & Harris, 1967), has been defined as the tendency to infer that people's behaviour is due to their internal disposition (personality or beliefs) rather than to the situation (external influences). This idea relates to one of the main findings of social psychology, that we tend to underestimate the powerful influence of social situations on our behaviour. Jones and Harris', (1967) seminal study demonstrated this bias utilising an experimental approach. It should be noted that the bias is more likely to occur in specific circumstances – for example, when consensus and distinctiveness are low and when predicting others' behaviour in the far-off future.

Actor–observer effect

Nisbett, Caputo, Legant and Marecek's, (1973) classic study (utilising questionnaire and experimental techniques) demonstrated the fundamental attribution error is not observed consistently. The cause of the same act will be interpreted differently depending on whether you are the person performing the behaviour (actor) or the person observing that behaviour (observer). We tend to apply dispositional causes for others' behaviour whereas we are more likely to focus on situational causes when explaining our own behaviour. 'John walked into the lamp post because he is clumsy', whereas 'I bumped into the lamp post because my friend distracted me'.

As with the fundamental attribution error, specific situations may affect the likelihood of an actor–observer effect. For example, when the behaviour is unusual or socially undesirable we are more likely to see an actor–observer effect. Harre, Brandt and Houkman, (2004) examined the actor–observer effect in relation to young drivers' attributions of their own and others' risky driving. Participants were asked to indicate the reasons why they may take risks when driving. Responses were coded by researchers and categorised as either dispositional or situational causes. The results showed that more dispositional attributions were made for others' risky driving (observer) but there were no differences in the number of dispositional or situational attributions made for their own driving (actor). Thus, only offering partial support for the actor–observer effect.

One of the proposed explanations for this finding was the difficulty in categorising responses as either dispositional or situational causes – for example, is 'showing off' due to disposition or situation? It could be that there were errors in the coding or, more fundamentally, the dispositional–situational dimension is inadequate on its own to explain the way we interpret and explain our own and others' behaviour (Malle, 2006; White, 1991).

Explanations for biases

Attribution biases have been explained from a cognitive perspective (see Table 2.3) or by examining our motivations. You may be motivated to see the world in certain ways because these views make you feel better about yourself (self-serving bias) or life in general (belief in a just world).

Self-serving biases

The attributions we make for our own behaviour may be dependent on whether we feel we have succeeded or failed. A tendency to attribute positive outcomes

Table 2.3 Cognitive explanations for attribution biases

Explanations for attribution biases	Fundamental attribution error	Actor–observer effect
Perceptual salience When trying to explain behaviour we focus on information that is most salient for us	We focus on the person rather than the surrounding situation People have greater perceptual salience than the situation	We are aware of situational factors affecting our behaviour but are not so aware of these external factors when observing others To explain our behaviour: situation has salience To explain others' behaviour: person has salience
Information availability	We lack information about the situation or this information may be difficult to interpret (we may not know the meaning of the situation for the person)	Actors' self-attributions often reflect situational factors because we know how our behaviour varies from one situation to the next, whereas we may not have that information about someone we are observing
Intimacy		If we know the actor well the actor–observer difference should be reduced or eliminated because we have information about how they usually act in a similar situation
Two-step process of attribution	The anchoring and adjustment heuristic suggests we take mental shortcuts, firstly assuming behaviour is due to an individual's disposition and only later considering the role of the situation	

to internal causes (our ability, personality, effort), but negative outcomes to external causes (chance, task, difficulty) is known as a self-serving bias.

Individuals may make self-serving biases:

- to protect their self-esteem or present a positive self-image – most people try to maintain self-esteem even if they need to distort reality by changing their thoughts or beliefs (see also Chapter 3, Self)
- as a result of personal knowledge about past performance or when they expect to succeed – individuals have a tendency to attribute expected outcomes to internal causes.

Belief in a just world

People may make attribution biases which defend them against the realisation that they are vulnerable to tragic events, such as rape or disease. One form of this attribution is the *'belief in a just world'* – the assumption that people get what they deserve and deserve what they get (Lerner, 1977).

These defensive attributions help keep anxiety-provoking thoughts about our own mortality at bay. Studies have shown people often blame victims of crime for causing their fate – rape victims are to blame for rape, battered wives are responsible for abusive husbands' behaviour (Abrams, Tendayi, Masser & Bohner, 2003). This clearly demonstrates an important real-world application of social psychology. We need to look carefully at the situation before drawing a dispositional inference to deter individuals from blaming the victim for random acts of misfortune.

Test your knowledge

2.4 Using relevant examples, explain what is meant by the fundamental attribution error and the actor–observer effect.

2.5 Compare and contrast the methods adopted by Harre et al. (2004) with those utilised by Ployhart et al. (2005). List the pros and cons or using closed rating scales versus open-ended questions for measuring attributions.

2.6 The actor–observer effect should be reduced or eliminated if we know the actor well. What is the evidence for this 'intimacy' explanation?

Answers to these questions can be found at: www.pearsoned.co.uk/psychologyexpress

? Sample question   Essay

When are attribution biases most likely to occur? Discuss with reference to psychological evidence.

Further reading Attribution biases

Topic	Key reading
Review of the evidence for the fundamental attribution error	Gilbert, D. T., & Malone, P. S. (1995). The correspondence bias. *Psychological Bulletin, 117,* 21–83.
Empirical study of the actor–observer effect	Harre, N., Brandt, T., & Houkman, C. (2004). An examination of the actor–observer effect in young drivers' attributions for their own and their friends' risky driving. *Journal of Applied Social Psychology, 34*(4), 806–824
Review of the evidence for the actor–observer effect	Malle, B. F. (2006). The actor–observer asymmetry in attribution: A (surprising) meta-analysis. *Psychological Bulletin, 132*(6), 895–919.
Belief in a just world	Abrams, D., Tendayi, V. G., Masser, B., & Bohner, G. (2003). Perceptions of stranger and acquaintance rape: The role of benevolent and hostile sexism in victim blame and rape proclivity. *Journal of Personality and Social Psychology, 84*(1), 111–125.

Critique of attribution research

Attribution biases are cited in all social psychology texts and are, arguably, a key to understanding the way individuals interpret human behaviour. However, there are a number of critiques you should be aware of. Figure 2.1 outlines four of the main areas of debate.

Artefact of research design

Ecological validity

Research has consistently demonstrated the actor–observer effect, but the majority of studies have small effect sizes. The experimental design has the advantage of determining cause and effect but we must be cautious in our extrapolation of findings. Often attribution experiments are limited to hypothetical or imagined scenarios. Some authors have questioned the external validity of these studies, suggesting explanations for actual events do not demonstrate a (fundamental attribution error) or an actor–observer difference.

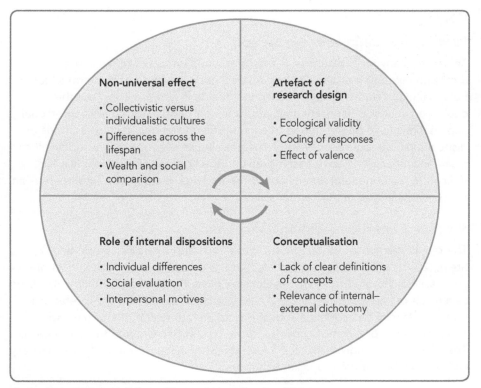

Figure 2.1 **Critique of the evidence for attribution biases**

Coding of responses

Many authors argue the internal–external dichotomy is too simplistic to capture significant variance in the way people explain behaviour. Perhaps natural text coding (in other words categorising freely elicited responses from open-ended questions) would be more sensitive than fixed rating scales in detecting actor–observer differences. However, the method of analysis is as important as the method of capturing attributions. Even if participants are allowed to indicate the perceived causes of behaviour in an open-ended manner, researchers may restrict these responses by imposing restricted categories in the analyses (e.g., all responses may still end up being categorised as internal or external causes; Malle, Knobe & Nelson, 2007).

Effect of valence

Attribution biases may be more prevalent when the outcome of an event is negative, the situation in the majority of published studies. Therefore it has been argued that attribution bias may be an artefact of bias in experimental design. We may need to add a caveat to the idea that biases are universal and fundamental. Indeed, we could argue there is no general actor–observer difference but a tendency towards the self-serving bias. See Malle (2006) for further explanations of the effect of valence.

Conceptualisation

Lack of clear definitions of concepts

There are many inconsistencies in the operationalisation of terms in the attribution literature and there is no agreed upon meaning of the term situation. Personal explanations refer to causes that reside inside the actor, but this could encompass personality traits, attitudes or mood. Consequently, personal explanations have been referred to as internal attributions, trait attributions or dispositional attributions. The interchangeable use of terms makes it difficult to make any meaningful comparison between the findings of research. It will be difficult to make generalisations about the findings in attribution until there is an accepted definition of the key variables.

Relevance of internal–external dichotomy

The real fundamental attribution error, as suggested by Sabini, Siepmann & Stein, (2001), is psychologists' beliefs that the causes of behaviour are simple and easily dichotomised. Many researchers have argued that the bias only occurs as a result of experimental demand characteristics and biased interpretations. Participants may believe behaviour is due to an interaction of internal and external causes or may not consider the causes of behaviour in this dimension. Therefore, asking individuals to infer whether behaviour is internally or externally caused may be imposing a false dichotomy.

Role of internal dispositions

Individual differences

Attribution theories are grounded in the idea that the situation is more important than internal dispositions when explaining behaviour. However, there is growing debate regarding the role of internal dispositions in the way individuals form attributions.

Some would argue social psychologists have not shown dispositions are significantly less important than laypeople believe them to be. For example, Milgram's studies (see Chapter 4, Social influence) are thought to demonstrate that behaviour is situationally produced, but the findings could also be explained by stating certain dispositions are stronger than others (obeying authority versus doing the right thing) or that particular situational factors (demands of experimenter) are more important than others (suffering of victim).

Additionally, evidence suggests the actor–observer effect may be dependent on specific individual differences, such as the degree of self-monitoring. High self-monitors expect themselves to behave differently across situations whereas low self-monitors expect their behaviour to be stable across situations.

Social evaluation

Studies which are frequently cited as demonstrating the situation is more important than dispositions when explaining social behaviour could, according to Sabini et al. (2001), be reinterpreted in terms of personality psychology. The central point of Sabini et al.'s (2001) article is that people in Western cultures underestimate the degree to which people's behaviour is affected by concerns with saving face and avoiding embarrassment.

Interpersonal motives

Leary (2001) suggests there is a need for increased attention on the role of self-presentation and the manner in which interpersonal motives (facework, impression management, desire for acceptance) shape the self and direct behaviour.

Non-universal effect

Despite the original proposition for universal laws of attributions, there is now little doubt that specific attributions can only be fully understood by taking into account the wider belief and value systems of individuals. Attribution biases may be dependent upon culture, your stage in the lifespan and social comparison.

Collectivistic versus individualistic cultures

Cross-cultural research has shown the fundamental attibution error is more prominent in individualistic cultures compared with collectivistic cultures (e.g., Blanchard-Fields, Chen, Horhota & Wang, 2007). Differences have also been found in the self-serving bias. Individuals from collectivistic cultures have been found to attribute successes to aspects of the situation and failure to internal causes. Interestingly, this would be described as a depressive attributional style in Western society, but is thought to strengthen interdependence of group members in Asian cultures.

Differences across the lifespan

Research has shown that older adults display stronger dispositional biases than do young adults. One explanation relies on the assumption that older adults have fewer resources to draw on and are therefore more likely to rely on a more accessible automatic process – in Western populations this would be a dispositional response. Blanchard-Fields et al. (2007) discuss the role of lifespan on attribution biases in a cross-cultural study, pointing out that this change over the lifespan wasn't apparent in a Chinese population. Chinese participants, regardless of age, showed a preference to examine the situational pressures on the behaviour of the target person.

Wealth and social comparison

In societies where people believe the world is a just place, economic and social inequities are considered fair. A just world attribution can be used to explain and justify injustice. People believe poor and disadvantaged have less because they deserve less. Interestingly, in cultures with extremes of wealth and poverty, just world attributions are more common than in cultures where wealth is more evenly distributed.

CRITICAL FOCUS

Social cognitive perspective

Evolutionary perspectives

The social cognitive perspective has led to some important and interesting findings in social psychology. However, some argue the dominance of social cognition has led to a proliferation of localised theories with limited utility and little emphasis on a more generalised theory. Baumeister and Leary (1995) propose we are alert to others' judgements due to a fundamental, universal, social motive –'the need to belong'. An evolutionary explanation for this need to belong suggests our behaviour is ultimately driven by a biological instinct (see also Chapter 9, Interpersonal attraction). Embarrassment is proposed to have evolved as one manifestation of the basic human need to seek inclusion and avoid rejection – and, as noted earlier, it is an important motive in influencing behaviour. Consequently, it is a motive that social psychologists may need to research further.

Phenomenological interpretation

Langdridge and Butt (2004) offer a critique of the social cognitive perspective and the fundamental attribution error in particular, based on a phenomenological approach. The fundamental attribution error rests on the assumption of dualism between the individual (i.e., internal dispositions) and the social (external influences). This suggests there is a clear division between them, whereas Langdridge and Butt argue psychological entities such as thought, emotion and behaviour cannot be measured as separate entities. Read Langdridge and Butt's paper for more on this perspective. The interrelationship between social and individual processes are also discussed in Chapter 11, Critical social psychology.

Test your knowledge

2.7 Explain how and why culture may affect the way we make attributions.

2.8 How might embarrassment play a role in attribution biases?

2.9 Select a number of empirical studies on the fundamental attribution error and determine how the authors have defined the internal–external dimension. Where the definitions vary, how does this affect our interpretation of findings?

Answers to these questions can be found at: www.pearsoned.co.uk/psychologyexpress

? Sample question   Essay

How 'fundamental' is the fundamental attribution error?

Further reading Critiques of attribution research

Topic	Key reading
Role of social evaluation in explaining the fundamental attribution error	Sabini, J., Siepmann, M., & Stein, J. (2001). The really fundamental attribution error in social psychological research. *Psychological Inquiry, 12*(1), 1–15.
Role of culture and lifespan in the fundamental attribution error	Blanchard-Fields, F., Chen, Y., Horhota, M., & Wang, M. (2007) Cultural differences in the relationship between aging and the correspondence bias. *Journal of Gerontology, 62B* (6), 362–365.
Evolutionary explanation of the fundamental attribution error	Andrews, P. W. (2001) The psychology of social chess and the evolution of attribution mechanisms: Explaining the fundamental attribution error. *Evolution and Human Behavior, 222,* 11–29.
Phenomenological critique of the fundamental attribution error	Langdridge, D., & Butt, T. (2004). The fundamental attribution error: A phenomenological critique. *British Journal of Social Psychology, 43,* 357–369.

? Sample question   Problem-based learning

Your friend has recently divulged to you that she is having difficulties in her marriage. She claims her husband doesn't understand the way she feels.

How could attribution theory explain the way your friend feels? (You may wish to refer to Chapter 9, Interpersonal attraction, for help with this question.)

Chapter summary – pulling it all together

→ Can you tick all the points from the revision checklist at the beginning of this chapter?

→ Attempt the sample question from the beginning of this chapter using the answer guidelines below.

→ Go to the companion website at www.pearsoned.co.uk/psychologyexpress to access more revision support online, including interactive quizzes, flashcards, You be the marker exercises as well as answer guidance for the Test your knowledge and Sample questions from this chapter.

Further reading for Chapter 2

Malle, B. F., Knobe, J. M., & Nelson, S. E. (2007). Actor–observer asymmetries in explanations of behaviour: New answers to an old question. *Journal of Personality and Social Psychology, 93*(4), 491–514.

Answer guidelines

✳ *Sample question*   *Essay*

The actor–observer effect is a widely accepted attibution bias in social psychology. Critically evaluate the evidence that this bias exists in reality.

Approaching the question

One way of approaching this question is to discuss whether the evidence for the actor–observer effect is ecologically valid. This means you need to gain a good understanding of the methods used to study the actor–observer effect. It may be useful to consult a research methods text to ensure you have a good understanding of the advantages of different methodologies.

Important points to include

The majority of studies have utilised an experimental paradigm and fixed response attribution scales. You could discuss how this limits the degree to which we can extrapolate the findings to real-life scenarios. You could also discuss the possibility that imposing an internal–external dichotomy on participants in attribution studies may introduce experimenter bias. You could consider how the types of scenarios that are most frequently utilised in studies of the actor–observer effect differ from naturally occurring situations. For example, the actor–observer effect is often demonstrated using laboratory-based behaviour with hypothetical situations, often with unknown or non-existent others. In reality, we often have some knowledge of the 'actor' and their past behaviour in a similar situation. Our explanations of observers' behaviour are also dependent on our attitude towards the actors – disliked actors, actors from out groups, tend to receive dispositional attributes, but otherwise we may make situational attributions.

Make your answer stand out

Many studies provide evidence in support of the actor–observer difference. The findings have been applied to a number of areas within psychology (relationships, occupational psychology, education) and outside (management, anthropology, politics). However, Malle in a series of papers (1999, 2006, et al. 2007) questions the strength of this evidence. A different approach to examining actor and observer differences is proposed: the folk–conceptual theory of behaviour explanation. The 2007 paper directly compares predictions made by the traditional actor–observer theory with those made using this new theoretical framework. When reading this paper you should note how adopting a different theoretical stance affects everything about the way a topic is studied, from the hypotheses, through the research design to the method of analysis. As Malle points out, the real differences in explanations made by actors and observers may only be determined by, firstly, allowing participants to articulate their explanations in a free-form response and, secondly, analysing these responses using a theoretical framework which goes beyond the internal–external dichotomy.

Explore the accompanying website at www.pearsoned.co.uk/psychologyexpress

→ Prepare more effectively for exams and assignments using the answer guidelines for questions from this chapter.

→ Test your knowledge using multiple choice questions and flashcards.

→ Improve your essay skills by exploring the You be the marker exercises.

Notes

Notes

3

Self

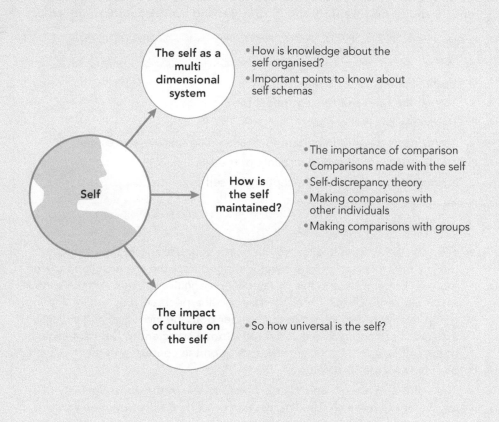

The self as a multi dimensional system
- How is knowledge about the self organised?
- Important points to know about self schemas

Self

How is the self maintained?
- The importance of comparison
- Comparisons made with the self
- Self-discrepancy theory
- Making comparisons with other individuals
- Making comparisons with groups

The impact of culture on the self
- So how universal is the self?

A printable version of this topic map is available from:
www.pearsoned.co.uk/psychologyexpress

Introduction

It could be argued that a sense of self is central to understanding the human condition. The ability to reflect on who we are is something which differentiates us from animals. Baumeister (1998) notes that the self has become one of the most commonly researched areas within psychology. Social psychologists have identified both individual aspects of self (e.g., traits, personal behaviours, states) and collective aspects (e.g., intra-individual group comparisons).

This chapter will focus on how the self is organised, maintained and how it regulates our behaviour. Both individual and collective aspects of self will be outlined, illustrating how comparisons with other people, other groups and even ourselves help to maintain a positive sense of self. We will also consider if the ways in which the self is viewed in the West are universal or if this might be an area of stark cultural differences. All of these elements are important in understanding how we think about ourselves and our relationships with others.

> ### → Revision checklist
>
> *Essential points to revise are:*
> - ❏ What the term self concept refers to
> - ❏ How the self is organised
> - ❏ Why comparison is important for maintaining positive self-esteem
> - ❏ Individual and collective accounts of the self
> - ❏ How culture may affect perceptions of self

Assessment advice

- The tasks are written to allow you to check your understanding of some of the key principles which have been identified from the research literature on the self. The emphasis in this chapter is on cognitive process and the ways in which our sense of self is mediated by social aspects such as culture and intra-group relations. It is important to consider both the individual and collective aspects of self and realise that the self is not a static entity. Different aspects of the self can become salient depending on the context, and these will affect both how we feel and behave.

- The self is also a topic which leads one to question the generalisability of psychological research. The final section on culture will encourage you to consider how a phenomenon might be global but experienced differently depending on country of origin.

- All these ideas are especially important for social psychological explanations, for if we are to understand human functioning in the social setting, the self needs to be at the forefront of our explanations.

Sample question

Could you answer this question? Below is a typical essay that could arise on this topic.

The self functions at both an individual and group level. Discuss social psychological findings which account for this.

Guidelines on answering this question are included at the end of this chapter, whilst further guidance on tackling other exam questions can be found on the companion website at: www.pearsoned.co.uk/psychologyexpress

The self as a multidimensional system

Baumeister (1998, p. 1) describes self as 'what you mean when you say I'. Whilst we may be able to relate to this statement, it does not capture the vastness of the self.

Psychological research reveals many different aspects to the self: a motivator of behaviour, a source of feedback of self-knowledge, an inter- and intra-group phenomenon, to name just a few.

A concise definition of the self has not been forthcoming within social psychology (Baumeister, 1998) and any student new to the area might feel overwhelmed by the vast amount of information available. It is useful therefore to think of the self not as a unitary concept, but as a multidimensional system.

Here, we consider a key player in the system – the self concept. The self concept is viewed as a cognitive representation of the self which seeks to provide coherence and meaning to our experiences. We discuss how it is organised, maintained and can regulate our behaviour.

How is knowledge about the self organised?

Developmental psychologists have established that we are not born self aware, but develop the ability at around 18 months. At this young age, self awareness represents little more than the knowledge we are an individual entity. However, as we grow and process more information, our bank of knowledge about our self develops and is cognitively organised in a structured way. These structures are known as self schemas (Markus, 1977), which are outlined in Figure 3.1.

Everyone has a number of self schemas which will relate to different aspects of themselves. For instance, I have a self schema about being a psychology lecturer; you, as a reader of this book, might have self schemas of being a

Contains	Where does it come from?	How is it stored?	Purpose?
• Knowledge about self	• Past generalisations	• As cognitive generalisations	• Helps organise and guide self-related information

Figure 3.1 **The self schema**

psychology student, whilst we both are likely to have self schemas about being family members.

Important points to know about self schemas

- A self schema can guide us by predicting how we expect to behave and feel in certain situations – e.g., a person with a self schema of being shy would have different thoughts about a forthcoming house party than being someone with a self schema of being outgoing.

- Our self concept comprises numerous self schemas, and it is suggested that these will be more complex than other schemas we have in our memory because we hold more information about the self than any other information we may store.

- Saliency of the self schema is especially relevant if the schema is to guide us and reduce uncertainty. Information which is congruent with a self schema will be processed more quickly, whilst incongruent information will be rejected (refer to Key Study below).

KEY STUDY

Markus (1977). The role of self schemas in processing information about the self

Based on responses to a self-report questionnaire about the dimension of independence–dependence, 48 students were selected to take part in an experiment. Those included were categorised as having either an independence self schema, a dependence self schema or being aschematic (neither independent nor dependent). They were then tested on their response times to trait adjectives, some of which were congruent with the independent self schema (e.g., ambitious) and some with the dependent self schema (e.g., submissive).

Participants indicated the perceived relevance of the adjective by either pressing a button labelled 'me' or 'not me' before being asked to provide examples of their behaviour from the past which would illustrate the self-reported typical trait behaviour. A number of schema-congruent and incongruent behaviours were also introduced, about which they were required to comment when asked 'How likely or how probable is it that you would react in this way?' These various tasks were used to provide information on both the content of participants' self schemas and how quickly congruent and incongruent information was processed.

Results offered empirical support for the self schema and its role in information processing self-relevant information. In terms of time, participants responded more quickly to adjectives they rated 'me' (i.e., those congruent with their self schemas). Also, a higher number of adjectives were categorised as 'me' from the independent congruent word list for independent self schematics and vice versa for the dependent schematics. The self schemas were also found to facilitate memories about examples of schema-congruent behaviours and increase predictions about their likelihood in the future. The aschematics, meanwhile, did not have different latency responses when pressing the 'me', 'not me' buttons. This led Markus to conclude that a salient self schema can protect the self against information which is schema-incongruent. Both the independent and dependent participants were less willing to accept incongruent information than the aschematics.

Further research into self schemas indicates that they can serve to motivate the self also, therefore acting in a self-regulatory way. Two examples are provided.

- Markus and Nurius (1986) coined the term 'possible selves'. These relate to thinking about yourself in the future in a situation in which you would like to be. It has been found that this can motivate the present behaviour towards the goal. For example, a student with a possible self of becoming a graduate could be motivated to complete an assignment. This is an example of a positive possible self. A negative possible self – such as not believing you could graduate – is unlikely to motivate you to complete the essay.
- Like Markus and Nurius, Chi-Hung Ng (2005) illustrated that self schemas are not just cognitive in nature but also have affective and behavioural implications. The study showed that students with a positive self schema for maths adopted a different learning style and better engagement with mathematical tasks – than those with a negative self schema. The negative group adopted a surface approach and exhibited a lack of persistence when doing mathematical tasks. Those in the negative category viewed maths as a source of embarrassment, anxiety and fear. For them, not engaging fully with the tasks protected their well-being. It was not a salient part of their self schema.

Test your knowledge

3.1 What is a self schema?

3.2 List three examples of self schemas which make up your self concept.

3.3 Discuss the ways in which self schemas might motivate our behaviour.

Answers to these questions can be found on the companion website at: www.pearsoned.co.uk/psychologyexpress

? Sample question   Essay

How can self schemas organise the way we think, feel and behave?

Further reading Self schemas

Topic	Key reading
The classic paper on self schemas	Markus, H. (1977). Self-schemata and processing information about the self. *Journal of Personality and Social Psychology, 35*, 63–78.
Self schemas and motivation for learning	Ng, C-H. (2005). Academic self-schemas and their self-congruent learning patterns: Findings verified with culturally different samples. *Social Psychology of Education, 3*, 303–328.
Possible selves	Markus, H., & Nurius, P. (1986). Possible selves. *American Psychologist, 41*, 954–969.

How is the self maintained?

Baumeister (1998, p. 139) describes the goal of perceiving the self positively as our 'master motive'. In order to promote a positive self it seems that we adopt strategies which can be categorised as self concept maintenance. A number of theories have been proposed to account for this.

The importance of comparison

Social psychologists suggest that a process of comparison is essential for understanding how the self is formed and maintained. Figure 3.2 illustrates the different types of comparisons we engage in and examples of corresponding theories.

Comparisons made with the self

Self-regulation refers to the ways in which we attempt to regulate our behaviour in a goal-directed manner.

Self	• Control theory of self-regulation • Self-discrepancy theory
Other individuals	• Self-evaluation maintance model • Motivated manipulation hypothesis
Other groups	• Social identity theory • Self-categorisation theory

Figure 3.2 Who do we make comparisons with?

In order to achieve the goals we set, Carver and Scheier (1981, 1998) suggest that we engage in an ongoing process of monitoring, evaluating and (if required) correcting goal-directed activities. Known as a 'control theory' of self-regulation, their model is based on the idea of a four-stage cognitive feedback system: The stages are:

1 **Test:** the self is compared either to private or public standard (people differ in the extent to which they are public or private self-monitors).

2 **Operate:** if the individual feels appropriate standards are not being, he or she will operate a behaviour change to address this.

3 **Retest:** this involves reflecting on the behaviour again, using the same points of comparison as Stage 1. If the self is still not reaching the desired standard, the feedback loop begins again. If it does, Stage 4 is adopted.

4 **Exit:** the self is in balance with the point of comparison. No need for any further feedback.

Points to consider

- There has been discussion about the amount of self-regulation which can take place. It seems that it requires a lot of energy, so focusing on one goal can deplete our resources to regulate other areas. Baumeister uses the term 'ego depletion' to describe this (Baumeister & Alquist, 2009).

- Self-regulation is related to our feelings about the amount of control we have over the environment and our ability to master important goals or, in other words, self-efficacy (Bandura, 1998). Individual differences will therefore exist in relation to the amount of self-regulation we engage in.

Self-discrepancy theory

Higgins' self-discrepancy theory (1987, 1989) illustrates how discrepancies between our self-comparisons can lead to different behaviours and feelings. He categorises comparisons into 'ought' or 'ideal' self-comparisons (we either compare our present self with how we feel we ought to be or how we would ideally like to be). These comparisons will regulate and guide our behaviour when seeking to resolve the discrepancy by setting relevant goals. If the discrepancy is unresolvable, and the goals not achievable, 'ought' self-comparisons will lead to agitation-related emotions such as anxiety. These are typically brought on by avoiding the activity which we feel we ought to be doing. When the goal is directed towards the ideal, perceived discrepancies lead to unresolved dejection-related strategies, such as sadness and disappointment.

Higgins has since identified two broader motivational orientations (promotion and prevention) and considered the role of situational demands, individual needs and the opportunities available in self-regulation (Higgins, 1999).

Making comparisons with other individuals

Festinger (1954) first introduced the idea of a social comparison. This stemmed from the idea that other people are a useful yardstick against which to measure and evaluate ourselves. It seems that we are particularly likely to do this in areas where we are uncertain. For example, having received a grade for an essay, we wish to find out how others did as a point of comparison for our own achievements.

You might think we would be seeking accurate feedback via these comparisons. However, evidence suggests we have a strong desire to view ourselves positively (Baumeister, 1998; Sedikides and Gregg, 2003), which accurate feedback might not provide. Imagine finding out in the example that your grade was in the bottom third of your cohort – comparing yourself with the two thirds above you (an upward comparison) would not enhance your self-esteem. Therefore, we engage in strategies of comparison which will protect our self-esteem. (Refer also to Chapter 2, Attribution theory, and consider the tendency towards self-serving attributions which play a similar role.)

Tesser (1988) developed the self-evaluation maintenance model. This identifies four strategies we adopt to protect our own self-esteem when engaging in upward comparisons with others:

1 exaggerate the ability of the successful target

2 change the target of comparison

3 distance the self from the successful target

4 devalue the dimension of comparison.

So, if the person in the example were to employ strategy 4, they might protect their self-esteem by stating, 'I might not be the most academic in my group, but I am doing really well in my part-time job, which is really important for gaining experience for future employment.'

Refer to Tesser (2000) for a discussion of the variety of self-enhancement techniques individuals employ to protect their self-esteem. This is important in illustrating how people manipulate information to maintain a positive self-evaluation. The Key Study outlined below offers an extension to the work on social comparison by looking at the processes involved in further detail.

KEY STUDY

Kiviniemi, Snyder and Johnson (2008). The motivated manipulation hypothesis

This hypothesis extends the work on social comparison by considering *how* representations of self are altered in relation to the target of comparison. Using the concept of psychological space (i.e., a cognitive structure representing the perceived distance between self and target), it is suggested that the space will be shrunk when making an upward comparison in order to manipulate a self-representation more similar

▶

to the target's. In this case, the superior performance will pose less threat. Downward comparisons will result in the space being stretched so the self-representation is of less similarity to the target with inferior performance.

Experimental manipulations involved providing participants with feedback representing either upward or downward comparisons on a dummy intelligence test score.

Findings showed that self-representation manipulation took place and self-esteem further mediated the effects (i.e., those with high self-esteem were more likely to shrink the psychological space in the upward comparison group). Results appeared particularly pronounced when engaging in upward comparison, suggesting that we are more motivated to protect self-esteem when engaging in social comparisons with other individuals. For a discussion of whether or not this is a universal phenomenon refer to the next section.

Making comparisons with groups

Tajfel and Turner (1979) first introduced the idea that our self can also be bound up in group membership and comparisons. As well as individual schemas (our personal identity), it is likely that we will have self schemas relating to group membership. For example, you might have a self schema of a psychology student from a specific university. Maybe you belong to a sports team? Are you a member of a society? Perhaps you view yourself as Welsh or English? All of these are different types of social identities.

As previously established, we have a number of schemas. The important determinant in activating them is saliency. You might feel like a student when sitting in a lecture, but, when at home in the evening watching the television, that part of your identity might not be activated. Therefore, the saliency of social identity is largely context-dependent. When the identity becomes salient, the dominant schema will guide our feelings and behaviour.

The way this works can be explained by a further theory called *self-categorisation theory* (Turner, Hogg, Oakes, Reicher & Wetherell, 1987). The focus here is on comparisons within (inter) and between (intra) groups. The categorisation works on the principle of meta-contrast. Intergroup contrast leads to highlighting *similarities* between the self and the group to which we belong. Intra-group contrast leads to emphasising any *differences* between our group and other groups.

Turner et al. used the term 'cognitive prototype' to describe the schema we hold in relation to the group. The prototype will guide our behaviour and feelings about the self as a group member. When such categorisation becomes psychologically salient, the self and other become depersonalised and the self is viewed as an embodiment of the prototype.

Social identity processes can also help to protect our self-esteem by highlighting positive aspects of the group to which we belong. The types of judgement made are likely to differ if one is a member of a high- or low-status group. Oldmeadow and Fiske (2010) found that high-status groups were more likely to focus on domains related to competence, whilst low status on domains related to warmth in order to emphasise areas of positive distinctiveness in their group. This process of categorisation is determined by people's motivations to reduce uncertainty about the self and others and protect self-esteem. Again, this illustrates how the self plays a role in cognition, emotion and motivation (Markus & Kitayama, 1991).

Test your knowledge

3.4 What types of behaviour might failure to resolve the discrepancies between 'ought' and 'ideal' self-comparisons result in?

3.5 Discuss the ways in which comparing the self to others might protect our self-esteem.

3.6 What happens to our personal self-identity when a group prototype becomes salient?

Answers to these questions can be found at: www.pearsoned.co.uk/psychologyexpress

---

? Sample question   Essay

Discuss the cognitive strategies used in upward and downward comparisons with other individuals to protect self-esteem.

Further reading Maintaining the self

Topic	Key reading
Self-esteem maintenance	Tesser, A. (2000). On the confluence of self-esteem maintenance mechanisms. *Personality and Social Psychology Review, 4*, 290–299.
Effects of self-regulation	Baumeister, R. F., & Alquist, J. L. (2009). Is there a downside to good self-control? *Self and Identity, 8*, 115–130.
Social comparison	Kiviniemi, M. T., Snyder, M., & Johnson, B. C. (2008). Motivated dimension manipulation in the processing of social comparison information. *Self and Identity, 7*, 225–242.
Social identity theory in high- and low-status group stereotypes	Oldmeadow, J. A., & Fiske, S.T. (2010). Social status and the pursuit of positive social identity: Systematic domains of intergroup differentiation and discrimination for high- and low-status groups. *Group Processes Intergroup Relations, 13*, 425–444.

The impact of culture on the self

As noted in the introduction to the previous section, the accepted position within mainstream psychology is that maintaining a positive sense of self is a master motive. However, this idea has been developed within the realms of

Western, largely North American, social psychological theorising and research settings. *Ethnocentrism* is a term for viewing another society based on the values and beliefs of your own. Has social psychology been ethnocentric in some of its thinking about the self?

CRITICAL FOCUS

The universality of positive self-regard

Maintaining positive levels of self-regard and self-esteem has been positioned as vital for a healthy self concept.

Heine, Lehman, Markus and Kitayama, (1999) offer a detailed review of research conducted in Japanese cultures and found that individuals here display an external frame of reference. The more hierarchical and collectivist structure of Japanese society means that focusing on a positive evaluation of the individual self would be to view the self as disconnected from the social context. Gaining the esteem of elders in the community, for example, is more desirable than one's own self-esteem. Empirical studies demonstrate that Japanese people tend to attribute their achievement more to effort than individual ability. The focus is on the collective rather than the individual. Important core concepts in Japanese culture are self-criticism, self-discipline, shame and the importance of others.

Much of the published psychological literature about enhancing the self, self-serving bias and positive self-esteem seem largely inappropriate for Japanese culture. These ideas, which have become central to psychological theorising about the self, seem to be artefacts of Western ways of being. The assumption that these aspects of the self are universal could be misplaced.

Culture seems to affect the ways the self is conceptualised and which aspects are viewed as the most significant in regulating behaviour. Markus and Kitayama (1991) identified two distinct ways of being or 'self-construals'. These are outlined in Table 3.1.

Table 3.1 Markus and Kitayama's construals of the self

Independent	Interdependent
Typically displayed in American and Western European cultures	Typically displayed in Japanese and other Asian cultures, African, Latin American and many southern European cultures
Individual the primary unit of consciousness	Self in relation to others the focus of individual experience
Self separate from others	Self connected to others
Autonomy and independence desirable attributes	Autonomy a secondary consideration – fitting in with relevant others is an obligatory part of interdependent relations
Inner attributes viewed as significant in regulating behaviour	Interpersonal harmony viewed as significant in regulating behaviour
Promote own goals	Promote the goals of others

Markus and Kitayama (2010) contend that construals of the self arise from our sociocultural experiences, which lead us to think about the self in specific ways. Individuals and sociocultural worlds are not separate. They use the term 'mutually constituted' to describe the relationship between the self and sociocultural experiences.

The self is viewed as a foundational schema which is shaped by the sociocultural experience. Such schemas guide us in interpreting the environment. They will function to regulate how we interact with others, how we feel and how we behave. The sense of self is viewed as the pivot around which other self-regulatory schemas are organised. From this perspective, the self constitutes people's thoughts, feelings and actions. This is illustrated in Figure 3.3.

Contemporary work within the field of neuroimaging has found that areas of the prefrontal cortex are activated when thinking about the self *and* the person's mother in China, but, in the USA, only when thinking about the self (Zhu, Zhang, Fan & Han, 2007). This provides further evidence for the interrelationships between culture and the self.

Points to consider

Voronov and Singer (2002) identify the following problems with pigeonholing a society into dichotomous categories such as independence and interdependence.

- Subtle differences and qualitative nuances more characteristic of that social entity may be lost.
- Descriptive labels evoke fixed and caricature-like mental impressions of cultures.

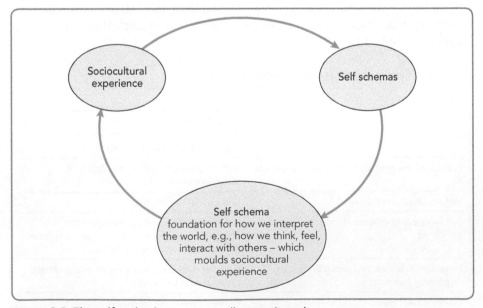

Figure 3.3 **The self and culture as mutually constituted**

- Presenting culture in such black and white terms can lead to good–bad comparisons.
- Such cautions highlight the danger of viewing these categories as fixed entities (which Markus and Kitayama's model does not do). Markus and Kityama (2010) note that the self-construals were not intended to be labels for whole groups of people – e.g., Japanese, Americans. Rather, they sought to illustrate how psychological processes may be implicitly shaped by the sociocultural system they inhabit.

So how universal is the self?

The work of Markus and Kitayama has been important in highlighting that some of the core ideas about the self might not be universal. This does not mean that the self is not experienced universally, but, rather, the ways in which it is experienced might differ depending on where in the world we live.

Test your knowledge

3.7 List three differences between interdependent and independent self-construals.

3.8 What impact might ethnocentric views of the self have on the validity of the research produced?

3.9 How might culture affect the ways in which we view the self?

Answers to these questions can be found at: www.pearsoned.co.uk/psychologyexpress

---

? Sample question   Essay

The self is an artefact of Western psychological theorising. Discuss this statement, drawing on the relevant cross-cultural research.

Further reading Culture and the self

Topic	Key reading
The relationship between the self and culture	Markus, H., & Kitayama, S. (2010). Culture and selves: A cycle of mutual constitution. *Perspectives on Psychological Science, 5*, 420–430.
Discussion of how universal positive self-regard might be	Heine, S. J., Lehman, D .R., Markus, H., & Kitayama, S. (1999). Is there a universal need for positive self-regard? *Psychological Review, 4*, 766–794.
Critique of labelling cultures in dichotomous fashion	Voronov, M., & Singer, J. M. (2002). The myth of individualism–collectivism: A critical review. *The Journal of Social Psychology 142*, 461–481.

? Sample question   *Problem-based learning*

John has received a grade C for his essay. His friend on the same course got an A. Based on some of the findings discussed in this chapter, what strategies might John employ to protect his self-esteem and sense of self in relation to his academic ability?

Chapter summary – pulling it all together

→ Can you tick all the points from the revision checklist at the beginning of this chapter?

→ Attempt the sample question from the beginning of this chapter using the answer guidelines below.

→ Go to the companion website at www.pearsoned.co.uk/psychologyexpress to access more revision support online, including interactive quizzes, flashcards, You be the marker exercises as well as answer guidance for the Test your knowledge and Sample questions from this chapter.

Further reading for Chapter 3

The following two books are from an edited series called *Key Readings in Social Psychology*. They cover classic and contemporary papers from many aspects of the literature on the self.

Baumeister, R. F. (1999). *The self in social psychology*. Hove, East Sussex: Psychology Press.

Postmes, T., & Branscombe, N. R. (2010). *Rediscovering social identity*. Hove, East Sussex: Psychology Press.

Answer guidelines

✳ Sample question   *Essay*

The self functions at both an individual and group level. Discuss social psychological findings which account for this.

Approaching the question

The question requires that you discuss both individual and collective views of the self. There is a lot of literature which you could draw on in order to answer this question, so you may wish to begin by selecting which specific theories or accounts you are going to consider.

One way of addressing the essay could be to focus on the role of comparison in the way the self is perceived. This would facilitate a clear structure, which could start by explaining why comparison seems to be important, before elaborating on the different functions of comparison in regulating behaviour and protecting self-esteem by using examples from both individual comparisons and group-level comparisons (e.g., control theory, social identity theory). The fact that there are different levels of analysis to consider when discussing the self illustrates that it is not a static entity, but flexible and context-dependent.

Important points to include

Some of the theories of the self have been written a considerable time ago. It would be important therefore to consider the current thinking in the field. For instance, have the theories been developed further? Have areas been contested? Have more in-depth studies focused on specific aspects? Such current knowledge in addition to the core concepts are the type of evidence that an examiner will be keen on finding. Examples of all of these have been noted within the chapter and the further reading boxes provide references for you to explore these findings in more depth.

Make your answer stand out

The majority of the research on the self has been conducted from a Western perspective. Consequently, there is much scope to critique this topic for being ethnocentric and guilty of cultural imperialism (viewing one culture's viewpoint as superior to those of others). Rather than adding this as a general critique, one way in which you could make your answer stand out would be to position culture as an example of a group-level analysis.

Explore the accompanying website at www.pearsoned.co.uk/psychologyexpress

→ Prepare more effectively for exams and assignments using the answer guidelines for questions from this chapter.

→ Test your knowledge using multiple choice questions and flashcards.

→ Improve your essay skills by exploring the You be the marker exercises.

Notes

Notes

Social influence

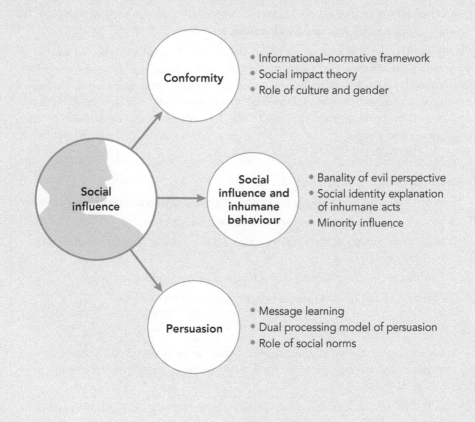

- **Conformity**
  - Informational–normative framework
  - Social impact theory
  - Role of culture and gender

- **Social influence**

- **Social influence and inhumane behaviour**
  - Banality of evil perspective
  - Social identity explanation of inhumane acts
  - Minority influence

- **Persuasion**
  - Message learning
  - Dual processing model of persuasion
  - Role of social norms

A printable version of this topic map is available from:
www.pearsoned.co.uk/psychologyexpress

Introduction

You may have noticed that the majority of social influence chapters in core social psychology textbooks focus on the classic experiments of Asch, Sherif, Milgram and Zimbardo. Despite their age, the findings of these now infamous pieces of research are still relevant today. The value of this work is enhanced because ethical considerations make it difficult to conduct similar studies today.

In this chapter, we will outline the main theoretical explanations for conformity and compliance. We will draw out when and who is most likely to conform, in particular situations, by examining the subtle variations of the Asch and Milgram paradigms. The informational–normative framework will be drawn upon to explain why we conform and obey instructions (even when this means harming others) and to understand how the minority may change the view of the majority. We will compare the 'conformity to roles' explanation for prison guard behaviour proposed by Zimbardo with the social identity explanation for tyranny proposed by Haslam and Reicher.

Finally, we discuss the manner in which organisations or individuals try to persuade us to change our views or behaviour. Research in this area is largely dominated by a cognitive response approach utilising dual processing models of persuasion, such as the elaboration likelihood model. We will evaluate this model and discuss the role of cognition, emotions and norms in the persuasion process.

> ### ➜ Revision checklist
>
> *Essential points to revise are:*
> - ❑ When and why we are likely to conform or comply due to normative pressure
> - ❑ Who is more likely to conform in different situations
> - ❑ How social psychologists have explained minority influence on attitudes and behaviour
> - ❑ The factors which determine the efficacy of persuasive messages
> - ❑ The role of cognitions, emotions and norms in persuasion

Assessment advice

- You should remember when discussing the classic research on social influence that tutors will be familiar with the set-ups of these experiments and the main findings of these studies.
- You should avoid describing the details of the experiments and, instead, depending on the question, focus on the explanations of the findings, the implications, discussion of the ethical issues, evaluation and critique.
- You should consider how the findings fit in with more recent studies and how historical and political context may affect the type of research conducted and the interpretation of the findings.

Sample question

Below is a typical essay that could arise on this topic.

---

* Sample question   *Essay*

To what extent does the psychological evidence support the claim that individuals will blindly conform or obey commands from an authority figure, even when this involves inflicting harm on others?

Guidelines on answering this question are included at the end of this chapter, whilst further guidance on tackling other exam questions can be found on the companion website at: www.pearsoned.co.uk/psychologyexpress

---

Conformity

Informational–normative framework

Conformity can be defined as 'changing one's behaviour due to the imagined or actual presence of others'. The most frequently cited theoretical explanation for this commonly observed phenomenon is that we conform as a result of informational or normative influences (Deutsch & Gerard, 1955). See Table 4.1 for an outline of the main features of these explanations, derived from the classic findings of Sherif and Asch. The conclusions in Table 4.1 represent the starting point of conformity research – you should note the caveats and critiques of these explanations which are discussed below.

Social impact theory

Social impact theory (Latané, 1981) suggests characteristics of the group members are likely to affect conformity rates, such as:

- **strength** – the importance of the group to you and the specific nature of the group will have differing influences on normative and informational influence (expertise being important for informational influence, whereas identity may be more important for normative influence)
- **immediacy** – the closer the group is to you in space and time, the greater the conformity
- **number of people in the group** – this is not a linear relationship – a small increase to a small group will have a greater effect on conformity than a small increase to a large group and research suggests increasing the group size beyond four or five doesn't significantly increase conformity.

Table 4.1 Informational–normative influence framework for understanding conformity

	Informational influence	Normative influence
Definition	Individuals see other people as a source of information to guide their behaviour	Attitudes and behaviour are guided by the need to be liked or accepted by other people or to avoid looking foolish
Classic empirical evidence	Sherif's (1936) study of the autokinetic effect – evidence of conformity with an ambiguous task	Asch's (1951) conformity studies using the 'line experiment' – evidence of conformity with an unambiguous task (as determined by control studies)
Acceptance level	Can lead to private acceptance where there is genuine belief others are correct	Public compliance is shown, but viewpoint is not always privately accepted
Type of task	Tasks perceived as highly important are likely to increase conformity	Tasks perceived as highly important are likely to reduce conformity

These ideas have been developed into a mathematical formula which purportedly predicts conformity rates (see Latané & Bourgeois, 2001). However, you should consider the extent to which this formula can be applied beyond an experimental setting. In these controlled settings participants are able to focus on one particular task. To understand conformity in real life, we would need to model how we make decisions when faced with competing priorities and how we may be influenced by the behaviour of people who are familiar to us. See Chapter 6, Prejudice and discrimination, for further discussions of how social identity may affect behaviour towards in group and out group members.

Role of culture and gender

Culture

It is generally accepted that collectivistic cultures are more likely to conform than individualistic cultures (Hodges & Geyer, 2006). However, there have been some contradictory findings – for example, Japanese participants have been found to be less conforming than US participants. In Japanese culture, cooperation is directed to the group to which you belong and identify with. Participants were therefore unlikely to conform with strangers (Williams & Sogon, 1984).

This demonstrates the biases our perspective may bring when applying a research paradigm to other cultures. It also highlights an important methodological point about the majority of conformity research. Generally, the group members are not known to the participants. To what extent can the findings of these studies inform us about conformity in real life?

Gender differences

Initially, it was thought that women were more conforming than men. However, reviews of conformity studies have shown the differences are not clear cut. On average, men are less likely to conform than women, but the differences are very small (Eagly & Carli, 1981). In addition, the differences in conformity depend on the type of normative pressure being applied. Sex differences are not apparent when participants give their responses in private. It has been argued that cultural expectations lead to gender-consistent behaviour, in that men are encouraged to be independent whereas women are encouraged to be agreeable and supportive.

The type of task also affects gender differences in conformity and can be determined by the gender of the researcher. Individuals are more likely to conform when confronted with an unfamiliar and unambiguous task. There may be unintentional sexism in the design of conformity tasks – for example, male researchers have been shown to be more likely to design studies with male-orientated tasks.

CRITICAL FOCUS

Interpretation of the Asch line paradigm?

Most commentaries on the findings of Asch have focused on the 28 per cent of participants who agreed with the majority incorrect response more than half the time. However, even Asch noted most people did not conform. Indeed, a typical participant dissented 75 per cent of the time. Findings are explained using the normative–informational influence framework, suggesting the greater conformity in public, as compared with private, is due to normative pressures – i.e., to avoid ostracism. But, since the majority dissented most or all of the time, it is difficult to comprehend how they avoided ostracism or ridicule. Researchers have questioned the idea that agreement on one trial labels that participant as conforming.

Hodges and Geyer (2006) argue that participants in Asch's study are not faced with a simple 'truth' versus 'consensus' dilemma, but need to balance multiple values. The values–pragmatics hypothesis proposes we agree with incorrect responses on some trials in order to resolve discrepancies between informational concerns ('What is true?') and normative concerns ('What ought to be done for the good of others and myself?'). In balancing these demands, many participants varied their responses, occasionally agreeing with the majority (demonstrating trust) and occasionally giving the accurate response (demonstrating truth). It is argued that this inconsistent behaviour may demonstrate rational behaviour in the circumstances.

Test your knowledge

4.1 How does social impact theory account for differential rates of conformity?

4.2 Complete the table, highlighting in each empty cell (using a normative–informational influence framework) how the interaction of task importance and task difficulty affects conformity rates.

	Task importance	
Task difficulty	Low	High
Easy		
Difficult		

4.3 Explain why researchers may have inappropriately concluded women are more conforming than men.

Answers to these questions can be found at: www.pearsoned.co.uk/psychologyexpress

---

? *Sample question*   **Essay**

Conformity is a universal phenomenon across cultures and genders. Discuss.

Further reading Conformity

Topic	Key reading
Social impact theory	Latané, B., & Bourgeois, M. J. (2001). Successfully stimulating dynamic social impact: Three levels of prediction. In J. P. Forgas & K. D. Williams (Eds.), *Social influence: Direct and Indirect Processes* (pp. 61–67). New York: Psychology Press.
Individualist and collectivist cultures and dissent	Hornsey, M. J., Jetten, J., McAuliffe, B. J., & Hogg, M. A. (2006). The impact of individualistic and collectivist group norms on evaluations of dissenting group members. *Journal of Experimental Social Psychology, 42*, 57–68.
Values/pragmatics explanation of conformity	Hodges, B. H., & Geyer, A. L. (2006). A nonconformist account of the Asch experiments: Values, pragmatics, and moral dilemmas. *Personality and Social Psychology Review, 10*(1) 2–19.

Social influence and inhumane behaviour

Banality of evil perspective

We are socialised to obey rules and norms and this is generally useful for society. However, on occasion, obeying authority figures has led to tragedy, including genocide across the world.

Classic research has demonstrated that ordinary people were willing to inflict electric shocks on an innocent fellow participant (Milgram, 1963). Milgram (1974) drew from Arendt's 'banality of evil' perspective to explain his findings, suggesting atrocities occur due to social norms for 'obedience' in the presence of authority figures without any questioning. Table 4.2 outlines the aspects of the Milgram experiment which may have increased the display of obedience.

Milgram's research did not tell us about interpersonal and group relationships over time, something which is crucial in understanding tyranny. The Stanford prison experiment (SPE) represented a general movement away from explanations of acts that rely on individual personalities to a focus on group processes (Zimbardo, 1989). The findings are well known – that the guards became ever more violent and the prisoners became more damaged and withdrawn. Zimbardo proposed a role conformity explanation for guard aggression and has more recently explained atrocities of military police in Abu Ghraib in a similar way (Zimbardo, 2007). The perceived power of the guards role and being a member of the group led individuals to lose their identity and feelings of responsibility (known as deindividuation).

Table 4.2 Factors leading to obedience in the Milgram experiment

Normative social influence	For society to operate effectively, the normative behaviour is to obey authority figures Evidence: when there were dissenters in the group, conformity with the experimenter decreased
Informational social influence	The participant used the experimenter to help them decide what to do Evidence: delivery of shocks was significantly reduced when the level of shock to give was proposed by a confederate of the experimenter rather than an expert and when experts showed disagreement about levels of shock to be administered
Conflicting norms	Initially, the norm of obeying an authority figure was appropriate, but the norm of not harming innocent people should have replaced this norm. It was difficult to switch norms in this situation due to key factors about the experiment, see below
No time for reflection	The experiment was fast-paced and involved many tasks (asking questions, determining whether or not the answers were correct and recording responses), preventing time for reflection
Self-justification	The small increments in delivering shocks created internal pressure to continue with the next shock. Once action has been taken on a difficult decision, we tend to internally justify that decision to reduce cognitive dissonance
Loss of personal responsibility	The experimenter is seen as taking responsibility for the participant's actions and any outcomes

Social identity explanation of inhumane acts

Reicher, Haslam and Rath. (2008) argue there is little evidence that authority figures induce a lack of awareness of what they are doing in those carrying out their orders. They suggest the banality of evil approach is not supported in experimental or historical case studies. In contrast, participants in Milgram's study did appear to be morally affected by their behaviour, as shown in interviews following the experiment. A blind 'conformity to roles' explanation is also critiqued. Firstly, Zimbardo appeared to play a significant leadership role in the SPE, secondly, not all the guards adopted a brutal persona and, finally, participants appeared to be aware and in control of their behaviour.

Reicher et al. (2008) suggest there has been an overemphasis on the perception of the out group and a lack of focus on understanding the participant's relationship with the in group. Acceptance of roles is likely to depend on whether individuals internalise group membership as part of their self concept. The authors draw on social identity theory and, particularly, self-categorisation theory (see Chapter 3, Self) to propose five steps which enable acts of tyranny:

1 creation of a cohesive in group through shared social identification

2 exclusion of specific populations from the in group

3 constituting the out group as a danger to the existence of the in group

4 representation of the in group as uniquely virtuous

5 celebration of out group annihilation as the defence of (in group) virtue.

KEY STUDY

Reicher and Haslam (2006). Rethinking the psychology of tyranny – the BBC prison study

The social cognitive perspective, with its focus on understanding individual beliefs, attitudes and motivations, has dominated research in social psychology in recent times. Ethical concerns have also limited the number of large-scale studies involving realistic social situations and examining group processes over time. This has resulted in explanations of social behaviour based on examinations of individual cognitive and biological phenomena. Researchers have argued that we cannot simply add up findings from individual studies in a linear fashion. To gain a full understanding of the social influence process we must pay attention to the social context (group membership, interpersonal relationships, cultural expectations) and study these processes in real-life scenarios over a significant time period (Mason, Conrey & Smith, 2007).

The BBC prison study – a partial replication of Zimbardo's prison study – is a rare recent attempt to capture social influence processes in an experimental field setting (Reicher & Haslam, 2006). The aim was to study interpersonal and group processes by examining the interactions between groups of unequal power and privilege. The study was grounded in a social identity theoretical framework and manipulations were put in place to test elements of this theory.

This experiment produced very different findings from those of the SPE. The guards were reluctant to impose their power and authority over the prisoners. Prisoners

▶

appeared to form a stronger group identity than in the previous study and overthrew the guards to form an egalitarian social system.

When reading about this study, you should consider how the theoretical approach and methodology affects the findings and ultimate conclusions of research. In addition, you should ask yourself to what extent the BBC prison study addresses the critique of social influence research highlighted by Mason et al. (2007). For example, the study was restricted to male participants and studied group processes within a prison scenario, not an everyday experience for the majority of us. The participants were also aware that they were being filmed for a television programme, which may well have influenced their behaviour. In addition, the researchers implemented interventions throughout the study to create feelings of power and privilege, which some argue added to the artificial nature of the study.

Test your knowledge

4.4 What are the main differences and similarities between the Stanford prison experiment and the BBC prison study. Organise your answer into the following themes:

- research design
- main findings
- theoretical explanations
- implications for reducing tyranny in real-world situations.

Answers to these questions can be found at: www.pearsoned.co.uk/psychologyexpress

? Sample question   Essay

Compare and contrast the 'conformity to roles' and the 'social identity' explanations for behaviour in groups.

Further reading Social influence and inhumane behaviour

Topic	Key reading
Stanford prison experiment and beyond	Zimbardo, P. (2007). *The Lucifer Effect: How Good People Turn Evil*. London: Random House.
The psychology of tyranny – methodological and theoretical discussions	*British Journal of Social Psychology* (2006) 45(1), 1–63. Four related papers: • the reporting of the BBC prison study by S. Reicher and A. Haslam; • commentary by J. C. Turner; • commentary by P. C. Zimbardo; • response by A. Haslam and S. Reicher.
Social identity explanations of tyranny	Reicher, S., Haslam, A., & Rath, R. (2008). Making a virtue of evil: A five-step social identity model of the development of collective hate. *Social and Personality Psychology Compass*, 2/3, 1313–1344.

Role of interpersonal relationships and dynamic interactions	Mason, W. A., Conrey F. R., & Smith, E. R. (2007). Situating social influence processes: Dynamic, multidirectional flows of influence within social networks. *Personality and Social Psychology Review, 11*(3), 279–300.

Minority influence

If individuals always conformed to the majority view, society would reach an equilibrium whereby we would all think and behave in a similar way. Obviously this is not the case. Indeed, research has shown minority views can have a substantial indirect influence on the attitudes and behaviours of others (see Wood, Lundgren, Ouellette, Buscerne & Blackstone 1994, for a review). Particular circumstances may lead strongly identified group members to deviate from the group norms. For example, the central tenet of Packer's (2008) normative conflict model is that strongly identified group members will dissent when they believe the current norm is harmful to the group.

Conversion theory (Moscovici, 1980) proposes majority and minority influence lead to different levels of public and private influence. Majority influence operates through social comparison processes and leads to public compliance with little private change. Therefore, changes in beliefs or behaviour, due to threats of censure and ostracism, are likely to be temporary.

Minority influence is more likely to lead to cognitive processing of messages due to their distinctiveness. This can lead to conversion behaviour – 'a subtle process of perceptual or cognitive modification by which a person gives up their usual response, without necessarily being aware of the change or forced to make it' (Moscovici & Personnaz, 1980, p. 271).

However, evidence that majority messages produce more private change than minority messages, is inconsistent with conversion theory. This has led to models such as the leniency contract model (Crano & Chen, 1998) and dual role model (De Dreu, De Vries, Gordijn & Schuurman, 1999) which integrate aspects of social impact theory, dual process models (see the next section, Persuasion) and conversion theory to explain majority and minority influence.

Leniency contract theory states that majority and minority influence are qualitatively different processes with qualitatively different results. Majority messages lead to compliance when threatening to the individual or when the majority is seen as an in group rather than an out group. Minority influence operates using different processes. Messages are analysed for threats. If the existence of the in group is threatened, the minority position will be ostracised (seen as an out group). Otherwise, majority members will systematically process messages, but it will not be immediately and overtly accepted. Minority influence occurs on related issues and in a delayed manner because too much change could lead to instability in the group.

In summary, evidence supports the following conclusions:

- majority-supported messages have greater influence than minority-supported messages on attitudes and beliefs expressed in public
- if minority-supported messages do have an influence, this is most likely for related rather than focal issues, on delayed rather than immediate observations and in private rather than public measures
- social impact theory, objective consensus and conversion theory do not explain all empirical findings
- leniency contract and dual role models may hold value as they are consistent with empirical evidence but require further direct testing.

Further reading Minority influence

Topic	Key reading
Dissenting from the in group	Packer, D. J. (2008). On being both with us and against us: A normative conflict model of dissent in social groups. *Personality and Social Psychology Review, 12*(1), 50–72.
Review of minority influence	Wood, W., Lundgren, S., Ouellette, J. A., Busceme, S., & Blackstone, T. (1994). Minority influence: A meta-analytic review of social influence processes. *Psychological Bulletin, 115*, 323–345.
Dissent and attitude change	De Dreu, C. K. W. (2007). Minority dissent, attitude change and group performance. In A. R. Pratkanis (Ed.), *The Science of Social Influence: Advances and Future Progress*. New York: Psychology Press.

Persuasion

Building on the ideas in Chapter 1, Attitudes, the following section will discuss the role of learning, cognition, emotions and norms on the efficacy of persuasive messages.

Message learning

The message learning approach to persuasion, led by Hovland, Janis and Kelley, (1953), is still widely adopted. The Yale model assumed learning and recall of persuasive messages occurs through a series of steps. More specifically, attention leads to comprehension, which in turn affords learning, yielding and ultimately behaviour change. Their research demonstrated that each of these steps has a decreased probability of success, known as the minimum effects model. The key to successful persuasion was to determine how we could ensure people travel through these steps. Research focused on four aspects of the persuasion process:

- message source – e.g. expertise, trustworthiness
- the message – e.g. length, structure

- recipient characteristics – e.g. self-esteem, intelligence
- the channel of communication – e.g. written, spoken.

Points to consider

- There was a lack of unifying theory which resulted in ad hoc explanations for a variety of effects, often conflicting with each other.
- The model assumed that attention to and comprehension of message would lead to persuasion – but there is no real evidence for a correlation between recall of a message and attitude change.

Dual processing model of persuasion

The cognitive response approach to persuasion asserts that mass communication and persuasion are dependent on the ability to change cognitive processes. The *elaboration likelihood model* (ELM) of persuasion (Petty & Cacioppo, 1986) incorporates two processing modes:

- the central route – persuasion is mediated by effortful scrutiny of message arguments
- the peripheral route – persuasion occurs through effortless processing via peripheral cues.

Figure 4.1 outlines the roles of motivation and ability when designing a persuasion campaign. Some of the most commonly identified factors affecting motivation and ability have been highlighted (see Crano & Prislin, 2006, for further information).

Which route is more effective in changing views and behaviour?

Attitudes formed by the *central* route are assumed to be more persistent, more resistant to counter-persuasion and more predictive of behaviour than those formed by *peripheral* mechanisms.

See Chapter 1, Attitudes, for a discussion of why message elaboration may lead to stronger and more persistent attitudes. It would also be useful to read Chapter 3, Self, and reflect on how arguments may be more convincing when they fit existing self schemas.

The *matching hypothesis* (Fabrigar & Petty, 1999) suggests cognitive appeals (for example, stressing price, efficiency or reliability) would be more effective in changing cognitive-based attitudes, whereas affective appeals would be more effective for affective-based attitudes. However, a review of the evidence has shown the matching hypothesis only applies to attitudes based on affect and not cognitive-based attitudes (Crano & Prislin, 2006). For example, for products where people have affectively based attitudes (e.g., designer jeans), adverts that stress values and social identity (associate product with sex, beauty, youthfulness) would more effective than encouraging cognitive processing (e.g., stressing the quality of the material or price).

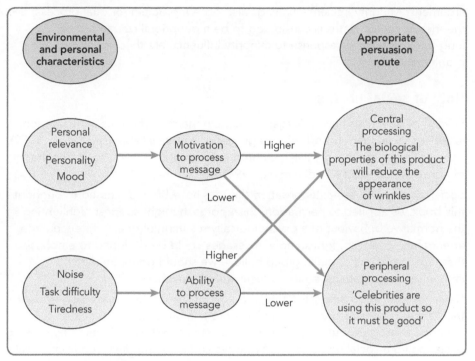

Figure 4.1 Elaboration likelihood model
Source: after Petty & Cacioppo (1986)

Furthermore, the *primary hypothesis* states that emotional associations with an attitude object are activated more quickly than cognitive associations. This hypothesis and the knowledge that we tend to be cognitive misers (see Chapter 2, Attribution theory) suggests peripheral route processing should be the default option. Researchers have since refined this argument, stating that to improve the efficacy of persuasion campaigns the emotional consequences mentioned in the appeal need to match the emotions experienced while receiving the appeal (Haddock & Huskinson, 2004).

Evaluation of the elaboration likelihood model

The ELM provides a comprehensive framework for the persuasion process and has been purported to explain complex and seemingly contradictory findings across a wide range of variables. For example, distraction has been found to both reduce *and* increase persuasion, which cannot be explained using the message-learning approach (see Bohner & Wanke, 2002, for a discussion of how the ELM explains the finding that distraction can sometimes lead to greater attitude change).

The ELM does not, however, explain *all* empirical findings and it has been critiqued for a lack of predictive power. It is not always clear whether a persuasion tactic will operate as a peripheral or a central processing cue – for example, will an attractive model serve as peripheral cue or a product-relevant argument? Minority influence findings also pose a problem for dual process theories as source status is considered to be a peripheral cue and, thus, long-term changes in response to minority influence are theoretically problematic.

Role of social norms

Several perspectives have emerged to explain the role of norms in persuasion, including social identity and self-categorisation theories (Abrams & Hogg, 1990), deviance regulation theory (DRT; Blanton & Christie, 2003) and the focus theory of normative conduct (Cialdini et al., 1991).

Social identity and self-categorisation theories have been discussed throughout this book. As applied to persuasion, this approach might suggest highlighting the normative behaviour of a psychologically meaningful group. To encourage attendance for flu jab, for example, messages could be designed to emphasise that most members of the in group believe we should go for influenza immunisation and attend clinics to receive their flu jab.

Deviance regulation theory (DRT; Blanton & Christie, 2003) is based on evidence that rare attributes are perceived to be more central to our identity than common ones. Individuals try to preserve or enhance their self-image by seeking deviation from social norms in positive ways and avoiding deviation from social norms in negative ways.

DRT predicts messages will be more persuasive if the message characterises people whose behaviours diverge from rather than conform to the norm. To continue with our example, if the normative behaviour is to get a flu jab, we should design messages linking the decision to *not* be immunised with negative characteristics. Equally, if the normative behaviour is 'not to get the flu jab' we should link decisions to be immunised with positive characteristics.

The *focus theory of normative conduct* (Cialdini et al., 1991) distinguishes between two different types of norms:

- descriptive – perceptions of what is done
- injunctive norms – perceptions of what ought to be done.

A norm will affect behaviour to the extent it is a focus of attention (salient).

Injunctive and descriptive norms influence behaviour via different routes:

- behaviour change influenced by injunctive norms is mediated by cognitive processing of the message.
- behaviour change influenced by descriptive norms will not require cognitive processing of the message.

Cialdini argues that campaigns have incorrectly utilised negative descriptive norms which may reflect reality (i.e., emphasis on the number of people who drop litter), but may inadvertently focus the message recipients on the prevalence rather than the undesirability of the behaviour. For example, removal of wood from a National Park actually increased when signs were posted alerting visitors to facts about the amount of wood that had been removed (descriptive norms) whereas signs asking them not to remove wood (injunctive norms) decreased removal compared to the situation in a control group (Cialdini et al., 2006).

You should note that highlighting descriptive norms is not always counter-productive. For example, students tend to overestimate peer consumption of drugs and alcohol. Highlighting the *actual* consumption rates can reduce consumption (Neighbours, Larimer & Lewis, 2004). However, evidence for the success of this social norms marketing approach to changing behaviour is mixed. When you find contradictory findings, you will need to examine the evidence carefully to unpick possible reasons for the differences. For example, placing normative information in a setting where behaviour change is required will ensure saliency of normative information (for example, in a bar rather than a health centre). It is important to examine the methodology of empirical papers in order to effectively compare and contrast findings and draw conclusions about theoretical explanations.

Test your knowledge

4.5 Given the information that the majority of older people do not attend for their flu vaccine, how would the focus theory of normative conduct suggest we design a persuasive campaign to increase uptake of this vaccination?

4.6 When would you utilise emotional messages to persuade your audience?

4.7 Collect a series of advertisements and health promotion campaigns from magazines and websites. Determine whether each promotion used central or peripheral processing and comment on the potential efficacy of the chosen technique.

Answers to these questions can be found at: www.pearsoned.co.uk/psychologyexpress

? Sample question   Essay

To persuade others, we should target their emotions. Discuss with reference to psychological evidence.

Further reading Persuasion

Topic	Key reading
Minority influence and persuasion	Crano, W. D., & Prislin, R. (2006). Attitudes and persuasion. *Annual Review of Psychology, 57*, 345–374.

Comprehensive summary of 107 social influence tactics	Pratkanis, A.R. (2007). Social influence analysis: An index of tactics. In A. R. Pratkanis (Ed.) *The Science of Social Influence: Advances and Future Progress.* New York: Psychology Press.
Focus theory of normative conduct	Cialdini, R. B., Demaine, L. J., Sagarin, B. J., Barrett, D. W., Rhoads, K., & Winter, P. L. (2006). Managing social norms for persuasive impact. *Social Influence, 1*, 3–15.
Social norms marketing	Neighbours, C., Larimer, M. E., & Lewis, M. A. (2004). Targeting misperceptions of descriptive drinking norms: Efficacy of a computer-delivered personalized normative feedback intervention. *Journal of Consulting and Clinical Psychology, 72*, 434–447.

? *Sample question*   *Problem-based learning*

Drawing on theoretical and empirical evidence, design a promotional campaign to encourage your fellow students to recycle more of their waste. Provide a rationale for the design of your campaign.

Chapter summary – pulling it all together

→ Can you tick all the points from the revision checklist at the beginning of this chapter?

→ Attempt the sample question from the beginning of this chapter using the answer guidelines below.

→ Go to the companion website at www.pearsoned.co.uk/psychologyexpress to access more revision support online, including interactive quizzes, flashcards, You be the marker exercises as well as answer guidance for the Test your knowledge and Sample questions from this chapter.

Further reading for Chapter 4

Cialdini, R. B., & Goldstein, N. J. (2004). Social influence: Compliance and conformity. *Annual Review of Psychology, 55*, 591–621.

Crano, W. D., & Prislin, R. (2006). Attitudes and persuasion. *Annual Review of Psychology, 57*, 345–374.

Forgas, J., & Williams, K. D. (2001). *Social Influence: Direct and Indirect Processes.* New York: Psychology Press.

Pratkanis, A. R (2007). *The Science of Social Influence: Advances and Future Progress.* New York: Psychology Press.

Answer guidelines

> ✳ *Sample question*   *Essay*
>
> To what extent does the psychological evidence support the claim that individuals will blindly conform or obey commands from an authority figure, even when this involves inflicting hard on others?

Approaching the question

The first thing to be aware of is there are limited studies which test the idea that people will voluntarily harm others. You should remember that a good essay doesn't necessarily need to draw on a vast number of empirical studies. However, you may want to discuss the reasons for the paucity of evidence and discuss the impact on the conclusions you can draw.

The question asks you to identify 'the extent' of the evidence, so you will need to discuss the validity and quality of the evidence. Describing the key classic studies will not tell the marker how well the evidence demonstrates we will blindly obey orders. You will need to evaluate the degree to which the evidence is robust, reliable and valid. For example, to what degree can we apply the findings to real-life scenarios?

To answer this question well, you will need to demonstrate an understanding of the social and political context of the research and it will be an advantage to have a grasp of current world affairs.

Important points to include

The question asks you to discuss both conformity and compliance. You should highlight the differences and similarities between these concepts, acknowledging normative explanations for obedience.

There are a number of main points you may wish to discuss. Firstly, how convincing is the evidence that people will harm others – not everyone obeyed or conformed in the key studies of social influence. Your essay should highlight the circumstances which are most likely to lead to obedience and conformity. You will need to discuss the degree to which we can apply the findings universally, across cultures and genders, and may wish to point to the lack of research into interpersonal processes over extended time periods. The two large-scale field studies which have attempted to understand group processes in social influence are both set within prison surroundings, not an everyday circumstance for the majority of the population. Additionally, these studies have both focused on the male population. It may be that you would want to argue for the need for further large-scale social influence studies which go beyond a male population within a prison scenario.

Make your answer stand out

Theoretical disagreements between Zimbardo (2006) and Haslam and Reicher (2006) have been articulated in four related papers in a special issue of the British Journal of Social Psychology. The researchers discuss the findings of the BBC prison study in detail. Additional commentary is also provided by John Turner (2006). This debate between key researchers is an extremely useful resource for considering how social psychologists can differ in their theoretical interpretations of experimental findings. The differences in opinion have far-reaching consequences for recommendations related to preventing atrocities in the future and a discussion of these implications would be valuable for this essay question.

Explore the accompanying website at www.pearsoned.co.uk/psychologyexpress

→ Prepare more effectively for exams and assignments using the answer guidelines for questions from this chapter.

→ Test your knowledge using multiple choice questions and flashcards.

→ Improve your essay skills by exploring the You be the marker exercises.

Notes

5

Decision making and productivity

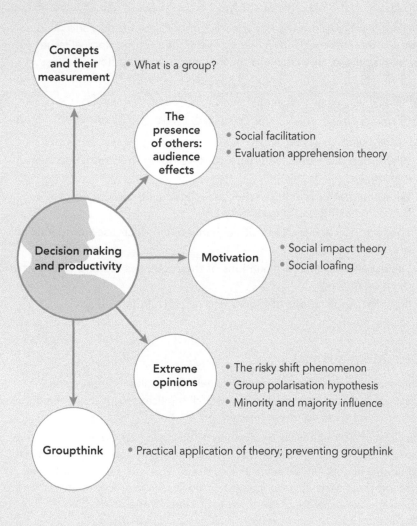

Concepts and their measurement
- What is a group?

The presence of others: audience effects
- Social facilitation
- Evaluation apprehension theory

Decision making and productivity

Motivation
- Social impact theory
- Social loafing

Extreme opinions
- The risky shift phenomenon
- Group polarisation hypothesis
- Minority and majority influence

Groupthink
- Practical application of theory; preventing groupthink

A printable version of this topic map is available from:
www.pearsoned.co.uk/psychologyexpress

Introduction

In social psychology, you cannot explore the processes involved in decision making and productivity without also exploring the processes that operate in groups. From reading the previous chapters, it can be seen that the way people think, feel and behave are constantly shaped by social forces, such as social influence. For this reason, much of the research into this topic explores how group interactions affect people's ability to perform tasks. Research typically contrasts individual performance with that of groups and attempts to identify faulty processes, which lead to poor performance. This theoretical emphasis on *group losses* at the expense of studying group *process* gains has been criticised.

This chapter will explore the key theories of decision making and productivity covered in the main social psychology texts, the methodological issues involved in measuring these concepts and the key debates in the field.

→ Revision checklist

Essential points to revise are:

☐ Why group processes are crucial to developing theories of decision making and productivity

☐ What the methodological issues associated with measuring group decision making and productivity are

☐ The factors which lead to both enhanced and decreased productivity in groups

☐ Social psychological explanations of the processes leading to defective decision making

☐ 'Real-life' applications of theory and research in this field.

Assessment advice

● This topic represents a mix of theory, with unresolved debates, and applied research, so consider 'real-world' implications of the research when constructing an assignment answer.

● Provide a comprehensive description of the theories you are referring to, but remember it is not merely enough to outline them – as a psychology student you need to critically evaluate the evidence you use. For example, was the methodology used appropriate, could there be other explanations for the phenomena observed or are there limitations to the theory?

● This topic is also highly related to previous topics, such as social influence and conformity, so think about how research from those fields may apply when constructing your response.

Sample question

Could you answer this question? Below is a typical essay that could arise on this topic.

> ✱ *Sample question*   *Essay*
>
> Critically review how group processes affect jury members' decision making in the courtroom. Discuss with reference to contemporary theory and research and the ecological validity of studies.

Guidelines on answering this question are included at the end of this chapter, whilst further guidance on tackling other exam questions can be found on the companion website at: www.pearsoned.co.uk/psychologyexpress

Concepts and their measurement

As stated, social psychological explanations of decision making and productivity focus heavily on group processes. For this reason, research into this topic tends to compare an individual's performance when working alone with his or her performance in a group.

At this stage, two concepts need to be examined:

● what is meant by the term 'group'?
● what the predominant methodology employed in this field entails.

What is a group?

Groups have been defined in numerous ways, including by common experience (e.g., Jewish people in Nazi Europe) or implicit social structure (such as within families or friendship groups). However, the definition adopted in this chapter is (Forsyth, 1998, pp. 2–3):

> a group exists when two or more people define themselves as members of it and when its existence is recognised by at least one other.

This definition captures the important feature of a group, which others do not – that of a shared awareness.

We each belong to numerous groups, from friendship groups to political groups and work teams to family. Understanding how these groups impact us will allow us to understand the processes which shape how we make decisions and behave.

CRITICAL FOCUS

Methodology

Steiner (1972) examined the methodology employed in group performance research and suggested tasks are either *maximising* (e.g., pulling rope as hard as possible) or *optimising* (identifying a specific object). They can also be subdivided into:

- **additive** – the sum of individual efforts
- **conjunctive** – all members must complete the task and performance is limited by the weakest member
- **discretionary** – the *group* chooses how to complete the task
- **disjunctive** – performance is measured by a single member, which involves an 'either/or' discussion between contributions.

Tasks can either also be *physical* (e.g., rope pulling) or *cognitive* (e.g., solving mathematical problems).

Much research, particularly early studies, focused on losses to productivity arising from individuals performing in groups. These studies often employed simple, additive tasks (often physical) and gave rise to numerous so-called *group deficit theories*.

Group deficit theories typically conceptualise productivity as (Steiner, 1972):

actual performance = potential performance – losses due to faulty processes

This approach involves identifying and calculating a group's potential performance and the processes leading to losses in order to explore its actual performance.

Points to consider

- The 'group deficit' approach to methodology has been criticised for suggesting group work always results in performance reduction. Shaw (1976) argues that Steiner's (1972) equation should be modified to include *process gains*.
- This methodology suggests *potential performance* and *losses* due to faulty processes can easily be identified, measured and calculated and are relatively fixed, which seems unlikely (e.g., individual differences).
- Research adopting this approach is usually conducted under laboratory conditions, which may artificially result in poor group performance. For this reason, some researchers have used 'real-life' case studies instead (Janis, 1971).

Test your knowledge

5.1 Why is it important to consider group processes when studying decision making and productivity?

5.2 Critically review group deficit theories.

5.3 What are the potential research methodological difficulties researchers have to overcome in order to increase our understanding of decision-making processes and productivity?

Further reading Group performance methodology

Topic	Key reading
Group processes and productivity	Steiner, I. (1972). *Group process and productivity.* San Diego, CA: Academic Press.
Researching groups	Forsyth, D. (1998). *Group dynamics*, (3rd ed., chapter 2). London: Wadsworth.

The presence of others: audience effects

Social facilitation

The concept of *social facilitation* was originally proposed by Triplett (1898), who asked children, either on their own or amongst a group of other children, to wind string onto a reel as fast as they could. Triplett found that the children who performed the task amongst others were quicker. He suggested that the mere presence of other people is enough to enhance task performance – an effect he called social facilitation. This is an example of an *audience effect* (Zajonc, 1965) similar to that of socially desirable responding.

However, it soon became apparent that the opposite effect could also be true. For example, researchers observed that people took longer to learn a finger maze and made more mistakes in the process when performing in the presence of spectators (Pessin & Husband, 1933). Triplett's theory could therefore only tell you that sometimes individuals' performance is enhanced by the presence of others and sometimes not.

The *evaluation apprehension theory*, proposed by Harkins and Jackson (1985), is useful in understanding this mechanism further.

Evaluation apprehension theory

Harkins and Jackson (1985) suggested that when people perform a task in the presence of others, they believe they are being evaluated. This leads to feelings of apprehension, which can motivate individuals to perform better.

Zajonc (1965) modified Triplett's social facilitation theory to explain the contradictory results outlined. He suggested that evaluation apprehension leads to physiological arousal, which enhances the *dominant response tendency* evoked by the task. So, for simple tasks where the desired response is clear (e.g., rope pulling), the arousal will lead to enhanced performance. However, for complex tasks where the desired response is not obvious (e.g., solving mathematical problems), the arousal will lead to increased anxiety, confusion and, ultimately, diminish performance.

Here we can see the implications that choice in methodology (e.g., simple v. complex tasks) can have in the interpretation of results and development of theory.

Further reading The impact of the presence of others on performance

Topic	Key reading
Critical analysis of social facilitation	Bond, C., & Titus, L. (1983). Social facilitation: A meta-analysis, of 241 studies. *Psychological Bulletin, 94*(2), 265–292.
Social facilitation effects in online environments	Sung, P., & Catrambone, R. (2007). Social facilitation effects of virtual humans. *Human Factors: The Journal of the Human Factors and Ergonomics Society, 49*(6), 1054–1060.
Individual differences and social facilitation	Uziel, L. (2007). Individual differences in the social facilitation effect: A review and meta-analysis. *Journal of Research in Personality, 41*(3), 579–601.

Test your knowledge

5.4 Explore the factors that help explain the social facilitation effect.

5.5 Considerable research into social facilitation is conducted under laboratory conditions. Critically review the advantages and disadvantages of such an approach.

Answers to these questions can be found at: www.pearsoned.co.uk/psychologyexpress

Motivation

In the late 1880s, Ringelmann examined the differences between individual and group performance in a rope pulling task (Kravitz & Martin, 1986). As this is a simple task with a clear desired outcome, the social facilitation theory suggests this would result in the enhancement of an individual's performance. However, the reverse was observed – individuals' performance was worse when performing in a group. Why should this be? According to Latané (1981) and Latané, Williams and Harkins (1979), this decrease in productivity can be explained in terms of motivational loss and the *social impact theory*.

Social impact theory

Social impact theory proposes that 'the amount of effort expended on group tasks should decrease as an inverse power function of the number of people in the group' (Latané et al., 1979, p. 830), so, as the number of people in a group increases, the social pressure on each person decreases (see Figure 5.1) and their inputs are disguised by the overall group effort. This loss of motivation results in *social loafing*, where members of a group are less productive when performing a task than if they were doing it individually.

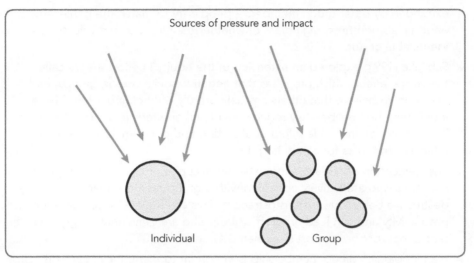

Figure 5.1 **Social impact theory**

Social loafing

According to Latané et al. (1979), social loafing occurs as a result of:

- individuals making incorrect attributions about how labour is divided in the group and wrongly adjusting their efforts accordingly
- goals being set lower than they should be, leading to them expending less effort
- individuals' unique contributions to the task being unidentifiable, leading individuals to either become lost or deliberately hide in the crowd.

The third point above is associated with the 'free-rider' effect (Kerr & Bruun, 1983; Suleiman & Watson, 2008), where individuals feel their efforts are unrecognised and so they expend less effort on a task when they perceive success can be still achieved through the efforts of other group members.

Evaluation apprehension theory (Jackson & Harkins, 1985) explains this by the fact that when people become group members, the potential for their individual performance to be observed and identified is reduced, leading to less apprehension and reduced effort.

Points to consider

- The concept of social loafing is controversial. Research exploring it is often conducted under experimental conditions, which are not reflective of 'real-life' decision-making and group processes. However, even when people know their group members and individual contributions are identifiable, social loafing and free-riding still occur (Karau & Williams, 1993; Kerr & Bruun, 1983).
- Jackson and Harkins (1985) proposed the *equity in effort theory*, which is that social loafing is mediated by an individual's perceptions of the levels of effort

expended by other group members – people try to match the perceived effort levels of others, *regardless* of whether their individual productivity is identifiable or not.

- Schnake (1991) explored an extension of the equity in effort theory called the *sucker effect*, which proposes that negative social cues in groups lead members to believe that others are deliberately withholding effort. These individuals then deliberately reduce their level of effort, to avoid appearing to be 'suckers'. Schnake identified goal setting and punishment to be the most effective strategies for combating this.

- The perception of social loafing, whether accurate or not, can lead group members who are actively engaging with a group task to engage in socially destructive behaviour, such as ostracism. This can reduce group cohesion and productivity and can lead group members who are genuinely struggling with a task to not receive support (Freeman & Greenacre, 2010).

- If an individual's group membership is *important* to them, they may work harder towards that group's goals (Dick, Stellmacher, Wagner, Lemmer & Tissington, 2009). For this reason Holt (1987) argued that social loafing should be renamed and divided into two concepts: *individual loafing* and *social labouring*.

- There is evidence to suggest that when a group's goals are important to an individual, but they perceived other group members are not exerting enough effort to achieve them, they will *increase* their efforts to balance this out. This phenomenon has been labelled *social compensation* (Todd, Seok, Kerr & Messé, 2006; Williams & Karau, 1991).

Test your knowledge

5.6 Critically review social loafing and the 'sucker effect'. What do research studies suggest could help reduce these effects?

5.7 Is it inevitable that people will lose motivation if they work as part of a group? Critically evaluate the literature and empirical evidence.

5.8 What significant issues might researchers have to confront when studying social loafing?

Further reading The causes and impact of motivational loss on productivity

Topic	Key reading
Social loafing	Kravitz, D., & Martin, B. (1986). Ringelmann rediscovered: The original article. *Journal of Personality and Social Psychology, 50*(5), 936–941.
Theory of equity in effort	Jackson, J., & Harkins, S. (1985). Equity in effort: An explanation of the social loafing effect. *Journal of Personality and Social Psychology, 49*(5), 1199–1206.

▶

The role of identifiability and dispensability of effort in social loafing	Price, K., Harrison, D., & Gavin, J. (2006). Withholding inputs in team contexts: Member composition, interaction processes, evaluation structure and social loafing. *Journal of Applied Psychology, 91*(6), 1375–1384.

Extreme opinions

The risky shift phenomenon

KEY STUDY

Stoner (1961). The risky shift phenomenon

Stoner (1961) asked 101 students to read through 12 vignettes and say how much risk they would advise the central character to take. There were two courses of action: the one decision had a known outcome; the other had an element of risk, but greater reward. One vignette described Helen, a writer, who has been given the opportunity to continue the books she was currently writing or write the novel she had always wanted to write. This latter option involved greater risk as it could have left her worse off financially.

Stoner observed that groups tended to give more risky advice than individuals, which became known as the *risky shift phenomenon*. However, other vignettes encouraged the opposite behaviour, such as one describing a single father who was considering selling his life insurance policy in order to invest money elsewhere.

It therefore appears that, rather than a 'risky shift', group decisions tend to amplify the dominant reaction tendency evoked by contextual information.

Group polarisation hypothesis

Myers and Bishop (1970) found evidence indicating that groups intensify opinions. They measured students' responses regarding issues concerning racial attitudes before and after discussion with other like-minded students. They found that opinions held by the groups became more extreme, that *group polarisation* occurred (Moscovici & Zavalloni, 1969). Moscovici and Zavalloni (1969) suggested that group polarisation may occur as a result of diffusion of responsibility across group members, resulting in people feeling able to be more daring in their decisions. A second route may involve *normative influence*, resulting from cultural values evoked by contextual information. For example, some cultures may be predisposed towards risk-taking. Normative influence may also result from *social comparison* (Festinger, 1954), where people evaluate their opinions and abilities against those of others. To encourage other people to like us, we express the views we share with them more strongly.

So, potentially, both positive and negative results may arise from group discussion.

Minority and majority influence

Nemeth (1986) suggested that minority influence is a mechanism which affects attitude change within groups and can produce greater diversity in perspectives, although this may be mediated by the perceived expertise of the source (Sinaceur, Thomas-Hunt, Neale, O'Neill & Haag, 2010). It operates differently from majority influence (which encourages shallow, convergent thinking) and can encourage greater consideration of alternative perspectives, greater creativity and lead to better-quality decisions (Kenworthy, Hewstone, Levine, Martin & Willis, 2008; Nemeth, 1986). However, this effect is subject to cultural differences. So, for example, there is evidence to suggest that group members who value collectivist beliefs are more likely to be influenced by the majority than the minority, and minorities which favour collectivism are also more likely to be influenced by the majority (Ng & Van Dyne, 2001; Zhang, Lowry, Zhou & Fu, 2007). This may explain why research conducted by Goncalo and Staw (2006) suggests that individualistic groups may be more creative than collectivistic groups.

Test your knowledge

5.9 Read through the Key Study again. Why do you think this risky–cautious advice behaviour might occur?

5.10 Discuss the key characteristics of group polarisation. How is this reflected in real-life situations?

5.11 Review why minority influence might result in more balanced group opinion decision making.

Answers to these questions can be found at: www.pearsoned.co.uk/psychologyexpress

---

Further reading The factors which may lead to the intensification of opinions in groups

Topic	Key reading
Group polarisation	Moscovici, S., & Zavalloni, M. (1969). The group as a polarizer of attitudes. *Journal of Personality and Social Psychology*, *12*(2), 125–135.
Polarisation and computer-mediated communication	Lee, E. (2007). Deindividuation effects on group polarization in computer-mediated communication: The role of group identification, public self-awareness, and perceived argument quality. *Journal of Communication, 57*(2), 385–403.

Groupthink

Groupthink is a theory of group decision-making processes, first proposed by Irving Janis (1971).

Janis suggested that a particular mode of thinking occurs in groups when concurrence-seeking behaviour overrides effective appraising of alternative courses of action. Janis argued this is most likely to occur if groups operate in isolation from alternative or dissenting views, they have a directive leader and are cohesive.

Groupthink has been suggested as the mechanism underpinning a number of famous and disastrous decisions, including Pearl Harbor (Janis, 1971). It may also have played a part in the development of the current economic climate, with groupthink suggested as a contributing factor to the WorldCom accounting fraud case (Scharff, 2005) and the Northern Rock bank's financial crisis (Kamau & Harorimana, 2008).

Janis identified a number of groupthink symptoms, including:

- ignoring warning signs because groups are overly confident in the success of their decisions
- ignoring ethical issues because the groups are assumed to be inherently moral
- discounting challenges and engaging in self-censorship to maintain the cohesion of the groups
- stereotyping others outside the groups and refusing to engage with them
- appointing *Mindguards* who 'protect' the groups from information which could lead to decisions being questioned.

Before reading further, attempt the case study task.

Case study

Imagine you are newly appointed as a team leader and are asked to enhance the decision making of a failing team, which has recently made a number of costly mistakes for your organisation. Team members appear to be unwilling to contradict each other, work with other teams or even share new ideas with the group.

From what you know about groupthink and other group processes, what steps could you take to enhance the group's performance?

Practical application of theory; preventing groupthink

Janis (1982) made a number of recommendations for combating groupthink, including:

- encouraging critical evaluation and impartiality (e.g., appointing a devil's advocate)
- dividing the group into smaller units to work and then reuniting them to encourage discussion and generation of ideas
- holding 'second chance' meetings and utilising advice from external sources, to ensure all members have had a chance to voice and discuss any doubts.

Does groupthink really exist?

Whyte (1989) suggests that groupthink is actually merely a collection of previously observed social psychological phenomena, such as group polarisation.

Janis retrospectively identified case studies for his theory, which may have been biased.

Not all cohesive groups lead to groupthink – for example, think of friendship groups. Cohesive teams can make members feel comfortable to voice different opinions and critically analyse alternative ideas. They can also be more flexible and innovative than individuals (Dick, Tissington & Hertel, 2009; Postmes, Spears & Cihangir, 2001).

Glick and Staley (2007) found that teams of physicians working together to form a diagnosis were more accurate than physicians working in isolation, suggesting that it is not inevitable that groups will lead to a loss of decision veracity.

Tetlock, Peterson, McGuire, Chang and Field, (1992) looked at other examples of real-life decision-making processes, such as the American hostage rescue attempt in Iran during the Carter administration, and argued that even decisions reached through 'good' group procedures could have disastrous consequences.

Test your knowledge

5.12 Review the evidence for the existence of groupthink.

5.13 Critically review whether or not groupthink exists under laboratory conditions.

5.14 Critically review the evidence for groupthink. How can it be avoided?

Answers to these questions can be found at: www.pearsoned.co.uk/psychologyexpress

Further reading Groupthink

Topic	Key reading
Groupthink	Janis, I. (1971). Groupthink. *Psychology Today*, 5, 43–46.
Critique of groupthink	Henningsen, D., Henningsen, M., Eden, J., & Cruz, M. (2006). Examining the symptoms of groupthink and retrospective sensemaking. *Small Group Research*, 37(1), 36–64.
Test of the replicability of the groupthink model	Park, W. (2000). A comprehensive empirical investigation of the relationship among variables of the groupthink model. *Journal of Organizational Behavior*, 21(8), 873–887.

? Sample question   Problem-based learning

You have been asked to develop an educational programme at the hospital in which you work, aimed at enhancing recently graduated nurses' clinical effectiveness skills, which involves good teamwork and decision-making skills. In a report outlining your proposal, identify what aspects of behaviour your educational programme will need to target and why, and what form the intervention will take.

Chapter summary – pulling it all together

→ Can you tick all the points from the revision checklist at the beginning of this chapter?

→ Attempt the sample question from the beginning of this chapter using the answer guidelines below.

→ Go to the companion website at www.pearsoned.co.uk/psychologyexpress to access more revision support online, including interactive quizzes, flashcards, You be the marker exercises as well as answer guidance for the Test your knowledge and Sample questions from this chapter.

Further reading for Chapter 5

Klehe, U., & Anderson, N. (2007). The moderating influence of personality and culture on social loafing in typical versus maximum performance. *International Journal of Selection and Assessment, 15*(2), 250–262.

Packer, D. (2009). Avoiding groupthink: Whereas weakly identified members remain silent, strongly identified members dissent about collective problems. *Psychological Science, 20*(5), 546–548.

Yardi, S., & Boyd, D. (2010). Dynamic debates: An analysis of group polarization over time on Twitter. *Bulletin of Science, Technology & Society, 30*(5), 316–327.

Answer guidelines

✳ *Sample question*   *Essay*

Critically review how group processes affect jury members' decision making in the courtroom. Discuss with reference to contemporary theory and research and the ecological validity of studies.

Approaching the question

The question is asking you to discuss the aspects of group processes that affect people's ability to work together and produce an accurate and balanced decision. Therefore, you will need to look at both productivity and decision-making theories and research. There are lots of good pieces of research to choose from to illustrate your answer, so pick studies carefully (possibly a mix of key classic research and modern applications of theory). However, there are a number of key concepts and debates which you should consider, such as how methodology choice has shaped theory development, what the mechanisms underpinning group processes are (such as social facilitation), what aspects of productivity and decision-making behaviour researchers have focused on and what factors potentially moderate observed phenomena.

Important points to include

Firstly, you need to define what a group is and briefly state why group processes are of particular importance in understanding individuals' productivity and decision-making performance. You could briefly bring in research from other topics, such as social influence and prejudice. However, remember that this is just the introduction to your answer and not the focus of the essay.

You will need to explore the aspects of decision making and productivity behaviour which are affected (both negatively and positively) by the presence of others and group work, such as problem solving, identifying maximal solutions, information seeking, critical analysis, risk acceptance and motivation. This is not an exhaustive list and it is up to you which factors to explore. Make sure that your answer has structure and avoid trying to look at everything as this will result in an essay which lacks depth and evaluation. You will need to explore the theories which have been proposed to explain these phenomena (such as social facilitation, social loafing, group polarisation, etc.), on what evidence they are based and whether or not other interpretations exist.

Make your answer stand out

Avoid spreading your focus too thinly and examining theories without depth. It may be useful to focus particularly on one concept, such as groupthink, to illustrate key issues and debates. For example, you could use real-life examples of the phenomena to illustrate the mechanisms which the theory specifies are in operation (or absent). Use explicitly examples of research to highlight the implications that research methodology has on understanding this topic, such as the issue concerning replicability of group processes under laboratory conditions. You could also illustrate that negative effects of group processes on productivity and decision-making performance can be prevented or mitigated – and provide evidence supporting this.

The key thing to remember is that a good essay will impartially present evidence both for and against the argument and then clearly state where the author's position in the debate lies and why, providing appropriately chosen supporting evidence.

Explore the accompanying website at www.pearsoned.co.uk/psychologyexpress

→ Prepare more effectively for exams and assignments using the answer guidelines for questions from this chapter.

→ Test your knowledge using multiple choice questions and flashcards.

→ Improve your essay skills by exploring the You be the marker exercises.

Notes

Notes

6

Prejudice and discrimination

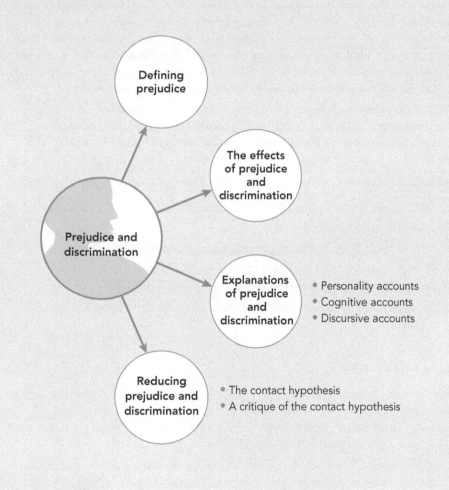

- Defining prejudice
- Prejudice and discrimination
- The effects of prejudice and discrimination
- Explanations of prejudice and discrimination
  - Personality accounts
  - Cognitive accounts
  - Discursive accounts
- Reducing prejudice and discrimination
  - The contact hypothesis
  - A critique of the contact hypothesis

A printable version of this topic map is available from:
www.pearsoned.co.uk/psychologyexpress

Introduction

This chapter will discuss prejudice and discrimination, a topic which has been widely researched within social psychology. Whilst it represents a topic of study in its own right, it also encompasses a number of areas – e.g., impression management, group processes and conflict reduction – so you are likely to find information about this topic appearing in different areas of social psychology textbooks. You might also find that aspects of other topic areas you learn about – e.g., attitudes and stereotypes – are also highly relevant to this topic; do not be afraid to integrate such information.

We have aimed to offer a summary of the key areas which are regularly discussed in relation to the topic of prejudice and discrimination here. Initially, definitions of prejudice and the effects it has on individuals at the receiving end will be identified. This will be followed by a discussion of the main accounts which have been posited to explain such negative beliefs and behaviour. The discussion will ask questions such as, is prejudice something which can be found in people with a certain personality type or do we all hold prejudiced stereotypes?

Having considered such contrasting approaches, the chapter will end with an applied angle, discussing a task which remains a significant challenge for psychologists around the globe: how might we use social psychological knowledge to reduce intergroup bias and conflict?

→ *Revision checklist*

Essential points to revise are:
- ❏ How to distinguish between prejudice and discrimination
- ❏ What the effects of prejudice and discrimination are
- ❏ The main explanations for prejudice and discrimination
- ❏ Social psychological accounts of contact as a way to reduce intergroup conflict

Assessment advice

- Because this is such a vast area, it is important that you can distinguish which information would be the most relevant to answer the specific questions asked. Think 'What?' (is it), 'Why?' (it occurs) and 'How?' (might it be reduced). The tasks are designed to help you do this.

- As ever, an evaluative edge is important, but remember that evaluate does not mean criticise! Consider the different evaluatory points offered after the accounts of prejudice, for instance – they do not just highlight the limitations of each one but also indicate their strength.

- It is likely that accounts coming from different viewpoints will focus on different aspects of the topic – consider how these different aspects fit together. Are they a total contrast or might they complement each other?

Sample question

Below is a typical essay that could arise on this topic.

> **✱ Sample question**   **Essay**
>
> Critically consider the accounts offered by social psychologists to explain the origins of prejudice.

Guidelines on answering this question are included at the end of this chapter, whilst further guidance on tackling other exam questions can be found on the companion website at: www.pearsoned.co.uk/psychologyexpress

Defining prejudice

In everyday conversation and in the media, you might find the terms *stereotyping*, *prejudice* and *discrimination* are used interchangeably. For social psychologists, however, clear distinctions have been made about the meanings and different components associated with these terms.

Points to consider

- You might have noticed that Table 6.1 maps onto the three-component model of attitudes (see Table 1.1) discussed in Chapter 1, Attitudes.
- Be careful not to assume that there is a linear relationship between these three components. Just because someone feels prejudiced it does not mean that they will automatically engage in discriminatory behaviour (see attitude–behaviour relationship in Chapter 1, Attitudes).
- Both the saliency and type of emotions experienced are likely to impact whether or not discrimination will occur and how it might be externalised. For

Table 6.1 **Definition of terms**

Stereotype	The beliefs about a particular group, i.e., what that group is like	Represents the cognitive component
Prejudice	How we feel about a particular group (typically the emphasis has been on negative feelings)	Represents the affective component
Discrimination	The action taken toward the group	Refers to the behavioural component

example, feeling strong anger towards the target might lead to expressions of violence, yet feeling disgust might lead one to avoid any type of interaction with them.

The effects of prejudice and discrimination

As already established, the cognitive component of prejudice is a *stereotype*. A *stereotype* represents a cognitive short cut, giving us access to a simplified set of beliefs about what people from certain groups might be like – known as *schemas*.

When it comes to prejudice and discrimination, stereotypes tend to contain largely negative and inaccurate beliefs about the traits and attributes of the target group. It is interesting to note that the literal translation of the word prejudice is 'prejudgement'.

Research indicates that the most common basis for our stereotypes are sex, age and race. You might be able to think of some further categories which form the basis of our stereotypes. Typically, the target is groups with a lower status in society.

Prejudice can have unfortunate outcomes for the individuals on the receiving end. Although it is not considered politically correct to overtly express prejudiced views in many countries, this does not mean that low-status groups are no longer being affected (see Critical Focus below for discussion of this). Feeling that you are being treated in a specific way because you are a member of a low-status group can impact how you feel and how you perform. For example, feeling that you are stigmatised by others can lead to an internalisation of these negative evaluations, which can then lower self-esteem. The effects that this can have are illustrated in Figure 6.1.

CRITICAL FOCUS

When being seen to be unprejudiced is insufficient

Are simple unprejudiced acts enough to alleviate such a widespread problem as discrimination? Some psychologists argue that such behaviour can be used as an excuse for not having to engage in any further antidiscriminatory actions. This is known as *tokenism* (refer to King, Hebl, George & Matusik, 2010, for research on this topic). Tokenism refers to a positive act towards members of a minority group, but it can be viewed as a token gesture (hence the name). An often-cited example is companies that employ a minority group member. At face value they seem to be engaging in non-discriminatory practices, but this can stop them employing any further measures to establish equal opportunities in the workplace. Consider how you would feel if you had been given your job because of your minority group status.

Research indicates that women who had reached management roles were less satisfied with their job and displayed less commitment to the organisation if they thought they

▶

had been hired as a token woman than if they felt that they had got their job based on their ability. Being perceived by others as a token or *affirmative action* employee can also lead to negative reactions. These might include resentment or lack of respect for the employee's abilities. The paradox of the situation is that, in acting in a manner which can be seen as reducing prejudice and discrimination, tokenism not only allows them to continue but could also make them worse.

Clearly, reducing prejudice is not an easy task (as discussed later).

Test your knowledge

6.1 How do social psychologists distinguish between the terms 'prejudice' and 'discrimination'? Why is it that employing a member of a minority group could cause them to feel stigmatised amongst the workforce?

6.2 What psychological effects might the scenario have on them?

? Sample question   Essay

Using evidence from the social psychology literature, discuss the potential consequences of prejudiced stereotypes on low-status groups.

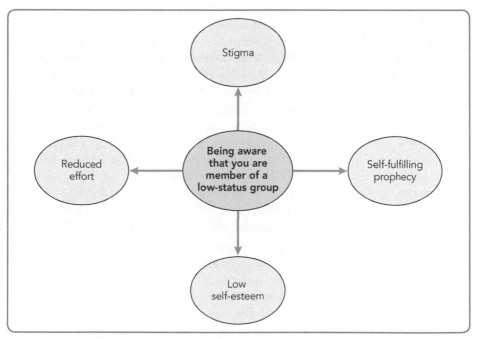

Figure 6.1 The effects of prejudicial attitudes

Further reading The effects of prejudice and discrimination

Topic	Key reading
Stereotyping	Fiske, S. T., Cuddy, A. J. C., Glick, P., & Xu, J. (2002). A model of (often mixed) stereotyping content: Competence and warmth respectively follow from perceived status and competition. *Journal of Personality and Social Psychology, 82,* 878–902.
Tokenism in the workplace	King, E. B., Hebl, M. R., George, J. M., & Matusik, S. F. (2010). Understanding tokenism: Antecedents and consequences of a psychological climate of gender inequality. *Journal of Management, 36,* 482–510.
Stigma	Major, B., & O'Brian, L. T. (2005). The social psychology of stigma. *Annual Review of Psychology, 56,* 393–421.

Explanations of prejudice and discrimination

Many different ideas have been posited for why people feel prejudice towards others. Three main psychological explanations offered come from personality, cognitive and discursive perspectives. These are considered both in terms of theory and method.

Personality accounts

One of the earliest accounts of prejudice came from a psychodynamic background and proposes that some individuals have a prejudiced personality. In the post-war period of the 1950s, Adorno contended that children brought up in overly harsh and disciplined households felt both love and hate towards their parents (Adorno, Frenkel-Brunswik, Levinson & Sanford, 1950). In an attempt to resolve this conflict, they repressed the feelings associated with hate towards their parents and, instead, displaced them on to weaker individuals. Parental figures then became idealised, which was generalised to any authority figure in later life. This approach is known as the authoritarian personality. More recent work in this area by Altemeyer (1981, 1996) has led to a re-elaboration of authoritarian personality to include measurement of the following constructs: conventialism, authoritarian submission and authoritarian aggression. This is known as right-wing authoritarianism (RWA) (see also Kriendler, 2005, for a discussion of RWA).

Both of these approaches use scales to measure these personality factors. For instance, an authoritarian personality is measured using the *F* (which stands for fascist) *scale*. This sought to identify individuals with potentially fascist/racist or more democratic leanings. However, all the statements were worded in such a way that agreeing with them was indicative of an authoritarian attitude. This is known as an *acquiescent response set*, where a high score can only be earned by agreeing with an attitude.

Social psychology adopts many different methodologies. Reflecting on the method in your assessments could also earn you marks for evaluation. Such methods are not exclusive to the topic of prejudice and discrimination, though, so aim to consider how the research was conducted in addition to the findings themselves.

Points to consider

- Personality approaches underestimate situational and socio cultural factors.
- Personality might dispose individuals to be prejudiced in some contexts, but societal norms which legitimise this are also a necessary condition.
- This approach suggests that only certain people have the potential to be prejudiced, yet prejudice can manifest itself in a whole population or at least a majority.
- Using the F scale confounds authoritarianism with acquiescence.
- This approach reflects the nature of social psychological theorising at the time: during the 1950s, authoritarianism became widely used as an explanatory concept.

Cognitive accounts

Remember from the Defining prejudice section early in this chapter that the cognitive component refers to stereotyping.

Cognitive accounts of prejudice are based on the idea of the individual as a cognitive miser (Fiske & Taylor, 1991). This means that, by having readily available categories about people (stereotypes), we can invest a lot less cognitive effort and reduce our cognitive load. Once we have attributed a category to someone (e.g., based on their sex, age or occupation), we can access information about their shared characteristics and, thus, anticipate how they might act in given situations. Here, categorisation has a distinct advantage. However, categorisation can also lead us to think in terms of in groups and out groups ('like us' or 'not like us'). Generalisations can then be made about groups which may be inaccurate, but, because it is a function of our cognitive system, categories and stereotypes are hard to change.

Categorisation is believed to be automatic and unreflexive, leading to implicit prejudice. Degner and Wentura (2010) found the automatisation of prejudiced attitudes evidenced amongst young adolescents of around 12 and 13 years of age.

A method known as an *implicit association test* (IAT) is often used to detect implicit prejudice. It is based on people's reaction times to paired words. For example, if wishing to detect stereotypes based on skin colour, the words 'black' or 'white' would be paired with both positive and negative words. Participants would then be shown them on a computer screen and asked to respond 'yes' or 'no' to whether they believe that the pairings are meaningful or not.

The response time is the crucial measurement in this procedure. The quicker the response, the more indicative it is of an existing attitude. Research of this nature has indicated that white participants were quicker to associate positive words with the word 'white' than with 'black'. Such responses indicate that, whilst at a conscious level we might think we are not prejudiced, we might automatically hold negative stereotypes towards certain groups.

Points to consider

● Cognitive accounts explain how everyone can be prejudiced – but not sharp rises and falls in prejudice.

● Having implicit prejudiced stereotypical beliefs does not necessarily mean that you will engage in negative behaviour towards the group concerned.

● More sophisticated tools of measurement than self-report scales have been developed.

● Categories are viewed as fixed – others' accounts (e.g., discursive) might see prejudice as more fluid and context-dependent.

● Much emphasis is put on the internal processes, but what about the social information required when constructing such widely shared stereotypes?

Discursive accounts

Is the idea that prejudice and discrimination are a function of perceptual biases and cognitive economy sufficient on its own to explain such belief systems? Discursive psychologists would suggest not, for they argue that language is required in order to jointly construct the meanings and ideas which makeup the categories cognitive psychologists focus on.

According to this perspective, we share a common language through which accounts of the social world are constructed. Our psychological lives are therefore shaped by linguistic resources which allow us to actively formulate versions of social reality. Rather than viewing prejudice as a belief 'in our head', this approach suggests that, via discourse, we perform public practices to give meaning to social relationships in particular contexts. These accounts can serve to provide evidence about how we position certain groups and often seek to legitimise our stance. This can be seen in this extract from Potter and Wetherell's (1987, p. 46) study of middle-class adults in New Zealand.

> I'm not anti them at all you know, I, if they're willing to get on and be like us; but if they're just going to come here, just to be able to use our social welfares and stuff like that, then why don't they stay home?

The participant is discussing Polynesian immigrants and starts with what's known as a *disclaimer*. This verbal device can be used to anticipate or reject possible negative attributions. In this example, stating 'I'm not anti them at all, you know' acts as a disclaimer for the comments which come later about 'why don't they stay home?'

Extreme case formulation is also used, where a claim or statement is taken to its extreme, providing an effective warrant for the speaker. The word 'just', which is repeated twice, is indicative of this here: 'but if they're *just* going to come here, *just* to be able to use our social welfares'. Such linguistic devices allow the participant to blame Polynesian immigrants for not getting on with white New Zealanders yet at the same time protect themselves from any charges of racism.

You will not be surprised to discover that the methods used to research this approach are based on language. Discourse analysis could be of a media account (e.g., analysis of a newspaper's report of a race riot), a political speech on the topic or an interview with someone involved in the riot. Linguistic devices such as those illustrated are identified. Such analysis extends accounts of prejudice further than fixed cognitive categories. Discursive accounts are more flexible and open to change based on the context in which the prejudice is occurring. (Discursive accounts of prejudice are returned to in Chapter 11, Critical social psychology).

Points to consider

- Can account for the role a collective belief system might have in specific situations
- Studies are based on real-life events.
- A subjective account (though many believe psychological research should be an objective endeavour).
- Less individualistic than the other approaches discussed in this chapter.
- Ignores any internal (e.g., cognitive) levels of processing.

Test your knowledge

6.3 Consider which account of prejudice would match these statements:
   (a) An account which indicates a stereotype might be an automatic process.
   (b) An account which considers how the individual speaks about a target population.
   (c) An account which views the type of parenting received as paramount.

6.4 Fill in the table overleaf. This will help you to clarify key points about each approach and be a useful revision tool.

   You do not have to draw exclusively from this chapter – in fact, we would advise you to look further. Some of the comments about methods or perspectives might be generic ones which you are aware of from other areas of your course or social psychology in general. Once completed, some of the points raised might be applicable to other topic areas also covered in this text.

Points to consider about each approach	How does this approach view prejudice?	How would prejudice be researched?	What are the limitations of this explanation of prejudice?	Why is this approach useful?
Personality				
Cognitive				
Discursive				

Answers to these questions can be found at: www.pearsoned.co.uk/psychologyexpress

---

? *Sample question*   *Essay*

Compare and contrast cognitive and discursive accounts of prejudice.

Further reading Explanations of prejudice and discrimination

Topic	Key reading
Prejudice and personality	Kreindler, S. A. (2005). A dual group processes model of individual differences in prejudice. *Personality and Social Psychology Review, 9,* 90–107.
Development of implicit prejudice in children and adolescents	Degner, J., & Wentura, D. (2010). Automatic prejudice in childhood and early adolescence. *Journal of Personality and Social Psychology 98,* 356–374.
A discussion of the discursive approach	Edwards, D. (1991). Categories are for talking: On the cognitive and discursive basis of categorization. *Theory and Psychology, 1,* 515–542.

Reducing prejudice and discrimination

Although specific acts of discrimination are more likely to occur towards individuals (rather than whole groups), prejudiced attitudes towards the individual are based on stereotypes of a group. Subsequently, when it comes to exploring ways of reducing prejudice and discrimination, social psychologists focus on intergroup processes. These processes in themselves represent a large area, so we have been selective in what is covered in this section. Further areas of this book might be relevant to understanding some of the underlying processes (e.g., social identity is covered in Chapter 3 on Self).

The contact hypothesis

A considerable amount of work has focused around the idea of contact, described by Dovidio, Gaertner and Kawamaki (2003, p. 5) as 'one of

psychology's most effective strategies for improving intergroup relations.'
Put simply, contact between groups is essential if we are to reduce prejudice
between them. However, this must not be taken at face value – mere contact
could result in *raising* prejudiced feelings. Lemos (2005) reported survey data
revealing inhabitants of the more multiracial areas of Britain were the most likely
to display negative attitudes towards members of other races. The contact
hypothesis, originally attributed to the work of Allport in his classic 1954 text *The
Nature of Prejudice*, suggests that contact in itself was insufficient for improving
intergroup relations. In order to be effective, certain prerequisites are required
(see Figure 6.2).

Another term which you might encounter is the *realistic group conflict model*.
Based on the social identity theory, this approach suggests that conflicts
occur because groups are seeking to maintain their shared or social identity.
Subsequently, they view their group as an in group and others as out groups.
Turned on its head, though, it suggests that working towards shared goals can
have the opposite effect (as predicted by the contact hypothesis) and allow
a common in group identity to be formed. Such intergroup dynamics were
masterfully illustrated in a series of now classic field experiments by Sherif and
colleagues in the 1950s (see Key Study below).

KEY STUDY

Sherif and Sherif (1953). The summer camp field experiments

A series of field experiments, each lasting three weeks, took place in actual summer
camps (Sherif and Sherif, 1953; Sherif, White & Harvey, 1955). Participants (adolescent
boys) were put into groups, unaware that they were part of a study. Experimenters
(posing as camp workers) observed as the different stages took place: group formation,
intergroup conflict and conflict reduction. Initially, as part of the group formation,
participants were involved in various activities which encouraged them to bond.

In stage two, contests between the groups were staged (such as tug of war), for which
prizes were awarded to the winning group. This introduced competition and with it
came intergroup conflict.

Groups that had initially coexisted became two hostile factions. The out group was
derided and, with meaningless tasks (such as picking up beans in a given time), in
groups tended to overestimate their performance.

Negative intergroup dynamics evolved very quickly (illustrating the flaws in personality
approaches to prejudice).

Stage three of the study involved reducing the hostility which had ensued. Both groups
were forced to engage in tasks which required them to work together for a shared
outcome (e.g., mending a water pipe). By jointly achieving a common goal, harmony
was restored.

Reviewing research on the contact hypothesis, Dovidio et al. (2003) report that
support still remains for the original formulation of the hypothesis. In addition, two
further concepts have been identified as critical for optimising intergroup contact:

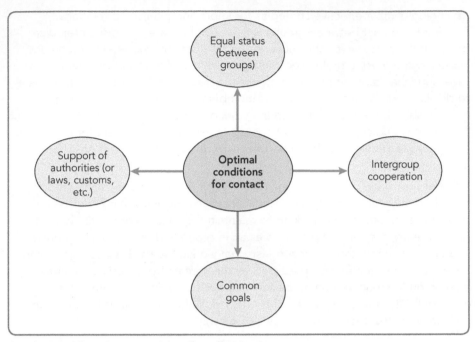

Figure 6.2 Allport's prerequisites for effective intergroup contact

- **personal acquaintances with out group members** – this can allow personalisation to occur.
- **developing intergroup friendships** – having a friend who is an out group member has been shown to reduce intergroup bias.

Such prerequisites tell us little about why these optimal conditions seem to work. Some critics have described them as a loosely connected list.

To address this, Dovidio offers accounts of the mediating mechanisms involved in contact. These mechanisms act to provide a unifying framework for many of the prerequisites, as well as a more comprehensive account around which to identify why conditions of optimal contact may (and may not!) be effective.

Pettigrew and Tropp (2008) identified the three most widely studied mediators of prejudice reduction by contact as:

- enhanced knowledge of the out group
- reduced anxiety about intergroup contact
- increased empathy and perspective.

Their meta-analysis of over 500 studies revealed that all three have positive mediational effects, but enhanced knowledge seems to be less strong than the other two mediators. A previous meta-analysis by the same authors in 2006 considered the general literature on contact (Pettigrew & Tropp, 2006). Like the study presented, it concluded that intergroup contact reduces intergroup

Table 6.2 **The mediating mechanisms of contact**

Functional relations	Behavioural factors
Focus: Cooperative interdependence as a mediator for attitudinal and behaviour and change	**Focus:** Group interaction has been seen as a form of behaviour modification. Can lead to the development of new norms
How does this mediate? When positive interdependence equates to cooperation. Favourable outcomes will be beneficial to both groups. Negative inter group attitudes reduced If interdependence is negative, it leads to competition. Unfavourable attitudes likely to be generated	**How does this mediate?** A favourable encounter leads to cognitive dissonance and need to rebalance our (previously negative) views of the out group. The new views lead to an acceptance of the out group which may be generalised to new situations and attitudes towards the group as a whole
Affective	Cognitive
Focus: The emotions expressed towards out groups	**Focus:** How we learn new information about the group and how this is represented
How does this mediate? Emotions such as empathy, likely to feel more positive towards the out group and motivated to help or be supportive of them Negative emotion often associated with intergroup bias is anxiety. Can cause distrust of the out group and *strengthen* stereotypes. Reducing anxiety identified as critical for enhancing intergroup contact	**How does this mediate?** Intergroup contact can enhance our knowledge about out group members, seeing them in individuated and personalised ways. Greater knowledge can also lead to less uncertainty about appropriate ways of interacting with the group

prejudice. Such reviews provide compelling evidence that, after more than 50 years of research, the contact hypothesis remains a robust idea.

Turner and Crisp (2010) have also presented evidence that imagining intergroup contact can contribute to reductions in implicit prejudice too.

A critique of the contact hypothesis

Not all social psychologists find the contact hypothesis the answer to reducing intergroup conflict. Dixon, Durkheim and Tredoux (2005) raise the following points:

- Is the literature detached from real-life scenarios in divided societies?
- Findings are based largely on short-lived laboratory manipulations or very localised interventions in the field.
- Is the idea that optimal conditions exist in everyday life a utopian position?
- Might the wider power structures which exist make optimal conditions such as cooperative interdependence difficult to implement?
- Is this perspective powerful enough to account for social change in areas where racial hatred and inequality are deeply embedded and part of the wider historical and political makeup of a society?

This critique also mirrors some of the limitations that critical social psychologists (see Chapter 11, Critical social psychology) have raised in relation to mainstream approaches.

Test your knowledge

6.5 Identify where Allport's prerequisites for successful contact can be observed in Sherif's summer camp studies.

6.6 Describe two of the mediating mechanisms used to explain why intergroup contact is effective.

6.7 If it were not possible for actual contact to take place, how else might psychologists try to reduce prejudicial attitudes towards an out group?

Answers to these questions can be found at: www.pearsoned.co.uk/psychologyexpress

---

? Sample question   *Essay*

Due to spending cuts, two small rural schools have been forced to amalgamate into one. However, teachers have experienced some conflict in the classroom between pupils from the former different schools. How might research on intergroup contact inform them about ways to reduce this conflict?

Further reading Reducing prejudice and discrimination

Topic	Key reading
A comprehensive review of research on contact	Dovidio, J. F., Gaertner, S., & Kawamaki, K. (2003). Intergroup conflict: The past, present, and future. *Group Processes and Intergroup Relationships, 6,* 5–20.
Studies on imagined contact	Turner, R. N., & Crisp, R. J. (2010). Imagining intergroup contact reduces implicit prejudice. *British Journal of Social Psychology, 49*(1) 129–142.
A critique of the contact hypothesis	Dixon, J. A., Durkheim, K., & Tredoux, C. (2005). Beyond the optimal strategy: A reality check for the contact hypothesis. *American Psychologist, 60,* 697–711.

✳ Sample question   *Problem-based learning*

A press article entitled 'Thugs rampage on the elderly' outlined how a group of youngsters had vandalised a daycare centre on an inner-city housing estate. It was thought that some of those attending the centre had previously complained to the police about the antisocial behaviour exhibited by the group of youths. The group took revenge by breaking into the centre, damaging equipment and spray-painting ageist graffiti on the walls. You have been asked to appear on a current affairs programme to provide a psychologist's view of why this might have happened and what the community might do to reduce the ensuing rift which has occurred between the two generations. Drawing on the evidence provided in this chapter, write a script of what you might say.

Chapter summary – pulling it all together

→ Can you tick all the points from the revision checklist at the beginning of this chapter?

→ Attempt the sample question from the beginning of this chapter using the answer guidelines below.

→ Go to the companion website at www.pearsoned.co.uk/psychologyexpress to access more revision support online, including interactive quizzes, flashcards, You be the marker exercises as well as answer guidance for the Test your knowledge and Sample questions from this chapter.

Further reading for Chapter 6

Brown, R. (2010). *Prejudice: Its social psychology.* Oxford: Wiley-Blackwell.

Whitley, B. E. Jr., & Kite, M. E. (Eds.) (2006). *The psychology of prejudice and discrimination.* Belmont, CA: Thompson-Wadsworth.

Potter, J. & Wetherell, M. (1987). *Discourse and social psychology: Beyond attitudes and behaviour.* London: Sage. (A discursive account.)

Answer guidelines

✱ Sample question   Essay

Criticaly consider the accounts offered by social psychologists to explain the origins of prejudice.

Approaching the question

There are two key components to this question: to identify the accounts offered for explaining prejudice; to critique these accounts. In order to address the whole question, make sure that you have not just outlined the different approaches. You may want to define terms, perhaps discussing the relationship between prejudice and discrimination, but essentially the bulk of the essay needs to be on the actual accounts. You need to be clear which approaches you intend to include and identify evaluatory points which can both illustrate ways in which these approaches are useful and where their limitations might be. The table you were asked to complete earlier in this chapter for Test your knowledge question 6.3 should act as a useful aid for this essay.

Important points to include

This is potentially a wide question and there is a danger that you might try to cover too much information. Note that the question is not asking you to discuss what can be done about prejudice, simply what its origins might be. Remember the idea of thinking of the topic in terms of 'What?' (is it), 'Why?' (it occurs) and 'How?' (might it be reduced) introduced in the Assessment advice at the beginning of this chapter? This essay is essentially the why! Examiners will not expect you to cover every account which has ever been offered. They will want to see succinct summaries of the approaches you have clearly identified as providing an explanation for why prejudice might occur. As always, these need to be supported with evidence.

Consider how many different accounts would be a sensible number to cover in a set time in an exam or within a specific word count for an essay. Whilst there is no definite figure for this, we would suggest that attempting more than three different perspectives might be a bit much. Try to avoid describing one, then offering a few evaluatory points, then the next and continuing in that vein. Whilst much of the relevant information might be covered, the structure would be a little formulaic and list-like. Are there some common dimensions of evaluation around which you can structure the essay and discuss in relation to each account you provide? See below for some suggestions. You might be able to think of others.

> **Make your answer stand out**
>
> *Consider areas which might provide an evaluatory framework for this essay. You could, for example, structure your essay around mainstream and critical approaches, within which discussions could ensue about the different methods which would be used and the different types of knowledge about the topic would be presented. What about a chronological account? It is always important to locate social psychology historically and the ideas which were being written in the post-war period about authoritarianism and personality constrast somewhat with the ideas offered in more contemporary social psychology.*

> Explore the accompanying website at www.pearsoned.co.uk/psychologyexpress
> → Prepare more effectively for exams and assignments using the answer guidelines for questions from this chapter.
> → Test your knowledge using multiple choice questions and flashcards.
> → Improve your essay skills by exploring the You be the marker exercises.

Notes

Notes

Prosocial behaviour

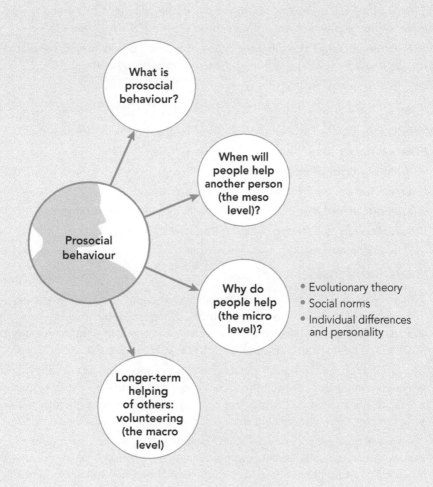

What is prosocial behaviour?

When will people help another person (the meso level)?

Prosocial behaviour

Why do people help (the micro level)?
- Evolutionary theory
- Social norms
- Individual differences and personality

Longer-term helping of others: volunteering (the macro level)

A printable version of this topic map is available from:
www.pearsoned.co.uk/psychologyexpress

Introduction

This chapter explores the field of prosocial behaviour – a term which, in its broadest sense, refers to behaviour involving helping others. There are many different types of situations this could cover – for instance, rescuing someone in an emergency situation to giving money to a charity for a country devastated by a natural disaster.

The literature on this topic is also wide, ranging from factors about the situation which might affect our willingness to help to evolutionary theories suggesting that helping behaviour may be genetically determined. The key areas of psychological research are the situational determinants of prosocial behaviour (or, in other words, questions about *when* people will help) and reasons *why* people might help (which encompass more theoretical explanations).

This chapter considers the different types of helping behaviour, the explanations for them and why some people might help long-term by engaging in volunteering.

→ Revision checklist

Essential points to revise are:
- ❏ What the term *prosocial behaviour* means
- ❏ Which factors might influence helping behaviour
- ❏ Theoretical and empirical evidence for why people help others
- ❏ Volunteering as a form of helping behaviour

Assessment advice

- As you read this chapter, you might notice that some information appears in other areas of the book, too. For example, Chapter 8, Antisocial behaviour, will discuss aggression, where some of the same theories are used as explanations. Evolutionary theory also appears in Chapter 9, Interpersonal attraction.

- The basic theories, limitations and strengths are the same so there is no reason why you cannot use some of the same information and apply it to both topic areas. This will facilitate a wider use of the points you might elect to revise, whilst at the same time allowing for a more succinct set of revision notes.

- The research on prosocial behaviour is dominated by social cognitive decision-making accounts, evolutionary and personality perspectives. When considering these different accounts, remember rarely does one offer an explanation of the phenomenon in its entirety. Some accounts may be incompatible with each other, although it is more likely that the ideas can be applied to explain different aspects of the same process. The tasks and essay questions are designed to help you establish reasoned arguments about each of the different areas.

Sample question

Could you answer this question? Below is a typical essay that could arise on this topic.

✳ *Sample question*   *Essay*

To what extent has social psychological research furthered our understanding of prosocial behaviour? Discuss with reference to empirical evidence and theoretical explanations.

Guidelines on answering this question are included at the end of this chapter, whilst further guidance on tackling other exam questions can be found on the companion website at: www.pearsoned.co.uk/psychologyexpress

What is prosocial behaviour?

Whilst helping behaviour encompasses prosocial acts, there are some specific terms used which you should be aware of. Penner, Dovidio, Piliavin and Schroeder (2005, p. 366) note that the term *prosocial*, 'represents a broad category of acts that are defined by some significant segment of society and/ or one's social group as generally beneficial to other people.' They divide the literature in this area into the three categories, outlined in Figure 7.1.

A term which you will come across in many textbooks is *altruism*. This refers to unselfish acts of helping behaviour motivated by a desire to benefit another person. Although the terms altruism and prosocial are often used

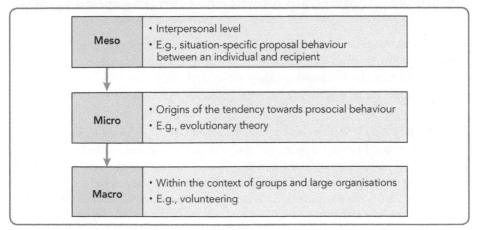

Figure 7.1 **Categories of prosocial literature**
Source: after Penner et al. (2005)

interchangeably, they are not the same: prosocial behaviour could include being rewarded for helping, whereas altruism describes the prosocial act as an end in itself, with no benefit to the altruist.

Test your knowledge

7.1 Which of the statements could be considered as prosocial behaviour and which could be considered altruism?

(a) Jumping into a cold river to help a stranger who had fallen in and was struggling to swim against the current.

(b) Donating money to a charity because you want to help, but also because it makes you feel good.

(c) Walking to work and stopping to help someone in distress who had lost their dog. This act will make you late for work.

7.2 Match the examples with Penner et al.'s (2005) levels of prosocial behaviour.

(a) Learning prosocial behaviour from modelling parental behaviour.

(b) Spending summer holidays while at university working for a voluntary organisation driving a lorry with aid to developing countries. You do not get paid for this.

(c) Describing the decision-making process involved in helping an elderly lady who had fallen over in a quiet lane.

Answers to these questions can be found on the companion website at: www.pearsoned.co.uk/psychologyexpress

---

When will people help another person (the meso level)?

Ironically, the original impetus for work on prosocial behaviour came from situations where people did *not* help. The killing of Kitty Genovese in New York in 1964 was the landmark incident which led Latané and Darley to seek an explanation for why so many became unresponsive bystanders to this brutal murder.

Their classic study (1968) involved male students being exposed to another student (a stooge) having a seizure and choking. Participants in different experimental conditions thought that they were either the only person aware of this mock emergency or one of two or five bystanders. They could communicate with others via an intercom. Helpfulness was measured both in terms of whether or not they attempted to get help and time elapsed before doing so.

The researchers hypothesised that the more bystanders there were, the longer the time it would take to respond and the less likely an individual would be to respond. The hypothesis was supported, and the idea of diffusion of responsibility now had empirical evidence. This has become known as the *bystander effect*.

Whilst media reports, such as that after the Kitty Genovese murder, are often quick to label unresponsive bystanders as callous, evil people, Latané and Darley's groundbreaking research indicated that *anyone* has the potential to walk on by. They developed a model to explain the decision-making processes which may occur in an emergency situation. The five stages, or choice points, are summarised in Table 7.1.

Further factors that can inhibit or enhance prosocial behaviour have been identified, including the following.

● **Who needs help.** If it is a friend or stranger we are quicker to help a friend.

● **Similarity.** We are more likely to help someone who we perceive to be similar to us – e.g., in terms of race, gender, dress.

● **Attribution of the cause of the distress.** If someone is perceived to be personally responsible for an incident (e.g., a drunk who has fallen in the

Table 7.1 The stages of decision making involved in Latané and Darley's (1968) model

The five stages (each is required for help to occur)	Possible outcome which could lead to bystander apathy
Stage 1 Notice something is happening	We might quite simply not notice the emergency situation. If someone is otherwise preoccupied, little help is likely to be given
Stage 2 Interpret the event as an emergency	We may have limited information about the situation, but have to make a decision about whether or not intervention is required. If there are others present, we may look to them for cues. However, if they do not know what is happening, pluralistic ignorance can occur, where no one does anything. This explains why more people can inhibit helping behaviour
Stage 3 Decide it is your responsibility to help	Unless you are a lone bystander (and therefore more likely to help) whose responsibility it is to help might not be clear. Typically, people perceived as being in leadership roles (e.g., a lecturer with students) or qualified for the task (e.g., someone thought to have medical training) are expected to take the lead
Stage 4 Decide that you have the necessary attributes to help	We need to know how to help. Even if we progress past Stage 3, we might not assume responsibility if we felt that we did not have the necessary knowledge or skills to help
Stage 5 Make a final decision to provide help	The final decision to engage in helping behaviour takes place here. We can still be inhibited at this final stage, though, by potential negative consequences. Fritsche, Finkelstein and Penner (2000) use the term *cognitive alegebra* to describe the process of weighing up the negative and positive aspects of helping which can occur

street as opposed to an elderly woman who has slipped on ice), we are less likely to help.

- **Alcohol.** Seems to reduce the anxiety about others' reactions, so we are less likely to be looking to them for cues. Consequently, when people have been drinking, they show an increased tendency to help.

- **Weighing up the costs and benefits.** As part of the decision-making process, it has been suggested that individuals weigh up the perceived cost helping will incur for them (e.g., time) against the perceived cost of not helping (e.g., feeling guilty). We will choose the response which incurs the smallest net cost, so are more likely to help if personal costs are low and the costs of not helping are high.

More recent studies have sought to establish if cognitively priming participants to think about the presence of others can also inhibit helping behaviour. This is known as an *implicit bystander effect*.

KEY STUDY

Garcia, Weaver, Moskowitz and Darley (2002). Do people need to be present for bystander apathy to occur (the implicit bystander effect)?

In a series of experiments, Garcia et al. (2002) hypothesised that priming the presence of others at an initial point will then affect behaviour on another unrelated task (even though the primed 'bystanders' could not play any direct role in the second task).

Students were asked to complete a two-page questionnaire. In the first condition, they were instructed to imagine that they had won a meal for themselves and 30 friends at a restaurant. Condition two cited that same prize, but in the presence of only 10 friends, whilst the control condition was a meal with one other. This was the primer.

Embedded in the later parts of the questionnaire were questions about what percentage of their earnings they would be prepared to give to charity once they had graduated and were working. They were given options ranging from less than 1 per cent to over 25 per cent.

Findings revealed that participants who had been primed to consider their meal in front of 30 friends stated that they would give less money to charity than those in the presence of 10, with the diners with only 1 person pledging to give more. It seems that the bystander effect was present here.

The intriguing thing about this study is that the dependent variable (amount given to charity) bore no relationship to the meal scenario. Also, the bystanders did not need to be physically present or even connected to the task for the diffusion of responsibility effect to occur.

Further studies sought to establish the psychological processes behind this effect. It is suggested imagining being in a group leads to lower levels of responsibility. Measured reaction times revealed that when participants imagined themselves in the social context of a group, they were quicker to react to the word 'unaccountable' than those in the control or one-person condition. People in a group may have associated notions of unaccountability which lead them to feel less responsible. Perhaps group stereotypes are at work here (refer to Chapter 6, Prejudice and discrimination, for evidence of implicit stereotyping).

▶

CRITICAL FOCUS

Bystander studies

As always, it is important that you maintain a critical edge when considering the research evidence provided for this topic. Here are some points you might wish to consider:

These studies are often based on students. How far can we generalise from such populations?

Look at the design of the Garcia et al. study in the Key Study above. One of the scenarios was to ask students about how much of their pay they would give to charity. This was a hypothetical question, the students did not have full-time jobs and were being asked to make a prediction about something in the future which had no consequences for them – they were not going to have to contribute any money to charity.

Giving to charity is also a very specific type of prosocial behaviour. Can findings from such scenarios be used to account for prosocial behaviour if an individual has fallen in the street, for instance?

Are there any alternative ways in which bystander behaviour could be researched? It is very hard to observe an *actual* bystander situation for a piece of research, so setting up a scenario is often a necessary part of such research. In a rare naturalistic study, Thornberg (2007) used an ethnographic approach to observe how children in a classroom reacted to a real-life situation in which a classmate was lying on the floor holding his arm and crying in pain. As this was a qualitative approach, the researcher did not set out to find evidence for a hypothesis. Instead, he observed the event and then explored the children's reasoning for either helping or not helping via individual interviews with them. Here, the findings were grounded initially in the accounts of the participants, representing a more inductive approach that that of an experiment. The findings are applied to the bystander literature towards the end of the research process. Whilst this has much higher ecological validity than an experiment, the method can only tap into their *conscious* accounts. *Implicit* accounts, such as those outlined in Garcia et al.'s study, are often automatic and *not* conscious.

These two studies offer accounts of different levels of human functioning. It is important to remember this when weighing up the relative merits of different studies. One is not necessarily better than the other – they ask and answer different questions about the topic and, consequently, have contrasting strengths and limitations.

Test your knowledge

7.3 Based on Latané and Darley's model, identify three points in the decision-making process which would inhibit helping in an emergency situation.

7.4 List four factors which could account for bystander apathy.

7.5 Explain how the implicit bystander effect might impact helping behaviour.

Answers to these questions can be found on the companion website at: www.pearsoned.co.uk/psychologyexpress

> ### ? Sample question   *Essay*
>
> Today's altruist could be tomorrow's bystander. Discuss.

Further reading When people help

Topic	Key reading
The classic paper on the bystander effect	Latané, B., & Darley, J. M. (1968). Group inhibition of bystander intervention in emergencies. *Journal of Personality and Social Psychology, 10*, 215–221.
More recent bystander paper	Fischer, P., Greitemeyer, T., Pollozek, F., & Frey, D. (2006). The unresponsive bystander: Are bystanders more responsive in dangerous emergencies? *European Journal of Social Psychology, 36*, 267–278.
An exploration of decision-making processes involved in helping	Fritsche, B. A., Finkelstein, M. A., & Penner, L. A. (2000). To help or not to help: Capturing individuals' decision policies. *Social Behaviour and Personality, 28*, 561–578.
Implicit bystander effect	Garcia, S. M., Weaver, K., Moskowitz, G. B., & Darley, J. M. (2002). Crowded minds: The implicit bystander effect. *Journal of Personality and Social Psychology, 83*, 843–853.
Qualitative study of accounts of bystander apathy	Thornberg, R. (2007). A classmate in distress: Schoolchildren as bystanders and their reasons for how they act. *Social Psychology of Education, 10*, 5–28.

Why do people help (the micro level)?

The previous section focused on determinants of the situation which influence *when* individuals might help. Another area of the literature – the macro level – has sought to provide theoretical accounts of *why* people help

Evolutionary theory

This approach contends that we are biologically predisposed to help those who share our genes. A parent will act altruistically if their child is in danger in order to facilitate species survival. We can increase the likelihood of our genes surviving if we act in ways to ensure the survival of our relatives. This is known as *inclusive fitness* (*direct fitness* being the procreation of offspring). Accounts of this approach appear in relation to other topics in this book (e.g., aggression, relationships).

Points to consider

● Why do people help in some situations and not others? Evolutionary theory would predict that we will selflessly help blood relatives.

- People help individuals other than family members – *evolutionary inclusive fitness* can not account for this.

- *Reciprocal altruism* could offer an explanation for both these. This is the idea that individuals will help each other if they feel the favour will be repaid in the future.

- Evolutionary theory has been criticised for failing to offer accounts of some kinds of helping we typically see in humans – e.g., giving to beggars, donating blood.

- However, Darwin's theory of *sexual selection* could apply. This suggests that we show a preference for certain traits in potential mates. Altruism is an example because it may be associated with positive qualities such as generosity, being kind and also having resources. Therefore, displays of seemingly altruistic behaviour could be a useful strategy for attracting a mate.

Social norms

Whilst evolutionary theorists view reciprocity as part of a shared genetic makeup, Gouldner (1960) suggests that the norm of reciprocity is a shared cultural norm. A more social psychological account of helping behaviour is to view it as a *social norm*.

As the name suggests, a social norm is a belief or type of behaviour which is considered normal and acceptable in a given group or society. Through socialisation processes, it becomes an internally held normative belief which can have a powerful effect on how we behave.

Points to consider

- Berkowitz (1972) noted that some people will help others in need *even* when they remain anonymous, so are not expecting praise or gratitude from others. This provides a contrast to evolutionary accounts and relates to the norm of *social responsibility* – the idea that helping others is something we *should* do, not be dependent on future reciprocity or whether or not the individual has helped us.

- Such a norm would suggest that potentially we would help anyone, but other research into attributions suggests not. A social cognitive explanation for this is the 'just world' hypothesis (see Chapter 2, Attribution theory). Lerner and Miller (1978) identified a heuristic tendency amongst individuals to believe that generally the world was just and fair. In order to protect this belief, we would also need to believe that good things happen to good people and bad things to bad people. Thus, we might be more likely to donate to a breast cancer charity (if we viewed sufferers as playing no role in developing the disease) than one for alcohol abuse (if we felt that the individuals' lifestyles impacted their situation).

- 'Just world' beliefs suggest that we might have a *fairness norm*, which affects the way in which we judge others' need for help and weigh up the costs to ourselves. If the perceived outcome of helping does not match up to our own standard of fairness, we are said to be *egoistically* motivated, rather than *altruistically*.

Individual differences and personality

This approach seeks to identify personality dispositions which might predict why some people are more helpful than others. Longitudinal data indicates that children who display prosocial tendencies early in life behave similarly in adolescence. Such dispositions are therefore considered relatively stable over time (Eisenberg et al., 2002).

Is there an altruistic personality?

Specific personality dispositions have been associated with prosocial behaviour.

Bierhoff, Klein and Kramp (1991) asked participants who had intervened in a traffic accident to complete a questionnaire containing personality dispositions which they felt may be relevant to such behaviour. A matched control of individuals who had observed but not intervened also completed the same task.

From their findings, they identified a combination of five dispositions associated with those who displayed prosocial behaviour:

- empathy
- belief in a just world
- social responsibility
- internal locus of control
- low egocentrism.

Data such as Bierhoff et al.'s is correlational. The authors are not claiming that having such dispositions will *cause* one to intervene in an emergency (correlation does not predict causality).

General predispositions were measured, which they then applied to a specific situation. There appeared to be a relationship between them. Is it appropriate to call this an altruistic personality? Will the participants also help in a host of other situations?

Empathy – 'A complex affective and cognitive response to another person's emotional distress' (Baron, Byrne & Branscome, 2007, p. 286) – has been widely associated with prosocial behaviour.

- The *affective* component has been identified as feeling distressed yourself when others are distressed and feeling sympathy and concern for the person, such that you wish to try to alleviate the distress.
- The *cognitive* component refers to an ability to consider the other person's viewpoint, often referred to as 'perspective taking'.

Empirical evidence for empathy comes from different sources. See Table 7.2.

Table 7.2 **Explanations for individual differences and empathy**

Biological	Biological differences are considered to account for around a third of the variation in affective empathy. Davis, Luce and Kraus (1994) found such evidence for hereditary effects on the *affective* components of empathy (personal distress and sympathetic concern). Their study, based on over 800 pairs of identical and non-identical twins, indicated no such influence for *cognitive* empathy.
Socialisation	We may be born with the capacity for empathy, but socialisation experiences could determine if this becomes a central component of ourselves. Studies reveal that highly empathic children have mothers who are empathic, good perspective takers, warm and comforting (e.g., Eisenberg, Fabes, Guthrie & Reiser 2000).
Motivation	Batson highlights empathy as a motivation for altruism. He distinguishes between *egoistically* motivated helping (which serves to benefit the helper) and altruistically motivated helping (the focus of which is the individual in need). The empathy altruism hypothesis links *altruistically* motivated helping with empathic concern. Experimental evidence indicates that participants who experience this affective state, rather than personal distress, are more likely to help a person in need (Bierhoff & Rohmann, 2004).

Test your knowledge

7.6 Describe accounts of reciprocal altruism offered from evolutionary and social norm perspectives.

7.7 Identify three personality dispositions which seem to correlate with prosocial behaviour.

7.8 Bierhoff et al.'s study found a correlation between helping behaviour in a traffic emergency and personality dispositions. What other reasons identified by psychologists might account for the behaviour demonstrated?

Answers to these questions can be found on the companion website at: www.pearsoned.co.uk/psychologyexpress

? Sample question   Essay

Compare and contrast the different psychological accounts of the origins of helping behaviour.

Further reading Why people help

Topic	Key reading
Evolutionary account of altruism and mate selection	Farrelly, D., Lazarus, J. & Roberts, G. (2007). Altruists attract. *Evolutionary Psychology*, 5, 313–329.

▶

Longitudinal research of personality dispositions	Eisenberg, N., Guthrie, I. K., Cumberland, A., Murphy, B. C., Shephard, S. A., Zhou, Q., & Carlo, G. (2002). Prosocial development in early adulthood: A longitudinal study. *Journal of Personality and Social Psychology, 82*, 993–1005.
Personality dispositions and intervention in *emergency situations*	Bierhoff, H. W., Klein, R., & Kramp., P. (1991). Evidence for the altruistic personality from data on accident research. *Journal of Personality, 59*, 263–280.
Genetic influences on empathy	Davis, M. H., Luce, C., & Kraus, S. J. (1994). The heritability of characteristics associated with dispositional empathy. *Journal of Personality, 62*, 369–391.
Empathy–altruism hypothesis	Bierhoff, H. W., & Rohmann, E. (2004). Altruistic personality in the context of the empathy–altruism hypothesis. *European Journal of Personality, 18*, 351–365.

Longer-term helping of others: volunteering (the macro level)

The majority of research covered in textbooks focuses on helping behaviour in one-off situations, such as intervening in an emergency (sometimes referred to as *spontaneous helping*), which can be reactive and automatic. Volunteering may be a different type of helping behaviour. It is planned, typically longer-term and considered less likely to be due to a sense of personal obligation.

Psychologists have sought to understand individuals' motivations for volunteering and the function such a role might play. Clary et al. (1998) developed the volunteering functions inventory (VFI). Six dimensions describe the functions volunteering fulfils, as shown in Table 7.3.

Table 7.3 The functions of volunteering measured in the volunteering functions inventory

Function	Definition
Values	To express or act on important values (e.g., humanitarianism)
Understanding	To learn more about the world or exercise skills that are often not used
Inventory enhancement	To grow and develop psychologically (by engaging in volunteering activities)
Social	To strengthen social relationships
Career	To gain career-related experience
Protective	To reduce negative feelings (e.g., guilt, loneliness) or to address personal problems

Matsuba, Hart and Atkins (2007) offer an integrative model of both psychological and social influences on people's commitment to volunteering. They differentiated between *enduring influences* (i.e., personality and socio-economic, cultural and demographic factors) and *mediating influences* (i.e., moral cognition, moral identity and social opportunity).

Their analytic survey of a large cross-sectional sample of American adults found higher levels of commitment was a combination of enduring factors (in this study, resilience as a personality trait, being older and more highly educated) mediated by the more malleable constructs of moral cognition, high helping identity salience and opportunities to volunteer.

Other factors which have been identified in relation to volunteering are the following.

- *Demographics*. Research indicates that women, older individuals and those who are more highly educated are likely to devote more hours to volunteering. However, women are more likely to display empathy and therefore have the traits associated with prosocial behaviour. Older people are more likely to have time to spare and the more highly educated are more likely to be members of groups, etc., which, the model suggests, are predictive of volunteer behaviour.

- *Personality*. As with research on the development of prosocial behaviour, a cluster of personality dispositions have been found to play a role in the decision to volunteer. These include empathy. Dispositional empathy has also been associated with a willingness to take part in certain volunteer activities.

- *Genetic component*. Son and Wilson's (2010) paper, based on data from over 500 sets of twins, is the first to find evidence for a genetic component for the transmission of prosocial behaviour in women. Gender differences in the heritability of aggression have long been suggested, so this might not be a surprising finding. However, it is probable that genes *encourage* the expression of personality traits such as empathy rather than there being a direct link between genes and helping behaviour.

In summary, this research indicates that volunteering is multiply motivated and different people might have different motivations for becoming volunteers.

Test your knowledge

7.9 Identify three ways in which volunteering might be different from the spontaneous helping behaviour noted in studies such as the bystander research.

7.10 Research seems to indicate that people might have different motivations for volunteering. What might these motivations be?

7.11 Who would we predict would be more likely to volunteer?

Answers to these questions can be found on the companion website at: www.pearsoned.co.uk/psychologyexpress

? *Sample question* *Essay*

Boris is 67 years of age and has been a volunteer for a charity for a couple of years – since he retired from his job as a teacher. The role involves working in the shop two mornings a week and sometimes standing in the foyer of a local supermarket with a tin to collect money for the charity. What can research on volunteering tell us about the possible reasons why Boris might engage in such work?

Further reading Volunteering

Topic	Key reading
Integrative approach to commitment to volunteering	Matsuba, M. K., Hart, D., & Atkins, R. (2007). Psychological and social–structural influences on commitment to volunteering. *Journal of Research in Personality, 41,* 889–907.
Genetic evidence	Son, J., & Wilson, J. (2010). Genetic variation in volunteerism. *The Sociological Quarterly, 51,* 46–64.
Motivations for volunteering	Clary, E. G., Snyder, M., Ridge, R. D., Copeland, J., Stukas, A. A., Hangen, J., & Miene, P. (1998). Understanding and assessing the motivations of volunteers: A functional approach. *Journal of Personality and Social Psychology, 74,* 1516–1530.

? *Sample question* *Problem-based learning*

A violent incident has taken place in broad daylight in a busy inner-city shopping centre. A young woman has been seriously injured and her handbag stolen. She was knocked to the floor, kicked and punched in an attack that lasted for a few minutes. There were many people in the vicinity at the time, but nobody intervened to try to stop the attacker. The newspapers have run headlines such as 'Heartless Shoppers Watch as Woman is Attacked' and 'Does Nobody Care About Others Any More?' You wish to write a letter to a newspaper highlighting some of the social psychological literature which can help us understand why people might not have intervened and that it does not necessarily mean people are uncaring. Identify some key points around which you will base your argument.

Chapter summary – pulling it all together

→ Can you tick all the points from the revision checklist at the beginning of this chapter?

→ Attempt the sample question from the beginning of this chapter using the answer guidelines below.

→ Go to the companion website at www.pearsoned.co.uk/psychologyexpress to access more revision support online, including interactive quizzes, flashcards, You be the marker exercises as well as answer guidance for the Test your knowledge and Sample questions from this chapter.

Further reading for Chapter 7

Dovidio, J. F., Piliavin, J. A., Schroeder, D. A., & Penner, L. A. (2006). *The social psychology of prosocial behaviour*. New York: Psychology Press.

Penner, L. A., Dovidio, J. F., Piliavin, J. A., & Schroeder, P. A. (2005). Prosocial behavior: Multi-level perspectives. *Annual Review of Psychology*, 56, 365–392.

Answer guidelines

✳ *Sample question*   *Essay*

To what extent has social psychological research furthered our understanding of prosocial behaviour? Discuss with reference to empirical evidence and theoretical explanations.

Approaching the question

This is a very broad question which potentially could encompass all the material covered in this chapter. Clearly that would not be feasible so you will need to decide which aspects of the evidence about prosocial behaviour you wish to use as illustrative evidence. We suggest that you do this initially, rather than start writing all you know and find that you run out of space. A mindmap could be a helpful aid to summarise the key information and select the areas to discuss.

'Discuss' is the term used in the question. In order to address this you will need to go further than outlining the evidence. Make sure that the relative strengths and limitations are accounted for, as well as highlighting what that specific evidence reveals. For instance, evolutionary approaches offer explanations of the origins of prosocial behaviour (why people help), whilst Latané and Darley's decision model accounts for situational determinants (when people help).

Explicitly stating such aspects could help you to structure your essay, but also indicate that you understand what the evidence tells us about the topic area.

Important points to include

Note that the question asks for both empirical *and* theoretical evidence, so make sure both of these appear. The more theoretical evidence tends to appear at the micro-level explanations drawn from approaches such as personality and evolution. These tell us less about the situational determinants, which is where the bystander research comes into its own. Whilst there is not a single way to answer this question, the examiner would expect to see evidence from both these levels of analysis in order to provide a rounded essay.

It is important that you address the specific question asked, which is 'to what extent'. A good tip is to use this actual phrasing in the conclusion when summing up your main arguments. Again, this could help your structure, whilst providing a tight focus on the set question.

Essentially, the research in this area aids an understanding of the many factors which might both constrain and enhance helping behaviour. This is important knowledge as inhibition of prosocial behaviour can constitute a serious social problem. However, as with any social psychological topic, one perspective cannot provide all the answers and this question gives you the opportunity to illustrate this. It might be worth noting also that prosocial behaviour comes in many forms and some approaches might be better suited to explaining certain types – e.g., an emergency situation – than others.

Make your answer stand out

Penner et al.'s (2005) paper offers a comprehensive summary, based around the three levels of analysis outlined earlier in this chapter. Acknowledging that such different levels of analysis exist and structuring your essay around them is a good way to tackle such a broad question. This will indicate a wide knowledge of the field. However, it will require very concise and precise writing skills in order to cover all aspects.

*Alternatively, tackling the question from the viewpoint that the literature focuses on **why** people help and **when** people help also provides a clear account of the core aspects of this field of research. This chapter has been structured around both these approaches in order to help you to classify the information available and make your answer stand out.*

Explore the accompanying website at www.pearsoned.co.uk/psychologyexpress

→ Prepare more effectively for exams and assignments using the answer guidelines for questions from this chapter.

→ Test your knowledge using multiple choice questions and flashcards.

→ Improve your essay skills by exploring the You be the marker exercises.

Notes

Notes

8

Antisocial behaviour

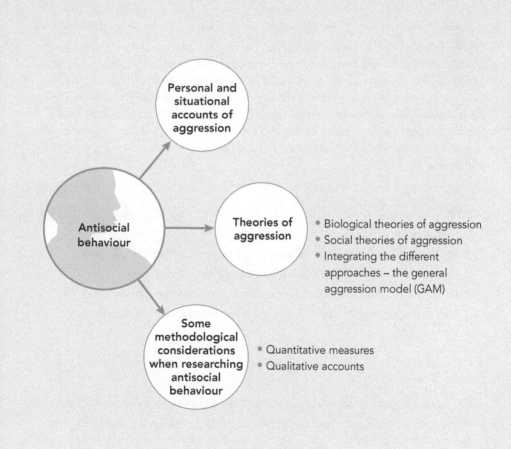

Personal and situational accounts of aggression

Antisocial behaviour

Theories of aggression
- Biological theories of aggression
- Social theories of aggression
- Integrating the different approaches – the general aggression model (GAM)

Some methodological considerations when researching antisocial behaviour
- Quantitative measures
- Qualitative accounts

A printable version of this topic map is available from:
www.pearsoned.co.uk/psychologyexpress

Introduction

The focus of this chapter is antisocial behaviour. Essentially, when psychologists use this term they are referring to aggression. Aggression is defined as 'any form of behaviour directed toward the goal of harming or injuring another living being who is motivated to avoid such treatment' (Baron & Richardson, 1994, p. 7). This definition covers a host of different types of aggressive behaviour, both verbal and physical. An important point to note is the *intention* to harm, even if harm does not actually take place.

You will find distinctions made by some researchers between *instrumental* and *hostile aggression*. Instrumental refers to aggression for a specific goal – e.g., taking someone hostage for a ransom, shooting someone in a war. Hostile aggression is motivated by a perpetrator's desire to vent negative feeling towards the target – e.g., feeling anger and shouting insults at another person.

Within this chapter, variables within the person and the situation which have been identified as influencing aggressive behaviour will be identified. Theories which have been suggested to account for aggression will also be discussed. Finally, we will raise some points about how psychologists might research this topic area. These illustrate some poignant ethical and methodological issues (which are pertinent to many of the topic areas covered by social psychology). Researching real-life social issues such as aggression is not a straightforward endeavour.

> **→ Revision checklist**
>
> *Essential points to revise are:*
> ❑ What psychologists mean when using the term antisocial behaviour
> ❑ How personal and situational influences affect aggression
> ❑ What the key theories used to explain aggressive behaviour are
> ❑ The methodological issues associated with researching antisocial behaviour

Assessment advice

● Theories of aggression inform us about how aggressive behaviour might start.
● The focus on biological and social factors reflects the wider psychological debate of nature versus nurture. When attempting to put all the information together, do not try to work out if it is only nature or purely nurture. Generally, psychologists suggest that it has an element of both components. Whilst there may be a strong innate drive for aggression, the extent to which we act on this is influenced by the social world. That is why we need also to understand the person and situational determinants. However, this does not

mean that there is only one way to answer each question. The advice on answering the essay question given at the end of the chapter illustrates this and will help you to consider the amount and type of information required.

- As ever, an evaluative edge is important, but remember that evaluation does not mean criticise! In this chapter we have included a section on methodology. The points raised could illustrate your wider awareness of how social psychological knowledge is constructed. They are not exclusive to this topic. You might want to consider applying them to other areas covered in this book.

Sample question

Could you answer this question? Below is a typical essay that could arise on this topic.

✱ *Sample question*	*Essay*

Aggression is an innate response in humans. Discuss using evidence from social and biological accounts.

Guidelines on answering this question are included at the end of this chapter, whilst further guidance on tackling other exam questions can be found on the companion website at: www.pearsoned.co.uk/psychologyexpress

Personal and situational determinants of aggression

Table 8.1 highlights some examples of what social psychologists label personal and situational determinants. Consideration of these helps us to understand why it might be that some people are more aggressive than others or, indeed, why any of us could be more aggressive in certain situations.

Some of these aspects are discussed in further detail below.

Personality

Distinctions have been made between Type A and Type B personalities. Type A's are described as competitive, irritable, in a hurry and lose their temper easily. Type B's are calmer and considered less likely to be aggressive. Type A's appear to exhibit especially high levels of hostile aggression. There do not seem to be significant levels of difference in instrumental aggression between the two personality types.

Gender

Observations of the amount and type of aggression displayed by both sexes indicate that males are more likely to engage in direct aggression (e.g., physical assaults), but

Table 8.1 Personal and situational determinants of aggression

Person-centred determinants	Situation-centred determinants
Personality Certain personality types are considered more aggressive than others, which suggests individual differences exist in aggressive behaviour	**Physical environment** Heat, overcrowding and noise are just some of the elements of our physical environment that seem to impact aggression
Gender Researchers of gender socialisation suggest that the gender-appropriate behaviour for females is more passive and less overtly hostile than that for males	**Social disadvantage** Feeling socially disadvantaged can lead to aggression. Aggression here is a reaction to a situation which is perceived as unjust
Cognition Attributions play a part in our reactions to others and there appear to be individual differences in the ways in which people's behaviours are interpreted. A hostile attribution bias has been associated with aggression. (Refer to Chapter 2 for a comprehensive account of attribution theory)	**Cultural influences** Contemporary research suggests that cultural norms remain prevalent, especially in relation to sexual infidelity, which is viewed as particularly threatening to a male's honour. In a *culture of honour*, aggression is viewed as an appropriate response when one's honour has been insulted

that females display higher levels of indirect aggression (e.g., spreading rumours). Males are more likely to aggress in situations where they are not provoked. If provocation is intense, however, such gender-related differences seem to disappear.

Heat

The impact of heat has been explored by looking at crime rates over a period of time to establish any correspondence between rises in temperature and rises in crime. An alternative method is to manipulate temperature in a laboratory setting and then to measure participants' responses when they thought they would have the opportunity to aggress.

Both types of evidence have shown a relationship between heat and aggression. However, the relationship is not a straightforward linear one. Whilst there are higher rates of aggression as the temperature rises, after a certain temperature they seem to drop. The relationship is curvilinear. This may be because if people are too hot they become lethargic and drained of energy. Longitudinal crime data has shown that not *all* crime increases with heat. For instance, rape and property crime do not seem to be affected. Violent crime does.

Social deprivation

If individuals believe that legitimate means won't work to improve their position, they may turn to aggression. At a collective level, a riot might ensue; vandalism at a more individual level.

Real-life examples of protests in reaction to people's situations can be found – e.g., race riots in the south of England occurred in 2001 as a consequence of

Asian youths protesting against a British National Party rally. A key factor seems to be the relative deprivation felt.

Test your knowledge

8.1 What is the difference between instrumental, hostile and indirect aggression?

8.2 Would an individual with a Type A or Type B personality be more likely to display hostile aggression?

8.3 Outline the relationship between heat and increased aggressive behaviour.

8.4 From wider reading or knowledge of this topic, can you identify any further examples of personal or situational determinants of aggression?

Answers to these questions can be found on the companion website at: www.pearsoned.co.uk/psychologyexpress

---

? *Sample question*   *Essay*

Discuss the role of situational determinants in inciting aggressive behaviour.

Further reading Person And Situational Determinants Of Aggression

Topic	Key reading
Role of gender in aggression	Richardson, D. S., & Hammock, G. S. (2007). Social context of human aggresssion: Are we paying too much attention to gender? *Aggression and Violent Behaviour, 12,* 417–426.
Relationship between heat and aggression	Bushman, B. J., Wang, M. C., & Anderson, C. A. (2005). Is the curve relating temperature to aggression curvilinear or linear?: Assaults and temperature in Minneapolis re examined. *Journal of Personality and Social Psychology, 89,* 62–66.
Honour as a cultural syndrome	Vandello, J. A., & Cohen, D. (2003). Male honor and female fidelity: Cultural scripts that perpetuate domestic violence. *Journal of Personality and Social Psychology, 84,* 997–1010.

Theories of aggression

Many different attempts have been made to theorise aggression. A useful way to group them is under the headings of biological and social accounts.

Biological theories of aggression

These approaches view aggression as an inborn tendency.

Psychodynamic accounts

Freud was a supporter of the view that humans are aggressive by nature. He believed that we have the two conflicting instincts of *eros* and *thantos*, or life and death. The aggressive urge was thought to stem largely from thantos. This death wish is initially aimed at self-destruction, but becomes redirected at others in the form of aggressive behaviour. The aggression is the result of tension which builds up in the body, eventually needing to be released to restore balance. This approach has similarities to the steam boiler model suggested by Lorenz.

Point to consider

- Although a dominant theory at the beginning of the twentieth century, the psychodynamic approach has very little empirical evidence to support its claims.

Ethology and evolution

The *ethological* perspective also suggests that humans have an instinct for aggression. Lorenz (1974), based on work with animals, believed that aggressive energy is continually produced, ready to be released when aggression-related stimuli (e.g., a rival mating partner) is present. If such stimuli are not present, it may burst out spontaneously, hence the label the steam boiler model of aggression! Once we have 'let off steam', our internal reservoir of aggression will be depleted. We will then need to rebuild this energy before engaging in any further aggression.

Points to consider

- Evidence exists that humans can perform more than one aggressive act in succession.
- A single aggressive act can serve to precipitate, not suppress, another aggressive act.
- Caution should be taken when directly relating studies from animals to humans (a point also relevant to evolutionary psychology).

Another biological approach based on studies of animals is the *evolutionary* theory of aggression. Here, aggression is viewed as having an important role in survival. In fighting for mating rights or to protect young stock, the ultimate goal is survival of the genes. Amongst humans, evolutionary psychologists see aggression as having social and economic advantages. For instance, in the workplace a manager might use aggressive tactics such as arguing with colleagues to maintain status or gain promotion.

Points to consider

- Evidence for evolutionary theories has been developed over thousands of years of adaptation. They are hard to test in laboratory settings, which require short timescales.

- Examples exist where humans show aggression towards their closest relatives (consider domestic violence towards partners and children). This is hard to explain in evolutionary terms, which state that we might use aggression to protect, not harm, them.

Hormones and genes

Hormones have also been associated with aggressive behaviour, especially in males. Links have been made between the increase in testosterone and aggressive behaviour displayed during male puberty. High cortisol levels have also been shown to predict aggressive behaviour in some studies.

Points to consider

- Evidence is mixed in this area.
- Meta-analyses have indicated only moderate positive correlations between testosterone and adolescent males' aggression.
- Conclusive evidence that hormones such as testosterone and cortisol cause aggressive behavioural patterns is yet to be found.

Genetic explanations can be found in a field known as *behavioural genetics*. Studies explore whether individuals with similar genetic makeup are also more likely to show similar levels of aggression than those who are not related genetically. Meta-analyses of twin and adoption studies indicate that genes can explain up to 50 per cent of the variance.

Points to consider

- Studies are often based on self- and parental ratings, which may be prone to bias.
- Meta-analysis of both genes and environment has found that, whilst there may be a genetic similarity, the environment seems to play a stronger role.
- A wide range of evidence seems to suggest that genes may predispose us to aggression, but the environment will play a strong role in either reinforcing or counteracting such behaviour.

Further reading Biological theories of aggression

Topic	Key reading
Evolutionary theory	Hilton, N. Z., Harris, G. T., & Rice, M. E. (2000). The function of aggression by male teenagers. *Journal of Personality and Social Psychology, 79*, 988–994.
Genetic and environmental influences	Rhee, S. H., & Waldman, I. H. (2002). Genetic and environmental influences on antisocial behaviour: A meta-analysis of twin studies. *Psychological Bulletin, 128*, 490–529.
A discussion of behavioural genetics and evolutionary approaches	Ferguson, C. J. (2010). Genetic contributions to antisocial personality and behavior: A meta-analytic review from an evolutionary perspective *The Journal of Social Psychology, 150*, 160–180.

| Hormones | Rowe, R., Maughan, B., Worthman, C. M., Costello, E. J., & Angold, A. (2004). Testosterone, antisocial behaviour and social dominance in boys: Pubertal development and biosocial interaction. *Biological Psychology, 55*, 546–552. |

Social theories of aggression

Social psychologists have suggested that our social situation can also impact the type and amount of aggressive behaviour we might display. Probably one of the best-known studies amongst psychology students is Bandura's Bobo doll (Bandura et al., 1961), which indicates that we can learn vicariously to act in an aggressive manner.

What follow are examples of some of the influential social theories that have been used to account for aggression. An exhaustive coverage is not offered here – rather, the aim is to illustrate chronologically the ways in which the field has developed and the types of questions and conclusions this has raised about aggressive behaviour.

Frustration aggression hypothesis

As the name of this theory suggests, it is argued that frustration is what leads to aggressive behaviour.

The idea stemmed from the work of Dollard, Doob, Miller, Mowrer and Sears, (1939), who claimed that when we feel frustration towards a specific person or event, aggression will ensue. If it is not appropriate to display aggression towards the specific target, the aggression will simply be redirected towards a more realistic target – known as *displaced aggression*.

Evidence for this approach initially came from observations of the lynching of black people in the American South during the 1940s. At the time, the country was in economic decline, which was thought to cause frustration. Individuals could do little about the economic downturn, so vented their anger on this minority group.

In a more recent meta-analytic review, Marcus-Newhall, Pederson, Carlson and Miller (2000) found robust evidence that, when frustrated, people displace their aggression on to less powerful or more accessible targets rather than the source of the aggression itself. However, the frustration aggression hypothesis as a unitary explanation for aggression has a number of weaknesses.

Points to consider

● An overemphasis on the idea that frustration *will* lead to aggression.
● Frustration can cause a whole range of responses – e.g., sadness, despair or motivate individuals to attempt to overcome the source of the frustration.
● Frustration can serve as a powerful determinant for aggression under certain circumstances, but there is insufficient evidence to suggest that it is either *necessary* for aggression to occur or a *unitary cause* of aggression.

- A meta-analysis of experimental studies (Marcus-Newhall et al., 2000) revealed that displacement of aggression remains a robust effect.

It appears that further variables in the environment which might affect whether or not we become aggressive need to be explored.

The weapons effect

Frustration was still being considered in the 1960s when Berkowitz began examining cues in the environment which might effect aggressive behaviour.

KEY STUDY

Berkowitz and LePage (1967). Does the presence of a weapon make us more aggressive?

In a study conducted by Berkowitz and LePage (1967), confederates angered and frustrated male participants by evaluating them on their task performance by giving them electric shocks. Participants were then allowed to evaluate the confederates' performance by the same method (i.e., electric shocks).

An important variable was manipulated at this stage – the aggressive cue. In the aggressive situational cue condition, a shotgun and revolver were placed on a nearby table. In the neutral condition, only a badminton racquet was present.

Results indicated that participants who had previously received shocks were more likely to administer more shocks in the aggressive cue condition than the neutral one. This became known as *the weapons effect*.

Note that it is not simply the *presence* of the weapon which elicits the aggression. Amongst a control group of participants who had not been given any electric shocks themselves, the presence of the weapon had no effect on the number of shocks administered. It seems that *when aroused* (as the participants who had received shocks would have been), an aggressive cue can incite further aggression.

Points to consider

- Mixed evidence has emerged from replications of studies such as these. Some have failed to find a weapons effect at all, whilst others found its presence even amongst *non-frustrated* participants.
- In 1990, Carlson, Marcus-Newhall and Miller concluded, based on a meta-analysis of 57 studies, that, in experimental settings, aggressive cues have been shown to increase aggression in those already angered, but to have a weaker effect on those in a neutral mood state.
- These findings suggest that frustration or anger might not be necessary for aggressive cues to have an impact. More contemporary approaches suggest that such cues might prime certain aggression-related cognitive schemas, thus increasing the saliency of the option to react aggressively.

Cognitive neo-associationist model

During the 1990s Berkowitz developed the frustration aggression hypothesis by considering the role of negative affect and cognitive appraisal. By this time, social psychologists had established that frustration was only one of a possible range of affective reactions to many different aversive stimuli. The cognitive neo-associative approach therefore represented a more general conceptualisation of the possible links between negative affect and aggression.

The basic premise of this model is that aversive stimuli will lead to negative affect. Our automatic reaction to this, of which we have no conscious awareness, is either fight or flight. This is known as a primitive associational reaction. However, our past experiences and the context itself will determine, on further more careful appraisal, the nature of the reaction which will ensue. This is illustrated further in Figure 8.1.

To give a fictitious example, imagine walking down your garden path and being hit by a stone thrown by your neighbour. Although not badly injured, this did hurt you. The pain you experience leads to negative affect and a possible combination of anger (you want to fight) and fear (urging you to retreat to the safety of your house). Context and past experiences will affect the nature of the appraisals made. Two possible appraisals of this hypothetical scenario are illustrated in Figure 8.2.

Of course, this is fictitious and I, my neighbour and my dog live in perfect harmony! However, one of the key concepts here is that the different emotional components activate or trigger a series of further responses and associations. A related concept is 'association', which can be used to explain the weapons

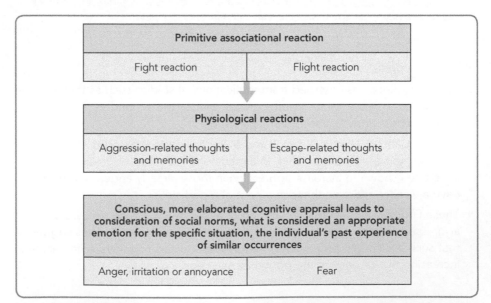

Figure 8.1 An illustration of the general components of the neo-associationist model

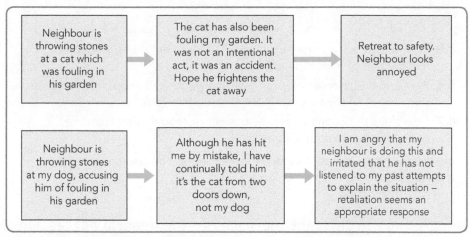

Figure 8.2 Two possible appraisals of the stone-throwing neighbour

effect. In such experiments, the weapon activated aggression-related associations which seemed especially salient in the condition when the individual was already aroused and angry.

Points to consider

- This approach subsumes the frustration aggression hypothesis.
- It offers a causal mechanism for why aversive events might increase aggressive inclinations.
- It is particularly well-suited to explaining hostile aggression.
- There has not been a proliferation of research into this approach since Berkowitz's book *Aggression: Its causes, consequences and control* in 1993. One exception is Pederson, Bushman, Vasquez and Miller (2008) (see Further reading below).

Further reading Social theories of aggression

Topic	Key reading
Using aggression as displacement	Marcus-Newhall, A., Pederson, W. C., Carlson, M., & Miller, N. (2000). Displaced aggression is alive and well: A meta-analytic review. *Journal of Personality and Social Psychology, 78,* 670–689.
Aspects of cognitive neo-associationist model	Pederson, W. C., Bushman, B. J., Vasquez, E. A., & Miller, N. (2008). Kicking the (barking) dog effect: The moderating role of target attributes on triggered displaced aggression. *Personality and Social Psychology Bulletin, 34,* 1382–1398.
General aggression model	Anderson, C. A., & Bushman, B. J. (2002). Human aggression. *Annual Review of Psychology, 53,* 27–51.

8.5 In what way is the steam boiler model of aggression flawed as an explanation of human behaviour?

8.6 Twin and adoption studies suggest that genes can account for what percentage of the variance in levels of aggression?

8.7 How does the cognitive neo-associationist model differ from the frustration aggression hypothesis?

Answers to these questions can be found on the companion website at: www.pearsoned.co.uk/psychologyexpress

Integrating the different approaches – the general aggression model (GAM)

Anderson and Bushman (2002) introduced this framework to bring together some of the ideas from the field of aggression. Previous approaches tended to be domain-specific, considering only single precursors (e.g., instinct, frustration) for aggression, so a more general theory of aggression was suggested.

The model describes a process with three main elements: inputs, routes and outcomes. It considers how both situational and individual difference variables can lead to aggression through their impact on arousal, affective states and cognition. Figure 8.3 offers a brief summary of the stages involved, whilst Anderson and Bushman's (2002) review paper provides a detailed account of this influential approach (see previous Further reading).

What's different about this model?

● GAM is a reflection of many years of research in the field of aggression and is viewed as the most comprehensive approach to date.

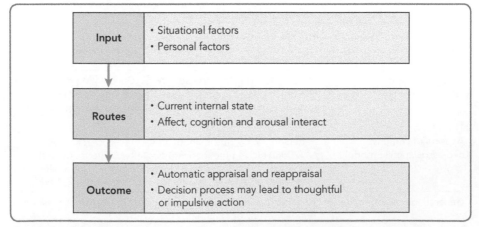

Figure 8.3 **The stages involved in the general aggression model**

- It shows how elements of previous accounts interact (e.g., much research has identified personal and situational factors, but here we see how they feed into current internal states). Cognitive features such as knowledge structures (e.g., behavioural scripts) are also part of the overall process.

- The person in the situation is considered. The process outlined in Figure 8.3 represents one cycle of social interaction, called an *episode*.

- GAM can explain how aggressive acts can be based on multiple motives.

? *Sample question*   *Essay*

Discuss the evidence that an integrative framework might be preferable to a domain-specific approach to aggression.

Some methodological considerations when researching antisocial behaviour

CRITICAL FOCUS

Researching aggression in the laboratory

Imagine that you have been asked to design a study to measure aggressive behaviour. Immediately there are ethical issues – is it OK to make someone behave in an aggressive manner? You cannot tell people to go and have an argument or a fight, so how do you simulate aggression in a laboratory situation?

Berkowitz and LePage (1967) allowed participants to administer electric shocks in their weapons effect study, but ethical guidelines have developed considerably since the 1960s and such studies would be unlikely to gain approval now. Despite this, laboratory studies remain the most popular method and researchers have devised a number of measures which act as aversive stimuli, but do not inflict actual harm. Examples include loud noise, cold water and even an extremely hot spicy sauce! (Refer to Krahe, 2010, for a comprehensive discussion of this.) The extent to which the participants are prepared to deliver the aversive stimuli to another person is the dependent variable, the measure of aggression.

A criticism often raised in relation to such artificial scenarios is that they are unrealistic in terms of mirroring real-life incidents of aggression and cannot be generalised to other populations and situations – they have low external validity. However, Anderson and Bushman (1997) provide a number of convincing arguments for the merit of lab-based studies.

- When studying aggression, a lab-based study can be the only ethical and affordable way to test theoretically driven propositions.

- Lab-based studies are typically designed to test *causal* theoretical propositions. In more real-world scenarios, variables are never sufficiently isolated to allow such precise examination.

▶

- If a lab-based study can capture a participant's intention to harm, then this can aid an understanding of the causes and correlates of aggression in real-world settings, such as violent crime.

- Their review of literature on both personal and situational determinants of aggression indicate that lab-based paradigms do have good external validity – i.e., the findings correspond with field-based (more naturalistic) studies if the *conceptual relations* between the two are considered. For instance, a study establishing that insulting 5-year-olds increased the likelihood of them displaying aggression towards another child is unlikely to have high external validity amongst a population of 35-year-olds if using the same name-calling anger manipulations. Here we are attempting to make a generalisation across participant populations. However, if we consider the general psychological process that is being studied – that insults increase aggressive behaviour – by using a different, but conceptually equivalent, insult manipulation, the external validity between the two can be tested. It is the *conceptual* relationship that is being generalised – an important distinction to make.

The third and fourth points in particular indicate that important links can be made between artificial scenarios and real-life acts of aggression and lab studies in the field of aggression can have external validity.

Below are some of the main methods used in aggression research, together with some points to consider for each of them.

Quantitative measures

Experiments

These allow hypotheses to be formed about why aggression might occur, under what conditions and the scale of aggressive behaviour shown to be measured.

Point to consider

- How generalisable are such studies are to 'real life'?

Behavioural self-reports

They provide information about the occurrence of aggression in more natural settings than is possible in an experiment. Standardised measures have been developed to measure both general levels of aggression and aggression within specific domains.

Points to consider

- Aggression is considered socially undesirable.
- Is there a possibility that individuals might underestimate their own levels of aggression?

Peer or other nominations

One way around the problems with self-reports is to collect reports from other people who know the person in question. They might be teachers, peers or parents, whose ratings can be compared with the self-reports to gain a more comprehensive picture. This method is often used in the field of behavioural genetics.

Point to consider

- Might parents be biased, too?

Qualitative accounts

The research discussed so far in this chapter tells us little about how it *feels* to be angry, yet this emotion is a central component of some types of aggression (e.g., hostile aggression). Such data is hard to capture using experiments or scales – qualitative approaches, such as phenomenology, are more appropriate for research of this nature.

Phenomenology considers how people experience certain phenomena. It gathers data from a smaller numbers of participants than experiments often via interviews, which seek to produce vivid and detailed accounts.

Point to consider

- Qualitative research does not attempt to establish any causal relationships or make generalisations to populations, which some (typically experimental psychologists) view as problematic.

KEY STUDY

Thomas (2003). A qualitative account of aggression

If you want to find out more about qualitative research, Thomas' (2003) phenomenological study of anger amongst a group of middle-class American men is a good place to start.

In this interview-based study, participants were asked to describe examples of incidents when they felt angry. Analysis revealed two key themes: the first, entitled 'right versus wrong', centred on how the men perceived their anger. Specifically, how they justified it when they felt it was necessary and, conversely, when it was considered inappropriate.

Theme two, 'being controlled versus having and maintaining control', discussed the ways in which they attempted (not always successfully) to control their anger.

Evidence was provided in the form of quotations from the interviews, which serve to illustrate how the men felt in their own words. Thomas suggests that such first-person narratives have previously been absent from research on anger. Through phenomenological accounts, an alternative approach to the laboratory study is offered. Here, the experience and meanings of anger play a central role.

Test your knowledge

8.8 What ethical issues might you need to consider if designing a laboratory study of aggression?

8.9 List two different ways in which aggression has been studied.

8.10 What is the difference between internal and external validity?

8.11 In what ways do qualitative and quantitative studies of aggression differ?

Answers to these questions can be found on the companion website at:
www.pearsoned.co.uk/psychologyexpress

? Sample question   Essay

Discuss the strengths and weaknesses of the different methods used to study antisocial behaviour. Support your answer with examples of studies from aggression research.

Further reading Research methodology and aggression

Topic	Key reading
The external validity of laboratory studies of aggression	Anderson, C. A., & Bushman, B. J. (1997). External validity of 'trivial' experiments: The case of laboratory aggression. *Review of General Psychology, 1*, 19–41.
Phenomenological study of male anger	Thomas, S. P. (2003). Men's anger: A phenomenological exploration of its meaning in a middle-class sample of American men. *Psychology of Men & Masculinity, 4*, 163–175.
Phenomenological study of female anger	Eatough, V., & Smith, J. (2006). 'I was like a wild, wild, person': Understanding feelings of anger using interpretative phenomenological analysis. *British Journal of Psychology, 97*, 483–498.

? Sample question   Problem-based learning

On a night out with some university friends who are not studying psychology, you mention that you had been to a lecture on aggression that day. One of them responds that, in their opinion, 'Aggressive behaviour can be explained purely as an expression of cultural norms.' They challenge you to provide some psychological evidence to convince them otherwise. Outline three other areas which psychological research has shown to influence aggression in humans.

Chapter summary – pulling it all together

→ Can you tick all the points from the revision checklist at the beginning of this chapter?

→ Attempt the sample question from the beginning of this chapter using the answer guidelines below.

→ Go to the companion website at www.pearsoned.co.uk/psychologyexpress to access more revision support online, including interactive quizzes, flashcards, You be the marker exercises as well as answer guidance for the Test your knowledge and Sample questions from this chapter.

Further reading for Chapter 8

Anderson. C. A., & Bushman, B. J. (2002). Human aggression. *Annual Review of Psychology, 53*, 27–51. (General summary of theories of aggression.)

Krahe, B. (2010). The social psychology of aggression. Hove, East Sussex: Psychology Press.

Answer guidelines

✳ Sample question   *Essay*

Aggression is an innate response in humans. Discuss using evidence from social and biological accounts.

Approaching the question

In order to fully answer this question, you need to be able to discuss evidence for both social *and* biological accounts of aggression. Initially, though, you should make it clear that the statement 'aggression is an innate response in humans' relates to the *biological* approach. It would be sensible to focus on this part of the question by outlining and evaluating the types of theories which exemplify the biological perspective. The essay could then develop with a discussion of more social accounts.

Important points to include

The key point to get across is that, although much biological evidence suggests humans have an innate tendency to aggress, the social context in which we exist is also important. Remember, you are writing from a social, not biological, psychology perspective, so ensure that a good balance between the two is maintained. Having said this, social psychologists do not deny that innate tendencies exist. Rather, they seek to explore how these tendencies are shaped and developed by the social environment.

Such distinctions are worth making and, as flagged up in the Assessment advice section at the beginning of this chapter, you are not being asked to decide if it is nature *or* nurture with questions of this type. Make sure that you have not just *described* the different approaches. Ideas for points of evaluation can be found throughout this chapter.

This is a big question and there is a danger that you might try to cover too much information. Be cautious about the number of theories you cover. The question states 'in humans', so you might elect to leave out accounts based on animal studies.

> ### Make your answer stand out
>
> *Don't forget the methodological points made in the final section of this chapter. Including a few of these within your essay will indicate an awareness of the wider issues which are pertinent when applying social psychological knowledge to specific topic areas.*
>
> *One way to bring the essay to an end could be the general aggression model. It is easy to see biological and social accounts as potentially competing views, but GAM illustrates how elements of both approaches interact (input variables include both biological and social factors). A brief acknowledgement of this model would also show your awareness of current thinking in the field of aggression research.*
>
> *Answering the other three sample essays in this chapter will help you with both of the suggestions.*

Explore the accompanying website at www.pearsoned.co.uk/psychologyexpress

→ Prepare more effectively for exams and assignments using the answer guidelines for questions from this chapter.

→ Test your knowledge using multiple choice questions and flashcards.

→ Improve your essay skills by exploring the You be the marker exercises.

Notes

9

Interpersonal attraction

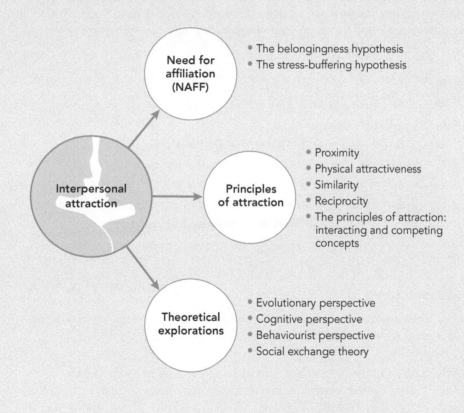

Interpersonal attraction

Need for affiliation (NAFF)
- The belongingness hypothesis
- The stress-buffering hypothesis

Principles of attraction
- Proximity
- Physical attractiveness
- Similarity
- Reciprocity
- The principles of attraction: interacting and competing concepts

Theoretical explorations
- Evolutionary perspective
- Cognitive perspective
- Behaviourist perspective
- Social exchange theory

A printable version of this topic map is available from:
www.pearsoned.co.uk/psychologyexpress

Introduction

This chapter will discuss relationships. Why do we need the company of other people and how do we choose our friends and lovers? Our need for affiliation, the factors influencing attraction and the theoretical explanations for relationship formation are presented as separate sections, but, of course, these are not separate entities. This chapter will consider how the influencing factors may support or refute the wider theoretical explanations. For example, how can an evolutionary explanation account for the importance of similarity as a key influencing factor in attraction?

You will also need to be aware of how knowledge from this chapter is linked with other parts of social psychology and consider the factors that sustain and deepen a relationship or lead us to end a relationship. Chapter 10 will discuss intimate relationships, love and the breakdown of relationships. Your assessments may require you to draw on your knowledge from both of these chapters and, indeed, draw on your wider knowledge of psychology.

→ *Revision checklist*

Essential points to revise are:
- ❏ Why and when we need the company of others
- ❏ The consequences if our need for affiliation is not met
- ❏ Which factors influence who we are attracted to
- ❏ How individual differences may affect the formation of relationships
- ❏ The main theoretical explanations of how we form relationships

Assessment advice

- The tasks are designed to get you thinking about the research in this area in a critically evaluative way to help you achieve a good grade in your assessments.
- Whilst it is important to know the key determinants of relationship formation, you also need to evaluate the applicability and strength of the supporting evidence. For example, what do we know about the formation of relationships at a later stage in the life course and do the principles of attraction apply to homosexual relationships?
- You should also note that some aspects of this topic may be fluid. For example, as we conduct more of our communication online, this may change the factors influencing the formation of relationships.

- Bear in mind that the hypotheses we generate will be influenced by a variety of factors, including our knowledge, beliefs, epistemology and social and cultural background. The research on interpersonal attraction is dominated by cognitive, behaviourist and evolutionary perspectives.

- When comparing the theories of attraction, remember, rarely does a theory account for a phenomenon in its entirety. Sometimes theories may be incompatible with each other, although, more likely, the ideas can be applied to explain different aspects of the same process.

Sample question

Could you answer this question? Below is a typical essay that could arise on this topic.

✳ Sample question   *Essay*

To what extent has social psychological research furthered our understanding of interpersonal attraction? Critically discuss with reference to empirical evidence and theoretical explanations.

Guidelines on answering this question are included at the end of this chapter, whilst further guidance on tackling other exam questions can be found on the companion website at: www.pearsoned.co.uk/psychologyexpress

Need for affiliation (NAFF)

Two main theories have been proposed to explain our need to affiliate (NAFF) with human beings in a friendly, cooperative way. An evolutionary perspective argues this biological instinct for forming relationships serves to protect the survival of our genes: the belongingness hypothesis. Others argue that when we are reminded of our mortality, such as in a natural disaster, there appears to be a natural desire to affiliate and help each other: the stress-buffering hypothesis.

The belongingness hypothesis

Many researchers claim to provide evidence to support the belongingness hypothesis, which proposes 'the need to belong is a powerful, fundamental, and extremely pervasive motivation' (Baumeister & Leary, 1995, p. 497). Support of this proposition comes, first, from research investigating attachment styles involving animal and human infants and, second, from research with adults showing the negative effects of short-term social exclusion and long-term isolation.

143

Attachment

The work of Bowlby (1969) and Ainsworth, Blehar, Watess and Wall, (1978) on maternal deprivation proposed an innate drive for affiliation which remains with us throughout our lifespan. Evidence to support this contention comes from studies showing that newborns are predisposed to look towards faces in preference to other stimuli (Mondloch et al., 1999). Furthermore, observational studies have shown that infants maintain physical proximity with their mothers or restore it if disrupted. Research has demonstrated the negative consequences if this need for social contact is not met appropriately (e.g., Rholes, Simpson & Friedman, 2006). Long-term social deprivation in children is psychologically traumatic and attachment styles developed in childhood affect relationships in adulthood (see how in Chapter 10, Intimate relationships). This demonstrates one of many areas where developmental psychology overlaps with social psychology.

Social exclusion and isolation

Social exclusion has been investigated through experimental manipulations of short-term rejection and correlational studies of self-reported loneliness (often as a result of long-term isolation). Generally, the research has shown negative outcomes when our 'need for affiliation' is not met (see Table 9.1).

Some researchers argue social exclusion may motivate individuals to affiliate and reconnect with others (e.g., Maner, DeWall, Baumeister & Shaller, 2007). The effect of social exclusion on emotion is debated widely, with some evidence that social exclusion leads to negative affect, whilst others suggest an emotion-numbing affect.

In a similar vein, authors do not agree on whether rejection affects self-esteem. Even two meta-analyses conducted at a similar time have made differing conclusions regarding the relationship between rejection and self esteem (Blackheart, Nelson, Knowles & Baumeister, 2009; Gerber & Wheeler, 2009).

Table 9.1 **Negative consequences of social exclusion and loneliness**

Negative consequences of rejection	Negative consequences of loneliness
Higher levels of negative affect	Higher rates of mental illness
Poorer cognitive functioning	Higher rates of mortality
Decreased prosocial behaviour	Life perceived as less meaningful
Greater conformity	
Greater antisocial behaviour	

KEY STUDY

Maner et al. (2007). Are people drawn to seek the company of others following rejection?

In a series of six experimental studies, Maner et al. (2007) attempted to determine how situational and dispositional factors affect how individuals respond to social exclusion. More specifically, when do socially excluded individuals feel a desire to seek the company of others?

Social rejection was manipulated using a number of standard techniques – e.g., participants were led to believe that others had rejected them as social interaction partners. Socially excluded individuals were found to perceive perpetrators of exclusion negatively, but were more positive about possible interactions with new partners.

Maner et al. (2007) suggest a social reconnection hypothesis – that is, social exclusion stimulates a desire to affiliate and reconnect with others. This seems to be contradictory to previous research, showing exclusion leads to withdrawal from interactions with people and even aggressive behaviour.

Maner et al. (2007) argue one's motivation to reconnect may vary with the perceived importance of a relationship. They speculate that if excluded by a romantic partner, this may lead to a strong motivation to reconnect with others.

Whilst reading this research, you should consider how far we can generalise from the experimental research on social exclusion. Participants are largely drawn from an undergraduate population in American universities. How does this affect the conclusions we can draw from these studies?

Real interactions are dynamic and ongoing and operate within a social and cultural context. Can we realistically study this complex dynamic in an experimental setting? How else could we study this phenomenon to address some of these concerns?

The stress-buffering hypothesis

The stress-buffering hypothesis suggests social support helps us to appraise a stressful event and formulate strategies to cope. Many studies have demonstrated the role of social support using an experimental paradigm (developed from Schachter's classic 1959 study). Participants, under a high-anxiety condition, are given the choice of interacting with others or not.

Findings suggest that, in these scenarios, we seek the company of those similar to ourselves or in a similar situation. More recent research has begun to further examine the characteristics we value in people when seeking support, including physical attractiveness, see Li, Halterman, Cason, Knight and Maner (2007).

There are two main explanations for our NAFF in stressful situations:

- Social comparison. Discussing the situation with others gives us 'cognitive clarity' – helps us make decisions about what to do – and 'emotional clarity' – gives us a better understanding of our own feelings and how to cope.
- Terror management theory. Affiliation raises self-esteem and reduces the terror of the inevitability of death.

CRITICAL FOCUS

Theoretical explanations of our need for affiliation

A number of studies investigating our need to affiliate are grounded in evolutionary theory, particularly experimental studies of social exclusion. How strong is the evidence for an evolutionary explanation for our need for affiliation?

As you read the research in this area, ask yourself how a researcher's overall perspective and beliefs about 'why we seek relationships with others' may influence the type of research questions they generate and the subsequent choice of research design to test these ideas. How much direct evidence is there that the need to affiliate is grounded in our biology? Indeed, can one perspective ever offer a full explanation for 'our desire to seek out relationships with humans'?

Kaschak and Maner (2009) propose an integrated framework. Reading this paper should help you gain an appreciation of how the perspectives do not need to be treated as separate and mutually exclusive. Which other perspectives could also offer an understanding of the 'need to belong' and why do you think these perspectives may be underrepresented in core psychology textbooks?

Test your knowledge

9.1 Describe two explanations for our need for affiliation and briefly outline three studies providing support for these explanations.

9.2 Outline how different attachment styles in infancy are thought to affect our relationships in adulthood.

9.3 List the advantages and disadvantages of:

(a) experimental research into social exclusion

(b) correlation research investigating feelings of loneliness.

Answers to these questions can be found on the companion website at:
www.pearsoned.co.uk/psychologyexpress

? *Sample question*   *Essay*

Critically evaluate the evidence that short-term rejection leads to individuals withdrawing from the company of others.

Further reading Need for affiliation

Topic	Key reading
Attachment styles and relationships in adulthood	Rholes, W. S., Simpson, J. A., & Friedman, M. (2006). Avoidant attachment and the experience of parenting. *Personality and Social Psychology Bulletin, 32,* 275–285.

Values attracted to in stressful situations	Li, N. P., Halterman, R. A., Cason, M. J., Knight, G. P., & Maner, J. K. (2007). The stress–affiliation paradigm revisited: Do people prefer the kindness of strangers or their attractiveness? *Personality and Individual Differences, 44*, 382–391.
Social exclusion and its effect on desire to affiliate	Maner, J. K., DeWall, C. N., Baumeister, R. F., & Shaller, M. (2007). Does social exclusion motivate interpersonal reconnection?: Resolving the 'porcupine problem'. *Journal of Personality and Social Psychology, 9*(1), 422–455.
Review of the experimental research on social exclusion	Gerber, J., & Wheeler, L. (2009). On being rejected: A meta-analysis of experimental research on rejection. *Perspectives on Psychological Science, 4*(5), 468–488.
Review of the experimental research on social exclusion	Blackheart, G. C., Nelson, B. C., Knowles, M. L., & Baumeister, R. F. (2009). Rejection elicits emotional reactions but nether causes immediate distress nor lowers self-esteem: A meta-analytical review of 192 studies of social exclusion. *Personality and Social Psychology Review, 13*, 269–309.
Theoretical discussion of how evolutionary and social cognitive theory can be applied so as to understand relationships	Kaschak, M. P., & Maner, J. K. (2009). Embodiment, evolution, and social cognition: An integrative framework. *European Journal of Social Psychology, 39*, 1236–1244.

Principles of attraction

So far we have considered *why* we need relationships. The rest of this chapter will discuss *who* we form relationships with. A number of key principles of attraction have been identified and extensively researched. These include proximity, physical attractiveness, similarity and reciprocity.

Proximity

Festinger, Schacter and Back's (1950) classic study of student friendships on a university campus demonstrated the importance of proximity as a facilitator of attraction. The people you see and interact with most often are the most likely to become your friends and lovers – known as the *propinquity effect*.

Evidence suggests the propinquity effect may be more a reflection of *functional* distance than *geographical* distance. In other words, it is not just about if you live close to someone but also if you are likely to meet that person regularly. Explanations of how the propinquity effect works include increased familiarity (through mere exposure), availability and expectations of continued interaction.

A number of experimental studies have shown that mere exposure to objects and people increases liking as compared to novel stimuli (see Attitude formation, Chapter 1). Evolutionary psychologists suggest it would have been adaptive for

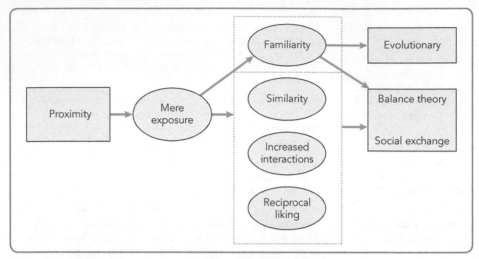

Figure 9.1 **Explanations for the role of proximity in attraction**

ancestors to be wary of approaching anything unfamiliar, whereas cognitive and reinforcement perspectives suggest interactions enable people to explore their similarities and sense each others' liking, see Figure 9.1.

The role of proximity has been called into question with the advent of long-distance communication via the Internet. The cues available during an online interaction are substantially different from those available in a face-to-face meeting. However, it appears even when people meet on the Internet, they do tend to meet up in real life (McKenna, Green & Gleason, 2002).

Physical attractiveness

A plethora of research has established that physical attraction is a major factor in initial attraction. Evolutionary theorists suggest we select attractive mates in order to improve the chances of our genes surviving (Buss, 2003). A number of points are made in support of this evolutionary position:

- attractive people fare better in life – they are judged more positively, have higher self-esteem, higher salaries, better physical and mental health
- individuals, regardless of race, class, age, share a sense of what is attractive
- the qualities we find attractive may be indicators of fertility and health
- very early on, babies prefer attractive faces (measured by time spent gazing at photos).

Many studies have shown physical attractiveness is a key factor in the prediction of date and mate selection. However, we do not always select the most attractive partner; there is fairly robust evidence to suggest that people tend to choose mates that match their own levels of attractiveness.

Evolutionary perspectives point to gender differences here. Men are thought to value physical attractiveness more highly than women and, thus, according to this perspective, would be less satisfied with a partner of perceived lower attractiveness than themselves. There is substantial evidence for this gender effect in stated preferences in laboratory studies of physical attraction (Buss, 2003).

Points to consider

- The majority of the research is conducted in controlled laboratory experiments.
- Participants very rarely interact with the supposed partner and will not form a relationship with that person in the future.
- Many studies focus only on the *early* stages of relationship formation.
- Limited research investigates the role of physical attractiveness in *established* relationships (see McNulty, Neff & Karney, 2008, for a rare example).

Studies of speed dating have consistently found that, although the gender effect discussed occurs in stated preferences, when following actual choices, both males *and* females select more attractive partners to the same extent (e.g., Luo & Zhang, 2009). This discrepancy between preferences in laboratory settings and real-life choices and the implication for evolutionary theory are discussed by Luo and Zhang (2009).

Similarity

One of the most robust findings in interpersonal attraction research is that we are attracted to those who are similar to ourselves – the *similarity–attraction effect* (SAE) (Byrne, 1971). We are attracted to people who are similar to ourselves in a number of ways – attitudes, personality traits, activities and demographics. As stated, we seem to end up with partners of a similar level of attractiveness. Furthermore, the greater the similarity between husband and wife, the happier they are and the less likely they are to divorce.

There are a number of proposed explanations for the SAE, but no strong evidence to universally support one particular theory to explain all aspects of attraction. Cognitive theory might suggest similarity renders a sense of familiarity. Interacting with similar people to ourselves validates our viewpoints and boosts our self-esteem. False consensus bias may add to this explanation. This bias suggests we assume that others share our attitudes. When we discover that someone has dissimilar attitudes, we may dislike the person as, otherwise, we have a problem with cognitive consistency. Choosing friends similar to ourselves makes us feel more comfortable. This may also explain why we become, or appear to become, more similar to our partners over time.

Jones, Pelham, Carvallo and Mirenberg (2004) propose a theory of implicit egotism, suggesting people generally see themselves in a positive manner, so anything reminiscent of the self could prompt automatic positive associations. *Social identity theory* (Tajfel & Turner, 1986) suggests people categorise themselves and others as belonging to various social categories form identities with specific social groups.

Is the similarity–attraction effect universal?

There are two reasons why we cannot state the SAE phenomenon is universal:

● there is no one clear explanation as to the mechanism responsible for the similarity effect

● much of the research is based around American university campuses.

Read Heine, Foster and Spina (2009) for a discussion of these issues.

Application of research on similarity

The SAE could have important implications beyond the realm of interpersonal attraction – see Devendorf and Highhouse's (2008) investigation of the role of similarity in job selection.

Further reading Similarity and attraction

Topic	Key reading
Link between similarity and personality in attraction	Tenney, E. R., Turkheimer, E., & Oltmanns, T. F. (2009). Being liked is more than having a good personality. *Journal of Research in Personality, 43,* 579–585.
Cross-cultural study of similarity–attraction effect	Heine, S. J., Foster, J., & Spina, R. (2009). Do birds of a feather universally flock together?: Cultural variation in the similarity–attraction effect. *Asian Journal of Social Psychology, 12,* 247–258.
Application of similarity–attraction effect to employment	Devendorf, S. A., & Highhouse, S. (2008). Applicant–employee similarity and attraction to an employer. *Journal of Occupational and Organizational Psychology, 81,* 607–617.

Reciprocity

The basic premise of reciprocity is that 'we like those who like us'. Self-esteem appears to be a key moderator of this effect. Specifically, individuals with high self-esteem are less affected by the responses of others. The *gain–loss hypothesis* suggests we are particularly attracted to those who initially dislike us but then gradually begin to like us.

Kenny (1994) distinguishes two different types of reciprocity: *general* reciprocal liking and *dyadic* reciprocal liking. Evidence for dyadic reciprocal liking appears to be more reliable, whereas evidence for general reciprocal liking is inconsistent.

The principles of attraction: interacting and competing concepts

Figure 9.1 has demonstrated that the principles of attraction are not likely to act independently. Tenney, Turkheimer and Oltmanns (2009) put forward competing explanations for the SAE, drawing on mere exposure and the complementarity hypothesis, thus demonstrating we still do not have a full understanding of the mechanism of attraction. Additionally, there are a number of important concepts that may play a key role in attraction which are not directly mentioned in the core principles of attraction. Cottrell, Neuberg and Li (2007) discuss the role of other valued characteristics, particularly the influence of trust.

Test your knowledge

9.4 What are the key determinants of attraction?

9.5 What are the main limitations of the research on determinants of attraction?

9.6 How does gender influence the key determinants of attraction?

Answers to these questions can be found on the companion website at: www.pearsoned.co.uk/psychologyexpress

? Sample question   Essay

Television shows that give viewers a makeover are very popular. Should viewers be encouraged to participate in such shows in order to improve their chances of attracting a suitable partner?

Further reading Principles of attraction

Topic	Key reading
Desirability of specific values, most notably trust	Cottrell, C. A., Neuberg, S. L., & Li, N. P. (2007). What do people desire in others?: A sociofunctional perspective on the importance of different valued characteristics. *Journal of Personality and Social Psychology, 92*(2), 208–231.
Physical attraction in established relationships	McNulty, J. K., Neff, L. A., & Karney, B. R. (2008). Beyond initial attraction: Physical attractiveness in newlywed marriage. *Journal of Family Psychology, 22*(1), 135–143.
Physical attraction in real-life settings	Luo, S., & Zhang, G. (2009). What leads to romantic attraction: Similarity, reciprocity, security, or beauty?: Evidence from a speed-dating study. *Journal of Personality, 77*(4), 933–964.
Internet relationships	McKenna, K. Y. A., Green, A. S., & Gleason, M. E. J. (2002). Relationship formation on the Internet: What's the big attraction? *Journal of Social Issues, 58*, 9–31.

Theoretical explanations

Evolutionary perspective

We have noted how the evolutionary perspective has been utilised to explain interpersonal attraction. Buss and colleagues have conducted numerous experimental studies which describe and explain gender differences in attraction. Roberts, Miner and Shackelford (2010) go further in contending that the evolutionary perspective could be of value in ensuring satisfactory relationships. In their paper, they discuss how increasing exposure to mass media, new technologies and cultural changes may have led to dissatisfaction in relationships, particularly via the effect on self-perception and partner perception. In other words, our expectations are inflated by the images of glamorous celebrities. They present a case for the value of evolutionary psychology in ameliorating the effects of these changes – for example, by ensuring more successful matching in online dating services.

Cognitive perspective

We saw in Chapter 1, Attitudes, that we are driven to achieve balance between our attitudes and behaviour to avoid dissonance. In a similar way, cognitive balance theory (Heider, 1946, 1958) suggests we are driven to achieve balance in our thoughts about an attitude object (see Table 9.2).

As applied to relationships, balance theory would suggest we are 'in balance', for example, when we like people we agree with. Conflict arises when a person we like disagrees with us (e.g., we believe it is important to recycle but the other person is unconcerned about it). We can resolve this situation by deciding to end the friendship, perceiving our friend does agree with recycling, or deciding we don't think recycling is really that important. Interestingly, it seems we do modify our attitudes to fit those of our partners in close relationships (Davis & Rusbult, 2001).

Attribution theory (see Chapter 2) can also help us to understand relationships. Research has shown that differences in the way couples make attributions are related to marital satisfaction scores. Happily married couples tend to attribute their partners' positive behaviour to internal, stable, global and controllable factors, whilst attributing negative behaviour to external, unstable, specific and uncontrollable factors. Thus, they give credit to their partners for the good things that they do, blaming the situation rather than them for any negative behaviour. It is also worth noting that men and women may differ in their attributional behaviour as regards relationships. Women tend to engage in attributional thought throughout the relationship, whereas men only do so when the relationship becomes dysfunctional (Holtzworth-Munroe & Jacobson, 1985).

Behaviourist perspective

The discussions about the formation of attitudes in Chapter 1 outline the importance of reinforcement and modelling in the development of our attitudes. This can be applied to attraction as studies have shown that we are more likely to judge someone as attractive if they are near to us when we receive a reward (Griffit & Guay, 1969).

Social exchange theory

Social exchange theory is an economic model grounded in behaviourist principles. The main tenet is that we form relationships when the benefits (rewards) outweigh the costs.

As applied to relationships, the theory also incorporates interactions and perceptions. How people feel about their relationships depends on their perceptions of:

- the rewards from the relationship
- the costs of the relationship
- the kind of relationship they deserve
- the chances of having a better relationship with someone else.

We will discuss this idea further in Chapter 10, Intimate relationships.

Test your knowledge

9.7 Describe the three main components of social exchange theory.

9.8 Outline how evolutionary and behaviourist theories of attraction are similar and how they differ.

9.9 Using Figure 9.1 as an example, create a mindmap showing how the overall perspectives, specific theories and principles of attraction are interlinked with each other.

Answers to these questions can be found on the companion website at: www.pearsoned.co.uk/psychologyexpress

---

Table 9.2 **Theories of attraction**

Cognitive perspective	Behaviourist perspective
Focuses mainly on our need to maintain consistency referring to concepts	Relies on the concept of reinforcement
Cognitive balance: we are attracted to individuals who are similar to ourselves to maintain balance	**Direct reinforcement:** we like those who are around when we receive a reward
Cognitive dissonance: disagreement causes tension and conflict, resulting in either one of you changing your views or dissolution of the relationship	**Reinforcement–affect model:** expanded to include the role of emotion

---

? *Sample question* **Essay**

Susie is 21 years of age and is just about to start her first year at university. She will be studying the history of art and is keen to continue painting in her spare time. Susie is keen to find a romantic partner. She is considering a variety of different options for meeting someone, including joining a dating agency, speed dating and joining a university club.

What advice would you give Susie to give her the best chance of meeting a compatible partner?

Further reading Theories of attraction

Topic	Key reading
Friendships and social exchange	Hand, L. S., & Furman, W. (2009). Rewards and costs in adolescent other-sex friendships: Comparisons to same-sex friendships and romantic relationships. *Social Development, 18*(2), 270–287.
Impact of mass media, on perception of the self and your partner	Roberts, S. G., Miner, E. J., & Shackelford, T. K. (2010). The future of an applied evolutionary psychology for human partnerships. *Review of General Psychology, 14*(4), 318–329.

✳ *Sample question* *Problem-based learning*

You have been employed as a consultant by a new dating agency called *'Find the Right Match'*. The agency wishes to base its initial questionnaire (from which it will match each of its clients with three possible dates) on factors drawn from psychological evidence about attraction and relationship formation. Having read this chapter, consider what areas the questionnaire might cover, then have a go at writing ten potential questions.

Chapter summary – pulling it all together

→ Can you tick all the points from the revision checklist at the beginning of this chapter?

→ Attempt the sample question from the beginning of this chapter using the answer guidelines below.

→ Go to the companion website at www.pearsoned.co.uk/psychologyexpress to access more revision support online, including interactive quizzes, flashcards, You be the marker exercises as well as answer guidance for the Test your knowledge and Sample questions from this chapter.

Further reading for Chapter 9

Collins, W. A., Welsh, D. P., & Furman, W. (2009). Adolescent romantic relationships. *Annual Review of Psychology, 60*, 631–652.

Peplau, L. A., & Fingerhut, A. W. (2007). The close relationships of lesbians and gay men. *Annual Review of Psychology, 58*, 405–424.

Whitty, M., & Carr, A. (2006). *Cyberrspace Romance: The Psychology of Online Relationships.* Basingstoke: Palgrave Macmillan.

Answer guidelines

✱ *Sample question*   *Essay*

To what extent has social psychological research furthered our understanding of interpersonal attraction? Critically discuss with reference to empirical evidence and theoretical explanations.

Approaching the question

The question requires that you evaluate and discuss the strength of the evidence, not just describe the research. The question asks about 'interpersonal attraction'. You may want to define this term, discussing the difference between friendships and intimate relationships. You could choose to focus on both types of relationships or on one particular type of relationship. Either way, you need to be clear about your aims and, as a consequence, select the most appropriate evidence.

Important points to include

There is no one way to answer any essay question, but an examiner would expect you to discuss the main principles of attraction, as well as theories of attraction. Try to avoid describing these in separate sections. A better answer would apply the theories to explain the empirical evidence or vice versa. The mindmap you drew for question 9.10 should help here.

A key part of this essay is to outline the current thinking and evaluate the quality and depth of the supporting evidence. Point out where there is robust evidence from multiple studies using different methodologies and identify gaps and weaknesses in the evidence. For instance, you could conclude there is considerable evidence that similarity is a key determinant of attraction for white, American undergraduate students. However, we still do not fully understand the mechanism behind this principle or whether the similarity–attraction effect is apparent in other groups. For example, there is limited research investigating the formation of relationships in late adulthood or the elderly.

Make your answer stand out

Online forms of communication have hugely increased since the advent of many of the concepts and theories covered in this chapter. Do we require alternative accounts for relationships which are formed via the Internet?

You might want to add a further dimension to your answers by considering what psychologists have found about relationships on the Internet. Initially, it was thought that online relationships were shallow – they were not a substitute for 'real' relationships, and could even make people lonelier in the long term. However, as this field of research has developed, much evidence has emerged to discredit such claims. It seems that the Internet can fulfil our need to affiliate, providing a medium through which both friendships and more intimate relationships are formed.

Some authors have suggested alternative theories to those presented in this chapter which account for computer-mediated relationships. Whitty and Carr (2006) provide a comprehensive coverage of the issues and debates in this area. Their work will provide you with a grounding in the ways in which relationships are different from and similar to those we develop offline. This book will serve as a useful evaluatory tool for parts of Chapter 11, too.

Explore the accompanying website at www.pearsoned.co.uk/psychologyexpress

→ Prepare more effectively for exams and assignments using the answer guidelines for questions from this chapter.

→ Test your knowledge using multiple choice questions and flashcards.

→ Improve your essay skills by exploring the You be the marker exercises.

Notes

Intimate relationships

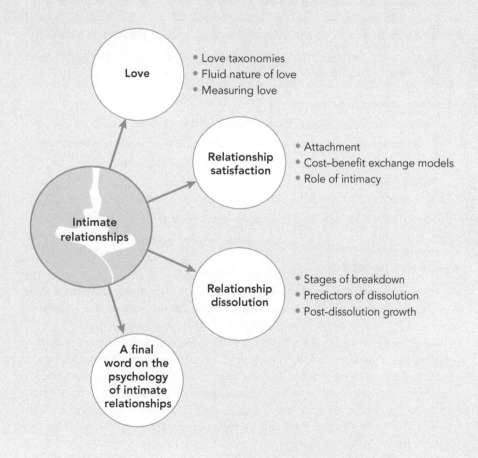

- Love
  - Love taxonomies
  - Fluid nature of love
  - Measuring love

- Relationship satisfaction
  - Attachment
  - Cost–benefit exchange models
  - Role of intimacy

- Intimate relationships

- Relationship dissolution
  - Stages of breakdown
  - Predictors of dissolution
  - Post-dissolution growth

- A final word on the psychology of intimate relationships

A printable version of this topic map is available from:
www.pearsoned.co.uk/psychologyexpress

Introduction

When talking about developing intimate relationships, the phrase 'falling in love' is often used, but what do we actually mean by this?

This chapter will discuss psychologists' attempts to define and measure love. We will also consider why some couples maintain happy, long-lasting relationships, whilst other relationships are short-lived. A number of factors may influence relationship satisfaction; here we look at attachment style, cost–benefit models and intimacy. Finally, why and how relationships break down will be discussed. Importantly, we will note that relationship dissolution is not always negative but can, for some, be a positive experience.

Whilst reading this chapter, consider how the theoretical perspective and sample selection may limit our current understanding of relationships (e.g., the bias towards studies of young, heterosexual couples in Western cultures).

> ### → Revision checklist
>
> *Essential points to revise are:*
> - ❏ How social psychologists have defined and measured love
> - ❏ The influence of attachment style on the quality of adult relationships
> - ❏ The role of interpersonal processes in determining relationship satisfaction
> - ❏ The process and predictors of relationship dissolution
> - ❏ How dissolution can lead to growth in some areas

Assessment advice

- Often, doing well in assessments is not just about demonstrating you have read widely about the topic but also that you can apply your knowledge selectively. For example, the principles of attraction (see Chapter 9, Interpersonal attraction) are relevant to the initial process of relationship formation. However, to fully understand long-term intimate relationships, you also need to be familiar with the role of emotions, love and intimacy. In addition, the ways we form, maintain and dissolve relationships throughout our lifespan could be important. Ensure that you learn about these different areas, but have thought through the types of questions each would be most pertinent to.

- To offer robust accounts of long-term intimate relationships, social psychologists also need to overcome the problematic nature of measuring feelings such as love, passion and intimacy. You might want to consider how well we are doing in this endeavour.

Sample question

Below is a typical essay that could arise on this topic.

> ✳ *Sample question*   *Essay*
>
> What is the role of love in relationship satisfaction?

Guidelines on answering this question are included at the end of this chapter, whilst further guidance on tackling other exam questions can be found on the companion website at: **www.pearsoned.co.uk/psychologyexpress**

Love

Love taxonomies

Acknowledging there is unlikely to be just *one* definition of love, researchers – notably Lee (1988) and Sternberg (1998) – have proposed taxonomies of love styles. Sternberg (1998) views love as a triangle, composed of passion, intimacy and commitment. These can be combined in numerous ways to produce an array of potential love experiences, shown around the triangle in Figure 10.1.

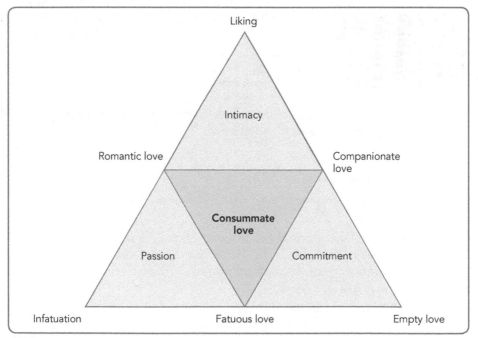

Figure 10.1 Taxonomies of love
Source: after Sternberg (1998)

Table 10.1 **Styles of love**

Styles of love	Definition
Passionate or romantic love	An intense longing for another person, characterised by the experience of physiological arousal and a confusion of feelings (e.g., anxiety, jealousy, elation, tenderness)
Companionate love	Feelings of caring, intimacy, affection and a concern for the welfare of another person (not accompanied by passion or arousal)
Compassionate love (care-giving, altruistic sacrificial love)	Feelings, cognitions and behaviours that are focused on caring, concern, support and understanding (particularly when the other is perceived to be suffering), given with no expectation of benefit in return
Adult attachment love	A strong affectional bond to a specific person, experiencing distress when involuntarily separated from that person and seeking proximity to that person when we feel under threat

The ultimate form of love, called *consummate love*, involves all three components.

The study of 'love' is still relatively new, so there is inconsistent evidence regarding many of the individual proposed love styles. However, support does seem to exist for *passionate* or *romantic love* and *companionate love* (Sternberg & Weis, 2006), whilst Berscheid's (2010) review proposes two additional types of love: *compassionate love* and *adult attachment love*. These are all outlined in Table 10.1.

Fluid nature of love

Note that these love styles are not considered stable traits, but context-dependent ideologies. Reasons for adopting different styles are discussed below.

Context-dependent ideas

Cultural and societal changes can influence our ideas and expectations about love and relationships.

- Evidence suggests our expectations of experiencing passionate love have increased in many cultures since the 1920s. Some claim marital dissatisfaction may be a consequence of unrealistic expectations of continued passionate love in relationships.
- Morgan (2011) outlines another conceptual shift away from passionate love towards assumptions of compatibility, soulmates and intimacy. This is purported to be related to societal shifts from a capitalist to an environmental discourse.

● Increases in life expectancy may lead to greater calls for compassionate love, with a greater likelihood that one partner will adopt the role of carer. This may have implications for relationship satisfaction in older couples.

Combinations of love styles

Hendrick and Hendrick (1995) present evidence that accounts of romantic love relationships are usually intertwined with companionate love. Our lovers are often our best friends.

Changes within relationships

It is commonly argued that in the initial stages of a relationship, we experience the strong emotions associated with passionate love, but this changes to a more stable love, more akin to companionate love. Evidence for this evolution comes from studies which observe the number of times spouses express affection for one another (e.g., Huston & Chorost, 1994).

Measuring love

Development of love taxonomies are based on inductive research techniques which elicit laypersons' subjective experiences of love. These are then used to form psychometric scales of love such as the LAS Agape Scale (Hendrick & Hendrick, 1986).

This mix of methodological approaches incorporates the power of quantitative analysis grounded in measures based on real-life experiences; a robust combination. However, such scales tend to adopt bipolar anchors which do not allow for separate assessment of positive and negative affect. Research indicates that we can experience love and conflict at the same time and they are not necessarily correlated with one another. This methodological design may have unwittingly led to the neglect of positive emotions in the study of relationships.

The majority of studies to date are cross-sectional or focus on the beginnings or ends of relationships. To fully understand the role of love in relationships we need to conduct longitudinal research, which maps how, when and why love changes over the life course of a relationship (Berscheid, 2010).

Test your knowledge

10.1 What is meant by a taxonomy of love styles?

10.2 How are the four types of love (passionate, companionate, compassionate and adult attachment) different and/or similar to each other?

10.3 Explain how love is a fluid concept.

Answers to these questions can be found on the companion website at: www.pearsoned.co.uk/psychologyexpress

> **?** *Sample question*   *Essay*
>
> Critically evaluate social psychologists' approaches to studying love in intimate relationships.

Further reading Defining love

Topic	Key reading
Review of love taxonomies	Sternberg, R. J., & Weis, K. (2006). *The New Psychology of Love*. New Haven, CJ: Yale University Press.
Changing role of romantic love in relationship satisfaction	Morgan, M. (2011). Soulmates, compatibility and intimacy: Allied discursive resources in the struggle for relationship satisfaction in the new millennium. *New Ideas in Psychology*, 29(1), 10–23.
Holistic, subjective experience of love	Watts, S., & Stenner, P. (2005). The subjective experience of partnership love: A Q Methodological study. *British Journal of Social Psychology*, 44, 85–107.

Relationship satisfaction

There are a number of factors that influence relationship satisfaction. We will discuss:

- the role of internal dispositions in the forming of attachment
- the role of interpersonal processes in the form of cost–benefit exchange models
- the importance of positive processes and love in the form of intimacy.

Attachment

Bowlby's (1969) and Ainsworth et al.'s (1978) theories of attachment suggest the way we form bonds with our primary caregivers influences our schema for forming and developing adult relationships. The relationship between attachment styles and quality of relationships has been shown in numerous questionnaire and interview studies (see Table 10.2 for the typical patterns).

Cost–benefit exchange models

A number of theories attempt to understand relationship satisfaction by considering the interpersonal processes of exchanges between partners, particularly the balance of inputs from partners.

Social exchange theory (see Chapter 9, Interpersonal attraction) contends that people participate in relationships where the rewards outweigh the costs.

Table 10.2 Attachment style in infancy and relationships in adulthood

Attachment style	Quality of relationship in infancy	Quality of relationship in adulthood
Secure attachment	• Caregiver – responsive to infant's needs • Infant – high level of trust, lack of concern about abandonment and high self-worth	• Easily forms close bonds with others • Ability to trust others • Ability to develop mature, lasting relationships
Avoidant attachment	• Caregiver – aloof, distant, rebuffing attempts at intimacy • Infant – suppresses need for attachment	• Uncomfortable becoming close to others • Difficulty trusting others • Least likely to enter into relationships • Lowest levels of commitment • Difficulty in developing close intimate relationships
Anxious/ ambivalent attachment	• Caregiver – inconsistent and overbearing • Infant – higher than average levels of anxiety	• Concern that others will not reciprocate attempts at intimacy • Likely to be obsessive and preoccupied with relationship • May enter into relationships quickly, but have short-lived relationships • Difficulty maintaining close, intimate relationships

Equity theory is grounded in social exchange theory, but is particularly concerned with expectations of exchanges in *close* relationships. The main principles of equity theory are:

- the outcomes of being in a relationship should be proportional to the input (e.g., in terms of love, emotional support, household tasks, financial support)
- *equitable* outcomes are not necessarily *equal* outcomes; equity is a perception
- inequitable relationships lead to feelings of discomfort: those contributing less feel guilt, those contributing more feel irritation
- relationship between inequity and marital distress is circular as feelings of inequity lead to distress and then there is a greater likelihood of perceiving the inequity
- in shorter-term relationships, exchanges are fairly rigid and fixed – favours are repaid immediately and we feel exploited if not repaid
- in longer-term relationships, exchanges are more varied – the need to reciprocate is less immediate and the perceived need to keep track of exchanges diminishes.

Social exchange and equity models have successfully predicted relationship satisfaction across cultures. However, these models cannot explain why people sometimes remain in relationships even when they perceive inequity.

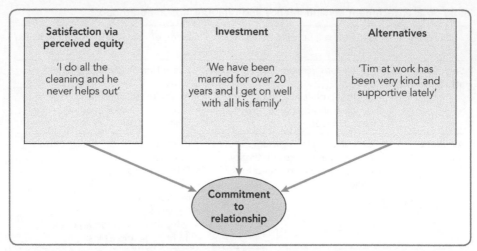

Figure 10.2 The investment model of close relationship
Source: after Rusbult (1983)

In the *investment model of close relationships* (Rusbult, 1983), satisfaction with the relationship is still thought to be determined by weighing up rewards against costs and then comparing this against our expectations of what we should receive by being in a relationship. However, our commitment to the relationship is also determined by our level of *investment* in the relationship and the quality of alternatives to this relationship (see Figure 10.2).

Evidence for this model came initially from a longitudinal survey (lasting seven months) of students' relationships. Satisfaction, quality of alternatives and level of investment were all significant predictors of commitment and likelihood of breaking up – the quality of alternatives being the strongest predictor in this case (Rusbult, 1983). Similar findings have since been demonstrated with married couples across age groups, lesbian and gay relationships, both collectivistic and individualistic cultures and abusive relationships.

Role of intimacy

Recall our earlier description of compassionate love, whereby interactions in intimate relationships are governed by a desire to be responsive to the other person's needs (Clark & Mills, 2001). This type of love cannot be explained through exchange models of relationship satisfaction. Indeed, there is evidence that people in happy, long-term relationships make efforts *not* to calculate exchange benefits (Buunk & Van Yperen, 1991) and feelings of intimacy may be more important for relationship satisfaction than equity (Cate, Lloyd & Long, 1988). Table 10.3 outlines four ways in which increased intimacy can lead to greater satisfaction in relationships.

Interdependence theory

This theory draws together the many facets of relationship satisfaction research.

Table 10.3 **Role of intimacy in relationship satisfaction**

Concept	Role in relationship satisfaction
Self-disclosure	We like those who disclose (reveal intimate aspects about themselves) to us and we disclose to those whom we like. This leads to trust, deep companionate love and greater relationship satisfaction (Sanderson & Cantor, 2001).
	In contrast, poorer satisfaction with married life is related to perception of concealment of information, lack of trust and intimacy (Finkenauer, Kerkhof, Righetti & Brange, 2009).
Overlapping selves	The more our self concept overlaps with the self concept of our partner, the greater our satisfaction, commitment and investment in the relationship (Smith, Coats & Walling, 1999).
Adopting approach relationship goals	Approach goals (goals focused on the pursuit of positive experiences in relationships, pursuit of intimacy, fun) rather than avoidance relationship goals (goals focusing on avoiding negative experiences, such as disagreements and conflict) increase positive emotions and lead to greater relationship satisfaction (Impett et al., 2010).
Perception that our partner knows how we feel	Believing our partner knows our goals leads to a feeling of being understood and cared for (closeness) which is related to relationship quality (Riediger & Rauers, 2010).

The contention is that, to understand what makes relationships successful, we need to consider how specific situational factors affect interpersonal processes (e.g., equity) and stable interpersonal dispositions (attachment style). The authors emphasise the importance of conducting longitudinal dyadic research to capture interactions within specific social contexts (Rusbult & Van Lange, 2003).

Test your knowledge

10.4 How does the investment model of close relationships address the limitations of equity theory in understanding relationship satisfaction?

10.5 What is the evidence that intimacy is important in marital satisfaction?

10.6 Outline how attachment styles in childhood may affect adult relationships.

Answers to these questions can be found on the companion website at: www.pearsoned.co.uk/psychologyexpress

? Sample question   Essay

A marriage is more likely to survive when each partner contributes equally to the partnership. Discuss with reference to psychological theory and empirical evidence.

Further reading	Relationship satisfaction
Topic	Key reading
Attachment styles and close relationships	Birnbaum, G. E., Reis, H. T., Mikulincer, M., Gillath, O., & Orpaz, A. (2006). When sex is more than just sex: Attachment orientations, sexual experience and relationship quality. *Journal of Personality and Social Psychology*, 91, 929–943.
Approach goals and relationship satisfaction – a longitudinal dyadic study	Impett, E. A., Kogan, A., Gable, S. L., Gordon, A. M., Oveis, C., & Keltner, D. (2010). Moving toward more perfect unions: Daily and long-term consequences of approach and avoidance goals in romantic relationships. *Journal of Personality and Social Psychology*, 99(6), 948–963.
Feeling that your partner knows you well and relationship satisfaction	Riediger, M., & Rauers, A. (2010). The 'I know you' and the 'you know me' of mutual goal knowledge in partnerships: Differential associations with partnership satisfaction and sense of closeness over time. *British Journal of Social Psychology*, 49, 647–656.
Interdependence theory	Rusbult, C. E., & Van Lange, P. A. M. (2003). Interdependence, interaction and relationships. *Annual Review of Psychology*, 54, 351–375.

Relationship dissolution

You might not be familiar with the term 'dissolution'. The literal meaning is to dissolve a partnership, hence its use in the relationship literature when discussing the ending of relationships.

Stages of breakdown

Intimate relationships rarely break down overnight, therefore much research has considered dissolution as a *process*. Various authors have offered models mapping the stages or phases of dissolution (refer to Vangelisti, 2006, for a comparison of the different approaches). One of the most prolific writers in this area is Steve Duck, whose model is discussed here.

Duck (1982) identifies four main phases of relationship dissolution. Each is qualitatively different and will be initiated when a certain threshold of dissatisfaction is reached. The initial model is summarised in Table 10.4.

Since introducing this model in the 1980s, Duck has further developed his work. In 2005, Duck himself described his model as at fault for ignoring everyday life communication, which plays a central role in managing relationships. The amended model considers the ways in which such (often seemingly mundane) communication patterns are an integral part of the process of managing the relationship in crisis (Duck, 2005).

Table 10.4 Duck's (1982) phase model of relationship dissolution

Name of phase	Description of threshold of dissatisfaction	Summary of phase
Intrapsychic	'I can't stand this any more'	One or both partners start to feel dissatisfaction. It is not verbalised within the relationship at this stage. Confiding in a close friend might be an option. The focus here is on the other partner who is the source of the dissatisfaction. Alternative relationships might be considered
Dyadic	'I'd be justified in leaving'	At this stage, the partner is confronted. Less formal, short-term relationships could end with a general 'See you around' type statement. In more established cohabiting or marriage relationships, serious discussions ensue. Outcomes might be to end the relationship or consider ways in which it might be changed or repaired
Social	'I mean it'	If dissolution reaches this stage, then the break-up 'goes public'. Stories of events are given by both parties which do not make them look culpable. Gossip is often a source of information dissemination in this and the next phase
Grave-dressing	'It's now inevitable'	Duck talks about dressing the grave – putting the relationship to rest. Accounts are given about the relationship history. In this phase (as in the previous one), the partners both need to protect their reputations. The term 'social credit' is used to describe the idea that we seek to take little or no blame for the break-up. We need to leave the relationship with our own reputation intact

The other significant amendment was to extend the model to look at what happens *after* the grave-dressing phase – labelled *resurrection processes*. Here, in preparation for a new relationship, a review of psychological beliefs about the self, others and relationships takes place. The outcome may be to adjust previously held beliefs in order to carve a 'better' future. The other process involves attempts to avoid areas which have proved problematic in one's relationship history – e.g., actively avoiding going out with someone who has attributes which you have determined to be problematic in your previous partner(s). Duck acknowledges that the nature and amount of readjustment to beliefs that take place will depend on the level of trauma experienced during the dissolution and personality differences, such as attachment style. However, the resurrection process is a form of psychological reconstruction which allows us to build a different worldview when it comes to relationships (Duck, 2005).

Advantages of stage approaches

Duck's work has been significant in widening the literature on interpersonal relationships from the predominant focus on formation and maintenance. As relationship dissolution has become more common and less stigmatised in many societies, it seems imperative to understand the lifecycle of relationships in their entirety. Dissolution needs to be seen as an important part of the research.

The model has practical implications for counselling and developing stage-based interventions. Duck has also identified strategies to repair relationships (e.g., in the intrapsychic phase, re-establishing a liking for your partner by keeping a record of his or her positive attributes would be more helpful than dwelling on the negatives).

The emphasis on possible repair strategies illustrates how the process of relationship maintenance and dissolution are not mutually exclusive.

Some limitations of stage approaches

Stage models suggest a linear progression through the different phases. Relationships might not always pass through these four stages in a neat fashion. Some people split up and then get back together again. Others might get to the dyadic stage on more than one occasion during the lifecourse of the relationship.

The idea that a relationship ends at a specific stage suggests partners no longer interact. This is unlikely to be the case when couples have children or joint finances and houses. Post-dissolution relationships (PDRs) can follow a number of different trajectories depending on the circumstances of the breakdown. Refer to Koenig Kellas, Bean, Cunningham & Yun Cheng (2008) for research in this area.

Predictors of dissolution

Models mapping the stages of dissolution also fail to inform us about the reasons why relationships break down. A useful way of examining the literature on this is to find review papers comparing the different variables which have been identified within lots of studies and conduct a statistical analysis on such findings to ascertain those having the strongest effect. From this, researchers can reach conclusions about trends in the literature and highlight which variables appear to be the strongest predictors. This method is known as meta-analysis.

Le, Dove, Agnew, Korn and Mutso, (2010) conducted a meta-analysis of the research relating to predictors of dissolution amongst non-married couples. They divided their study of 137 studies into three different groups of variables:

● *Individual-level factors.* These incorporate individual difference measures, such as personality measures, and those more specifically associated with relationship research, such as attachment.

● *Characteristics of relationships.* These relate to many of the areas discussed earlier on in this chapter, such as love, commitment and satisfaction.

- *External factors.* The final group is factors each person can draw on which are external to the relationship – social networks would be an example.

The meta-analysis revealed that individual differences are not good predictors of break-ups. A moderately sized negative predictor was network support. This means that those who have a stronger support network are more likely to stay together. Overall, characteristics of the relationship were the most robust predictors of dissolution. The strongest effects arose for the variables of positive illusions, commitment and love (the more individuals experienced these factors towards their partners, the less likely they were to dissolve their relationships).

Findings were also moderated by participants' gender. The variables which were identified as being more likely to predict dissolution amongst males were satisfaction, adjustment and ambivalence, whilst, for females, they were self-disclosure, closeness and conflict. Such studies indicate the complexity in understanding relationship processes.

Test your knowledge

10.7 What determines whether the relationship will move into the next stage of dissolution as outlined in Duck's model?

10.8 What might the real-life applications of Duck's work be?

10.9 What are the main differences in terms of the type of information provided between a stage theory of dissolution and a meta-analysis of the predictors of dissolution?

Answers to these questions can be found on the companion website at: www.pearsoned.co.uk/psychologyexpress

? Sample question   Essay

Discuss the relative merits of stage approaches to relationship dissolution.

Further reading Relationship dissolution

Topic	Key reading
Duck's revised model	Duck, S. (2005). How do you tell someone you're letting go? *The Psychologist, 18*, 210–213.
Post-dissolution relationships	Koenig Kellas, J., Bean, J. D., Cunningham, C., & Yun Cheng, K. (2008). The ex-files: Trajectories, turning points, and adjustment in the development of post-dissolutional relationships. *Journal of Social and Personal Relationships, 25*, 23–50.

Comparison of different stage modes	Vangelisti, A. L. (2006). Relationship dissolution: Antecedents, processes, and consequences. In P. Noller & J. A. Feeney, *Close relationships: Functions, Forms and Processes* (pp. 353–374). Hove, East Sussex: Psychology Press.
Meta-analyses of the predictors of dissolution	Le, B., Dove, N. L., Agnew, C. R., Korn, M. S., and Mutso, A. A. (2010). Predicting nonmarital romantic relationship dissolution: A meta-analytic synthesis. *Personal Relationships, 17*, 377–390.

Post-dissolution growth

Much of the literature about post-dissolution states has been written from a distress perspective, yet research suggests that there can also be positive out-comes from the dissolution process (Park, Cohen & Murch, 1996). In primarily focusing on distress, have relationship researchers only painted half the picture?

Tashiro and Frazier (2003) looked exclusively at post-dissolution growth and found positive changes to participants' sense of self was the most commonly cited area of growth. Such findings are consistent with the crisis–growth model (Tashiro, Frazier & Berman, 2006), which acknowledges that, although dissolution is a potentially traumatic and upsetting experience, it also provides opportunities for a reassessment of one's self, to discover new abilities and meet challenges. Not all relationship dissolutions will require crisis management, as can be seen from the Key Study below.

KEY STUDY

Lewandowski and Bizzoco (2007). Growth following the dissolution of a low-quality relationship

This study was based on the idea that if a relationship has been of a low quality (e.g., undesirable or damaging), its dissolution might *not* be upsetting. In this circumstance, the individual is able to experience growth through the subtraction of a relationship which had been limiting for him or her. This fits with the idea of a stress-relief pathway, where a state of relief which compares favourably to the feelings experienced when in the relationship is a salient dissolution experience. It is probable also that low-quality relationships provide limited opportunities for self-expansion (an area where romantic relationships have been identified as playing a key role).

A total of 155 participants who had experienced relationship dissolution during the previous 6 months completed various measurements. A self-expansion questionnaire measured the quality of their relationship pre-dissolution, whilst any post-dissolution growth was assessed via scales measuring loss of self, rediscovery of self, positive and negative emotions, growth and coping involving positive reinterpretation and acceptance.

The authors were seeking to establish if individuals who had been in relationships low in self-expansion would report substantial post-dissolution growth. Further, they hypothesised that less pre-dissolution self-expansion would be associated with higher

▶

levels of self-rediscovery, less loss of self, more positive emotions and more coping involving reinterpretation and acceptance when recorded post-dissolution.

The results indicated support for all of the above hypotheses, with the exception of reinterpretation and acceptance (although the trends were in the direction hypothesised).

This study expands our knowledge of the dissolution process by focusing on low-quality relationships and highlighting factors which mediate growth. Here self-rediscovery and positive emotions seem to be especially strong.

? Sample question   Essay

Critically consider the idea that relationship dissolution may also produce positive outcomes.

Further reading Post-dissolution growth

Topic	Key reading
One of the first studies to discuss this topic	Tashiro, T., & Frazier, P. (2003). 'I'll never be in a relationship like that again': Personal growth following romantic relationship breakups. *Personal Relationships, 10*, 113–128.
Growth after low-quality relationships	Lewandowski, G. W., & Bizzoco, N. M. (2007). Addition through subtraction: Growth following the dissolution of a low-quality relationship. *Journal of Positive Psychology, 2*, 40–45.
Moderating factors for perceived and actual growth	Gunty, A. L., Frazier, P. A., Tennen, H., Tomich, P., Tashiro, T., & Park, C. (2010). Moderators of the relation between perceived and actual posttraumatic growth. *Psychological Trauma: Theory, Research, Practice, and Policy*. No pagination specified. doi: 10.1037/a0020485.

A final word on the psychology of intimate relationships

Let us return to Le et al.'s (2010) meta-analysis of predictors of relationship dissolution. The study covers a sample of 37,761 participants, drawn from 137 studies conducted over a period of 33 years. This is clearly an impressive sample size. However, take a look at the demographics of the research reviewed: across all these samples, 81 per cent were white, 96 per cent heterosexual and the average age was 25 years old. Four studies were conducted in Europe, 15 in Canada and the rest in the USA. The demographics listed are not unusual for such mainstream research publications. Think back to our discussion of attempts to define love – what types of relationships do we actually know about?

- Young adults – especially students, but how much relationship experience will they have? Are they likely to share certain demographics?

- Dyadic, love relationships. What do we know about arranged marriages? Polygamy still exists in some societies.

- Western conceptions of relationships. Cross-cultural studies have revealed areas of similarity in non-Western cultures, but also differences (further reading suggestions on this are given at the end of this section).

- Heterosexual relationships. Less is known about lesbian and gay relationships, research on bi- and transsexual relationships is even more scarce (see Critical Focus below).

CRITICAL FOCUS

The heterosexual bias in relationship research

The majority of research on relationships has focused on heterosexual relationships. This can lead to the 'normativity' of such relationships (which refers to viewing such relationships as the 'norm' and being presented as an applicable model around which to consider all relationships). Lesbian, gay, bisexual, trans and queer (LGBTQ, see Chapter 11, Critical social psychology) researchers would argue that moulding other types of relationships according to this normative model is problematic. Any behaviour which does not conform to the norm could be overlooked (Clarke, Burgoyne & Burns, 2005).

It is important to note that lesbian and gay relationships have been historically marginalised. Psychological research can be used to raise awareness and inform policymakers. It should represent diverse perspectives, not just heterosexual ones.

Research on same-sex relationships is a growing field, still in its infancy. Much early comparative work sought to debunk stereotypes, such as those which viewed same-sex relationships as unhappy and dysfunctional (Clarke, Ellis, Peel & Riggs, 2010). More recent comparative studies of lesbian, gay and heterosexual relationships have focused on topics such as the division of labour, relationship satisfaction and quality and conflict (see Peplau & Fingerhut, 2007, for a review).

So, when discussing relationship literature, be aware of the heterosexual bias and the implications this has for assumptions we might make about the nature of intimate relationships. Even amongst LGBTQ research there has been a predominance of samples drawn from white middle-class gay men and lesbians. Less is known about trans- or bisexual relationships. There is still much to be learned beyond the normative heterosexual couple.

Further reading A final word on the psychology of intimate relationships

Topic	Key reading
Similarity from an Eastern perspective	Chen, H., Lou, S., Yue, G., Xu., D., & Zhaoyang, R. (2009). Do birds of a feather flock together in China? *Personal Relationships*, 16, 167–186.
Cross-cultural study of attachment in relationships	Friedman, M., Rholes, W. S., Simpson, J., Bond, M., Diaz-Loving, R., & Chan, C. (2010). Attachment avoidance and the cultural fit hypothesis: A cross-cultural investigation. *Personal Relationships*, 17, 107–126.

LGBTQ relationship research	Clarke, V., Ellis, S. J., Peel, E., & Riggs, D. W. (2010). *Lesbian, gay, bisexual, trans & queer psychology: An introduction* (Chapter 8). Cambridge: Cambridge University Press.
US research on lesbian and gay relationships	Peplau, L. A., & Fingerhut, A. W. (2007). The close relationships of lesbians and gay men. *Annual Review of Psychology, 58*, 405–424.

✳ Sample question   *Problem-based learning*

A professor in a psychology department in a university in New York has approached a professor of psychology in a London-based university to work together on a large survey-based study about the lifecycles of intimate relationships. It is proposed that formation, maintenance and dissolution of relationships will be considered. The sample will comprise students in the respective universities. Reflecting on the nature of research on intimate relationships discussed in this chapter, list the reasons why such a study might be potentially limited in capturing relationship trajectories.

Chapter summary – pulling it all together

→ Can you tick all the points from the revision checklist at the beginning of this chapter?

→ Attempt the sample question from the beginning of this chapter using the answer guidelines below.

→ Go to the companion website at www.pearsoned.co.uk/psychologyexpress to access more revision support online, including interactive quizzes, flashcards, You be the marker exercises as well as answer guidance for the Test your knowledge and Sample questions from this chapter.

Further reading for Chapter 10

Duck, S. W. (2011) *Rethinking Relationships*. London: Sage.

Noller, P., & Feeney, J. A. (2006) *Close relationships: Forms and processes*. Hove, East Sussex: Psychology Press. (A wide discussion of the field of relationships, covering areas discussed in Chapter 9 in addition to those covered this chapter.)

Answer guidelines

Approaching the question

There are numerous ways of tackling this question. You could choose to narrow the question by, for example, specifically focusing on a particular population. For example, you might state that the majority of the research has been conducted on a young adult student population in Western society. Therefore, you will address the question with this population in mind. Alternatively, you could discuss what we know about love and relationship satisfaction in a wider sense and critique the evidence on the basis of the sample biases in the research.

Important points to include

One of the first things you will need to address is how to define love. You will recall that there is no agreed definition and the existing taxonomies suggest love styles may be combined in a fluid array, rather than discrete entities.

You may wish to comment on the need to develop a temporal model of love to gain a full understanding of the role of love in relationship satisfaction across the lifespan of relationships. Berscheid's (2010) paper would be useful here.

You could comment on the dominance of exchange models and individual differences in the study of relationship satisfaction, pointing out that this doesn't tell us much about the role of love and intimacy in relationship satisfaction.

Research which has looked at the role of intimacy includes discussions of the contributions made by self-disclosure, overlapping selves and the development of closeness (e.g., Riediger & Rauers, 2010). You could also point to Le et al.'s (2010) research on relationship dissolution, which demonstrated that love was one of the most important predictors for relationship survival. Finally, you could note that our expectations of relationships may have changed over time. Essentially, acknowledge that the study of love and relationships is culturally, socially and temporally dependent.

Make your answer stand out

Much of the research linking love with relationship satisfaction is grounded in measuring love using psychometric scales. Some psychologists argue that psychometric scales are an inappropriate tool for measuring love. An alternative approach is offered by Watts and Stenner (2005), inclusion of which could offer a strong critical edge to your essay.

Explore the accompanying website at www.pearsoned.co.uk/psychologyexpress

→ Prepare more effectively for exams and assignments using the answer guidelines for questions from this chapter.

→ Test your knowledge using multiple choice questions and flashcards.

→ Improve your essay skills by exploring the You be the marker exercises.

Notes

Notes

Critical social psychology

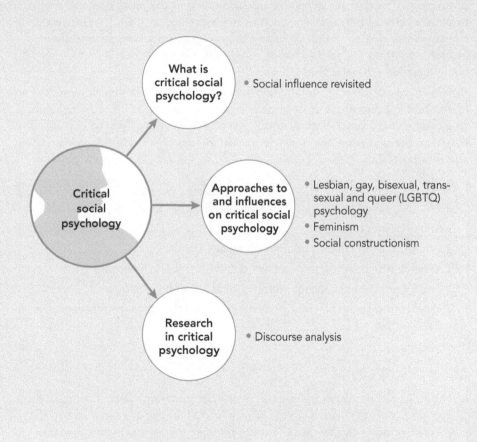

A printable version of this topic map is available from:
www.pearsoned.co.uk/psychologyexpress

Introduction

This chapter will discuss critical social psychology, a branch of the discipline which has grown in popularity in the UK during the past two decades. Many introductory textbooks now exist (e.g., Gough & McFadden, 2001; Stainton Rogers, 2011; Tuffin, 2005) about critical social psychology and references will be drawn from such sources in order to enhance your understanding of the basic premises of this approach. It will facilitate an appreciation of journal articles written from this perspective.

The chapter will begin by explaining what critical social psychology is and how it challenges some of the assumptions of the more traditional approaches to social psychology. We will then illustrate how these ideas have been translated into research to offer a contrasting way of researching topics central to social psychology. The chapter will also introduce some of the more politically orientated critical perspectives, such as feminism and lesbian, gay, bisexual, transsexual and queer (LGBTQ) psychology to provide an insight into the awareness raising and social change remit which is a part of the endeavour for some located within the field.

However, do not view this as an 'add on' or standalone – critical approaches are mentioned in other areas of this book. The ideas discussed can also be useful to evaluate social psychological enquiry and will encourage you to consider the nature of the discipline and how the 'social' in social psychology is constructed and interpreted.

> **→ Revision checklist**
>
> *Essential points to revise are:*
> - ❏ What the term critical social psychology refers to
> - ❏ Ways in which critical approaches differ from the mainstream
> - ❏ The influential approaches within critical social psychology
> - ❏ How critical social psychologists might research topics within social psychology

Assessment advice

- The tasks are designed for you to check your understanding of some of the key ideas of critical social psychology. It is vital that you grasp these so that you can make links between the underpinning theoretical stance and the research conducted from this perspective.
- We have found when teaching this approach that students often try to outline critical and mainstream approaches and then struggle to list the evaluatory points of each. This is how many of the other topics in this book have been

presented and the model often adhered to in textbooks. However, it is better to approach this topic from a slightly different stance. In discussing critical accounts you are evaluating; as their name suggests they offer a critique. When employing a critical social psychological stance, you are, by the very nature of the arguments presented, analysing both what social psychology is and the way in which social psychological knowledge is constructed.

● Any approach, be it cognitive, evolutionary or critical, will be influenced by a variety of factors, including our social and cultural background, belief systems and epistemology (theory of knowledge). The critical approach to psychology is one of the few that explicitly acknowledges this within its research.

● Writing assignments from this perspective requires an engagement with the epistemological stance of the critical approach and how this links to the research produced. Answering the essay questions will help you to articulate such ideas. Use the Answer guidelines advice offered at the end the chapter for further guidance on this.

Sample question

Below is a typical essay that could arise on this topic.

> ✱ *Sample question*   *Essay*
>
> Discuss the ways in which critical social psychology differs from mainstream approaches.

Guidelines on answering this question are included at the end of this chapter, whilst further guidance on tackling other exam questions can be found on the companion website at: www.pearsoned.co.uk/psychologyexpress

What is critical social psychology?

On one level, a critical approach to social psychology has existed for a long time. If you have read anything about the history of social psychology, you will have come across the so-called 'crisis' which occurred in the late 1960s and early 1970s when questions were raised about the ways in which social psychology should be researched and the type of science it represented.

Classic papers such as Kenneth Gergen's 'Social psychology as history' (1973) drew attention to the argument that social psychological knowledge should be culturally and historically located. In the 1980s, however, texts such as Henriques, Hollway, Urwin, Venn and Walkerdine's, (1984) *Changing the subject* offered essays from a more interpretive and politically informed stance and Potter and Wetherell's (1987) *Discourse and social psychology: Beyond attitudes and behaviour* suggested that more attention should be paid to the way in which language is used to construct meaning rather than focus on static cognitive entities such as attitudes.

The debates raised by the aforementioned authors provide a flavour of some of the concerns of critical social psychology. Critical social psychology has largely evolved from challenges to what is referred to as the *mainstream*. By 'mainstream', writers typically mean research which adheres to the view of social psychology as a *science* – one similar to the natural sciences. (You will find some texts use the term 'experimental' rather than 'mainstream'. For the purpose of this chapter, 'mainstream' will be used because it is considered to mean more than just the method.) The mainstream approach uses a hypothetico-deductive method (methods based on making a deduction by testing a hypothesis) which is problematised by critical social psychologists both in terms of the knowledge it provides and the power it holds as the dominant force within psychology.

Although 'critical psychology' is an umbrella term for different perspectives (some of which are discussed later), psychologists who subscribe to this approach tend to share similar concerns. Stainton Rogers (2011) suggests that there are three main challenges that the critical approach provides for the mainstream (see Figure 11.1 and Tables 11.1–3 for more detail). Essentially, these are interrelated points and influence the ways in which critical psychologists conduct their research and the types of questions they ask.

In Tables 11.1–3, more detail is provided about the critical approach as you will probably already be familiar with the mainstream perspective, which is the main one covered in the standard textbooks.

Method	Ideology	Social world
• Should social psychology be treated as a natural science?	• Is social psychology value-free and objective? • Does it promote a specific ideology?	• Is the social something 'out there' to be measured? • Can individual and social be separated?

Figure 11.1 **Challenges posed by the critical approach**

Table 11.1 **The challenge relating to method**

Mainstream position	Critical position
Social psychology should be treated as a science, like the natural sciences. The discipline should be objective, neutral, value-free. This can be achieved by adopting an experimental approach, which can provide facts	Social psychology should be aligned to the social sciences. The scientific method is only one approach to knowledge construction. Knowledge is a product of human meaningmaking, which is constructed and culturally and historically positioned

Table **11.2** The challenge relating to ideology

Mainstream position	Critical position
Social psychology should not be ideologically positioned. The scientific approach allows it to provide objective knowledge, to discover facts, irrespective of politics and values	Social psychology is ideologically positioned. Mainstream approaches are not neutral (as claimed), they adopt an elitist ideological position which addresses the interests of the most powerful, e.g., white, Western, able-bodied, male establishment (Stainton Rogers, 2011). This can leave the less powerful groups without a voice and add to their oppression. Critical social psychologists feel their work should challenge social institutions and practices which lead to oppression and inequality of certain groups. In order to do this, it needs to be ideologically positioned

Table **11.3** The challenge relating to the social world

Mainstream position	Critical position
Mainstream social psychology takes an individualist stance. It outlines processes which explain the functioning of the individual (e.g., cognitive processes). It can then establish laws of human behaviour which are generalisable (also called *nomothetic*). The 'social' is seen as something separate from the individual which may (or may not) have an effect on his or her behaviour (see Critical focus of conformity experiments below)	Critical social psychology focuses more on the interrelationship between individual and social contexts. These two are not viewed as separate. Individuals are seen as situated in a social setting where they interact with other individuals, institutions and social practices. The broader social structures are acknowledged by the critical approach (e.g., class, culture). Behaviour may differ depending on situation and context; it is not viewed as fixed and generalisable. The critical social psychologist will be more interested in the ways in which meanings are constructed in specific locations and situations by certain groups (often those with less power in society). Their approach will be smaller-scale and searching to unfold the meanings of particular situations (also called *idiographic*)

You can see that critical social psychology has a broad remit. This is summarised well in Hepburn's (2003, p. 1) definition:

> critical social psychology is critical of society or at least some basic elements of its institutions, organisations or practices. But critical social psychology is critical in another basic sense: it is critical of psychology itself. It asks questions about its assumptions, its practices and its broader influences.

Engaging with the critical approach will lead you to consider the purpose of social psychology, the types of topics it covers and how these might be investigated.

Social influence revisited

In order for you to see how these critiques might be applied to published topics within mainstream social psychology, this section will illustrate a critical approach to social influence.

Asch's study of conformity

Asch's work on conformity, originally conducted in the 1950s, represents a key study of social influence. It is cited in core textbooks, taught in undergraduate courses and is the most frequently replicated social psychology study cross-culturally. The study, in which individuals conformed to the opinions of others in a room of six on an unambiguous task (represented by lines of equal length), is heralded as robust evidence that, in a group situation, people will conform. In what ways might the critical approach challenge such research? Some examples are provided.

The adherence to an experimental approach might be one area of critique. This is a laboratory study where 'social' is represented by the presence of others. Hepburn (2003) notes behaviour might be very different in *actual* situations, depending on what is happening in the specific situation. A critical social psychologist would not, therefore, view conformity as a universal given in the presence of just any group.

Asch's work is presented in the following way:

individual + others in agreement = conformity

Conformity is viewed as something we do (or do not). It is a fact to be discovered. From a critical viewpoint, there is insufficient attention given to the context and dynamics of who was present. Even replications using the same method have illustrated this may alter the effect – e.g., Williams and Sogon (1984) found that the error rate differed when groups knew each other from that when they were strangers. For the critical social scientist, the individual and social cannot be so easily separated.

Critical social psychologists might argue that we have been presented with an interpretation rather than facts. For example, the figure of 33 per cent is often highlighted as evidence that people conform. However, only 5 per cent conformed on each trial, which suggests that 95 per cent of participants do not conform most of the time. Gergen (2008) suggests that statistics represent a scientific tool which can be used to silence those who do not understand such evidence. The power remains with the scientist, whilst those who cannot understand such interpretations are powerless to dispute the evidence presented.

For the critical social psychologist, social influence is not something 'out there' to be discovered. Disentangling the social from the individual is not considered fruitful. How might the critical social psychologist illustrate social influence if it is such an integral part of the social world and, therefore, the individual? Consider the Key Study below.

KEY STUDY

Sandfield and Percy (2003). How heterosexual women talk about marriage

Sandfield and Percy (2003) undertook semi-structured interviews with 12 heterosexual British women of varying relationship status (at time of interviewing, 7 were single). They considered the ways in which the participants spoke about themselves and other women who were not married.

A thematic analysis identified two interrelated themes of 'single youth versus spinsterhood' and 'constructing fault, blame and accountability'.

The first described the ways in which the women viewed being single as something which was accepted when younger, but took on very different connotations when older. Older single women were viewed as 'flawed' or 'deviant' in some way. The term 'spinster' was used and perceived as a fate to avoid. It was hoped that being single was a temporary state.

Such negative associations with the single relationship status were further developed in the second theme, 'constructing fault, blame and accountability'. Here participants engaged in narratives of self-blame, recounting previous relationship dissolutions as 'failures' and the consequence of some 'fault' on their part. Other women in their lives (e.g., family members) also appeared to reinforce negative images of singlehood.

The authors take a feminist stance, noting that such narratives can eclipse a woman's agency and selfhood beyond heterosexual relationships and marriage (i.e., the female identity is constructed around relationships with men). The women's perceptions reflect cultural images of the unmarried woman as desperate and flawed. Being single is positioned not as a lifestyle choice but as a lifestyle failure.

What does this tell us about social influence? The broader aim of the study was to explore the extent to which personal relationships featured in the women's discussions about their identity. The word conformity is nowhere to be seen in the title. However, the participants in Sandfield and Percy's study were seen as conforming to traditional discourses of the female life course. Within these, heterosexual romance and marriage are equated with successful trajectories for women to follow. Such discourses were then shaping their own identities and views of how women 'should' behave when it came to relationships.

Test your knowledge

11.1 Mainstream approaches are aligned with the natural sciences. Critical approaches are more aligned with what type of science?

11.2 How do critical social psychologists view the relationship between the social world and the individual?

11.3 Discuss the reasons why the mainstream's contention that their work is neutral and value-free might be viewed as problematic by critical social psychologists.

▶

11.4 Read the account of Sandfield and Percy's work and answer the following questions.

- What are the women conforming to?
- What does the study reveal about the relationship between individual and society?

Answers to these questions can be found on the companion website at: www.pearsoned.co.uk/psychologyexpress

? *Sample question*   *Essay*

Compare and contrast critical and mainstream accounts of social influence.

Further reading Critical social psychology

Topic	Key reading
Development of and key concerns of the critical approach	Stainton Rogers, W. (2011). *Social psychology* (Chapters 1–3). Maidenhead: Open University Press.
Clear account of the critical approach	Gough, B., & McFadden, M. (2001). *Critical social psychology: An introduction* (Chapter 1). Basingstoke: Palgrave Macmillan.
Social influence from a critical perspective	Sandfield, A., & Percy, C. (2003). Accounting for single status: Heterosexism and ageism in heterosexual women's talk about marriage. *Feminism & Psychology, 13,* 475–488.

Approaches to and influences on critical social psychology

Earlier, it was suggested that critical social psychology is an umbrella term for a number of voices. It has been influenced by approaches both within and outside of psychology – e.g., psychoanalytic thought, Marxist approaches, social theory, sociology and philosophy.

This section highlights two examples of approaches which are often cited as being influential within critical psychology and aligned with many of its concerns. It is important to view them as branches of psychology in their own right also.

Lesbian, gay, bisexual, transsexual and queer (LGBTQ) psychology

LGBTQ arose from a critique of mainstream psychology, which historically pathologised gay and lesbian individuals (especially psychiatry), and highlights mainstream psychology's tendency to research heterosexual individuals only and the normalisation of this. In other words, to be heterosexual is seen as the norm and other types of relationships are then considered in comparison to this.

Furthermore, it suggests that, if social psychology is to offer an account of all people, the experiences of LGBTQ individuals should also be considered in research.

This approach relates not just to sexualities but also other topics, such as stigma and prejudice, and seeks to raise awareness and fight for social change.

Feminism

Feminism considers that there are unequal power structures within society based on gender and views women as worthy of study in their own right. It suggests that experiential approaches are important in understanding the plight of women (experiential research considers individuals' experiences and how they describe the meanings of these; this is likely to be qualitative). The feminist approach is avowedly political, seeking to raise awareness and work towards a non-patriarchal society.

Whilst feminists have a different specific focus, jointly their work reflects many of the themes important within critical social psychology, such as power relations, a critique of mainstream approaches, desire to raise awareness of certain groups within society. You may be able to think of more.

Social constructionism

Many of the ideas noted so far are also reflected in social constructionism – a paradigm often supported by critical social psychologists and a perspective on which they base their work. Social constructionism is concerned with meanings rather than facts and does not view meanings as static. For example, take the word 'love'. Have you used the term this week? In what context? What did you mean by it? Consider the different meanings it might have in these sentences.

'I love my daughter.'
'I love watching films.'
'I love my dog.'
'I love the weekends.'
'I love ice-cream.'
'I love getting under a duvet.'

The accounts here range from a deeply felt emotion towards a relative, to the joy of eating and the warmth and comfort gained by covering yourself with a duvet! All these things have been derived from one word.

An important point about social constructionism is that meanings and interpretations are socially situated. They reject the idea of one 'truth' or reality, which is the essence of science. For them, there are potentially multiple meanings, which might change, based on time, cultural location and the individual's situation.

Consider the term marriage. This might have a different meaning for a heterosexual male and a homosexual male living in Britain. The latter would be excluded from the full legal rights marriage accords heterosexual couples. If he wished to hold the ceremony in a church, he would be unable to do so. From his perspective, the civil ceremony as a same-sex 'alternative' to marriage could be viewed as a ceremony which positions him as a second-class citizen. The two do not seem to be equal.

For the social constructionist, meanings are ideologically situated and are associated with power (as the example illustrates). Rather than 'facts' and 'truths' about the world, we offer interpretations, which are shared via discourse. To quote Gergen (2008, p. 2), 'Together we construct our worlds'. Objective truths are rejected by social constructionists; in their place are subjective realities.

How can such ideas be captured within research? It is worth highlighting that social constructionists such as Gergen are not calling for an abandonment of the scientific method and experimentation. Instead, they view this as a certain form of knowledge (and, in itself, a social construction). Constructionist approaches, and most critical social psychologists, therefore adopt different methods of research from the experiment, which pervades mainstream approaches.

Test your knowledge

11.5 List three of the concerns that feminist and LGBTQ approaches have in common with critical social psychology's critique of the mainstream approach.

11.6 Nelson Mandela has been described as a 'freedom fighter' and a 'terrorist'. Outline how a social constructionist account might reconcile such seemingly opposing views of the same person.

Answers to these questions can be found on the companion website at: www.pearsoned.co.uk/psychologyexpress

? Sample question   Essay

Discuss feminist approaches to psychology, evidencing how it might relate to critical social psychology.

Further reading Approaches to critical social psychology

Topic	Key reading
LGBTQ	Clarke, V., Ellis, S. J., Peel, E., & Riggs, D. W. (2010). *Lesbian, gay, bisexual, trans & queer psychology: An introduction.* Cambridge: Cambridge University Press.

Example of a journal article written from LGBTQ perspective	Crowley, S. (2010). how r u??? Lesbian and bi-identified youth on MySpace. *Journal of Lesbian Studies, 14,* 52–60.
Feminism	Wilkinson, S. (1996). *Feminist social psychologies.* Milton Keynes: Open University Press.
Example of a journal article written from feminist perspective	Sheriff, A., & Weatherall, M. (2009). A feminist discourse analysis of popular press accounts of postmaternity. *Journal of Feminism and Psychology, 19,* 89–108.
Social constructionism	Gergen, K. J. (2008). *An invitation to social construction.* London: Sage.
Social constructionism	www.swarthmore.edu/x20607.xml Papers written by Kenneth Gergen can be found here.

Research in critical social psychology

It has been established that critical psychologists view the experimental approach as a specific type of knowledge. In contrast, critical social psychologists suggest that behaviour emerges via meanings and practices that are culturally and socially organised. For this, they require an approach to research which:

● focuses on language

● explores human meaning making

● considers how meanings are shared, constructed and reconstructed through language.

A qualitative analysis is suitable for this. Many forms of qualitative analysis are used in such work – e.g., grounded theory, thematic analysis and phenomenological analysis. These are different methodological ways to achieve the three points listed above. The approach probably most widely used within critical work is discourse analysis, which is considered in more detail next.

Discourse analysis

The term discourse within this approach refers to the way particular meanings are constructed within language. It is not about the psychology of language per se, but how people use language in their everyday lives. Sources of data can be interviews, accounts given in counselling sessions or written accounts, such as newspaper articles or parliamentary policy documents. A key point is that language is not viewed as neutral, but as a vehicle to present different versions of objects which will be context-dependent. Discourse analysis considers how people use language to present a version of an event, which will often maintain or construct a particular position.

Discursive studies of prejudice are used to illustrate how these ideas are translated into research (return to Chapter 6, Prejudice and discrimination, and read the section entitled Discursive accounts). Here, the research of Potter and Wetherell (1987) illustrates the linguistic devices used by middle-class New Zealanders to position themselves as non-prejudiced when talking about Polynesian immigrants. This shows how a discursive approach offers an analysis of what language does and how people use language to present and legitimise a certain stance on a given topic. For another example of how discourse analysis has been used to examine prejudice, read the Key Study, below, about Chiang's (2010) study of the debates about illegal immigration aired on the American TV channel CNN.

KEY STUDY

Chiang (2010). A discourse analytic study of hate speech

The study analyses two extracts from the Lou Dobbs show (a CNN host who has been accused of racist talk), of him in conversation with Janet Murguia (a prominent civil rights leader). The research questions asked are: 'What specific procedures are used to deny racism so as to maintain a positive face in US public discourse?' and 'How do the various forms of racism denials help to position selves positively and others negatively?' The exchange between the two is confrontational and discourse analytic techniques serve to illustrate how the speakers attempt to position each other negatively, whilst projecting a positive self-image of themselves to the audience.

Murguia positions Dobbs as a racist and proponent of hate speech. The paper highlights the rhetorical devices each use. Rhetorical devices are strategies used to persuade the audience of a specific viewpoint. They are another example of the linguistic devices which discourse analysts look out for when analysing language. These are highlighted here in italics – remember, the speakers are using them to persuade people of their viewpoints. Murguia accuses media hosts of spreading a 'wave of hate' and uses the rhetorical device of *exemplification* (i.e., she provides a graphic account of racist terms use by a radio host) as a source of evidence. However, Dobbs uses a further rhetorical device of a *discounting strategy*, suggesting that her example is an extreme case, which he describes as 'contemptible'. In order to further undermine her account, he appeals to facts, asking her to quantify the number of talk show hosts who have used such inflammatory language. Her failure to do this facilitates Dobb's *act denial* (a further rhetorical device). He suggests the example Murguia gives is an 'exception'. The linguistic strategies used by Dobbs here then allow him to refute the idea that there is a 'wave' of hate (the accusatory term originally used by Murguia about media hosts such as Dobbs), but, at the same time, he is not denying that examples of racist speech have taken place. By doing this, he manages to present himself positively (by showing that he does not agree with such talk), but, at the same time, illustrates that it is not as big a problem as Murguia insinuates. Murguia's accusations are to a certain extent refuted.

Consider how this research illustrates the linguistic resources drawn upon and strategies people use to construct versions of events. Think also how this and Potter and Wetherell's study show us how prejudice can become justified via the language used and, therefore, continue in our social interactions. Chiang's study reveals specific examples of accusations and denial of racism in the US media.

Test your knowledge

11.7 What is discourse analysis?

11.8 What is a rhetorical device?

11.9 Potter and Wetherell's (Chapter 6) research of prejudice is written from a critical perspective. Describe how that study fits with a critical approach.

11.10 From the evidence presented across this chapter and your wider knowledge of research methods make a list of the reasons why qualitative research is well suited to a critical approach to social psychology.

Answers to these questions can be found on the companion website at: www.pearsoned.co.uk/psychologyexpress

---

? **Sample question**   *Essay*

Select a topic area covered in this text (e.g., aggression, prejudice, social influence) and discuss how a critical social psychologist might research this topic. Use examples of critical research studies to support and illustrate your answer (some can be found in Further reading, below).

Further reading **Research in critical social psychology**

Topic	Key reading
Prejudice	Shiao-Yun, C. (2010). 'Well, I'm a lot of things, but I'm sure not a bigot': Positive self-presentation in confrontational discourse on racism *Discourse & Society, 21*, 273–294.
Special edition on critical approaches to racism	*Journal of Community and Applied Social Psychology* (2006), 15.
Aggression	Day, K., Gough, B., & McFadden, M. (2003). Women who drink and fight: A discourse analysis of working-class women's talk. *Feminism and Psychology, 13*, 141–158.
Relationships	Sandfield, A., & Percy, C. (2003). Accounting for single status: Heterosexism and ageism in heterosexual women's talk about marriage. *Feminism and Psychology, 13*, 475–488.

? **Sample question**   *Problem-based learning*

A study published in 2011 reveals that there is still a feeling of stigma and discrimination amongst gay and lesbian couples who have had a civil ceremony in the United Kingdom. As a critical social psychologist, you have

▶

been asked to comment on a current affairs programme about why this might still be the case and how psychological research might help explore this further. What arguments might you present?

Chapter summary – pulling it all together

→ Can you tick all the points from the revision checklist at the beginning of this chapter?

→ Attempt the sample question from the beginning of this chapter using the answer guidelines below.

→ Go to the companion website at www.pearsoned.co.uk/psychologyexpress to access more revision support online, including interactive quizzes, flashcards, You be the marker exercises as well as answer guidance for the Test your knowledge and Sample questions from this chapter.

Further reading for Chapter 11

Gough, B., & McFadden, M. (2001). *Critical social psychology: An introduction*. Basingstoke: Palgrave Macmillan.

Stainton Rogers, W. (2011) *Social psychology*. Maidenhead: Open University Press. (Acknowledges both critical and mainstream approaches.)

Tuffin, K. (2005). *Understanding critical social psychology*. London: Sage.

Answer guidelines

* Sample question   Essay

Discuss the ways in which critical social psychology differs from mainstream approaches.

Approaching the question

The question requires you to consider the ways in which critical social psychology differs from mainstream approaches. As this is asked within a chapter on critical approaches, this is an opportunity to evidence your understanding of it. We would suggest, therefore, that more emphasis be placed on *how* the critical differs and *why*, rather than attempting to maintain an equal balance between critical and mainstream approaches. For instance you might highlight the fact that critical approaches acknowledge the ideological positioning of their approach, whilst the mainstream does not. This could be further developed by discussing the critical view that all research is ideologically positioned, even 'neutral' scientific knowledge. Such a debate would allow you to engage with the mainstream account, but also explain fully why the critical takes a different stance (as opposed to just listing what the differences are).

Important points to include

There is no one way to answer any essay question, but an examiner would expect you to discuss some of the key ideas of critical social psychology and establish that they are not just a reaction to the methods of mainstream approaches but also the ways in which the 'social' in social psychology has been viewed by this dominant perspective.

Try to avoid describing the mainstream and critical approaches within separate sections. A better answer would be able to highlight a key issue and explain how the mainstream would see this and how the critical social psychologist might respond to this point (with more emphasis on the critical, as already suggested). The three challenges identified by Stainton Rogers outlined at the beginning of this chapter (see also Figure 11.1 and Tables 11.1–3) could be a good starting point for this.

> ### Make your answer stand out
>
> *Although this question does not explicitly ask you to provide examples of research from a critical stance, this would be a good way to enhance your work. You might select a feminist journal article, briefly outline the feminist position (as an example of a perspective aligned to the critical approach) and then use the study to illustrate the points you have made when explaining how the critical and mainstream approaches differ. Here are some ways in which this might be done:*
>
> - *As feminist research, it will be written from a particular viewpoint (in other words it will be ideologically positioned – your first link with the critical approach)*
> - *What methods have been used? Is it looking at language or experiential accounts rather than conducting an experiment? Does it offer a more social science approach?*
> - *How is the individual being viewed in relation to society? It is likely to be a study of women – are they being viewed as an oppressed group within society?*
>
> *The three points raised here map directly on to the three challenges in the tables mentioned above. This will show that you not only understand some of the key issues but are also able to apply them.*

Explore the accompanying website at www.pearsoned.co.uk/psychologyexpress

→ Prepare more effectively for exams and assignments using the answer guidelines for questions from this chapter.

→ Test your knowledge using multiple choice questions and flashcards.

→ Improve your essay skills by exploring the You be the marker exercises.

Notes

And finally, before the exam . . .

How to approach revision from here

You should be now at a reasonable stage in your revision process – you should have developed your skills and knowledge base over your course and used this text judiciously over that period. Now, however, you have used the book to reflect, remind and reinforce that material you have researched over the year/ seminar. You will, of course, need to do additional reading and research to that included here (and appropriate directions are provided) but you will be well on your way with the material presented here.

It is important that in answering any question in psychology you take a research- and evidence-based approach to your response. For example, do not make generalised or sweeping statements that cannot be substantiated or supported by evidence from the literature. Remember as well that the evidence should not be anecdotal – it is of no use citing your mum, dad, best friend or the latest news from a celebrity website. After all, you are not writing an opinion piece – you are crafting an argument which is based on current scientific knowledge and understanding. You need to be careful about the evidence you present: do review the material and from where it was sourced.

Furthermore, whatever type of assessment you have to undertake, it is important to take an evaluative approach to the evidence. Whether you are writing an essay, sitting an exam or designing a webpage, the key advice is to avoid simply presenting a descriptive answer. Rather it is necessary to think about the strength of the evidence in each area. One of the key skills for psychology students is critical thinking and for this reason the tasks featured in this series focus upon developing this way of thinking. Thus you are not expected to simply learn a set of facts and figures, but to think about the implications of what we know and how this might be applied in everyday life. The best assessment answers are the ones that take this critical approach.

It is also important to note that psychology is a theoretical subject: when answering any question about psychology, not only refer to the prevailing theories of the field, but also outline the development of them as well. It is also important to evaluate these theories and models either through comparison with other models and theories or through the use of studies that have assessed them and highlighted their strengths and weaknesses. It is essential to read widely – within each section of this book there are directions to interesting and pertinent papers or books relating to the specific topic area. Find these papers, read these papers, and make notes from these papers. But don't stop there. Let them lead you to other sources that may be important to the field. One thing that an examiner hates to see is the same old sources being cited all of the time: be innovative, and as well as reading the seminal works, find the more obscure and interesting sources as well – just make sure they're relevant to your answer!

How not to revise

- **Don't avoid revision.** This is the best tip ever. There is something on the TV, the pub is having a two-for-one offer, the fridge needs cleaning, your budgie looks lonely ... You have all of these activities to do and they need doing now! Really ... ? Do some revision!
- **Don't spend too long at each revision session.** Working all day and night is not the answer to revision. You do need to take breaks, so schedule your revision so you are not working from dawn until dusk. A break gives time for the information you have been revising to consolidate.
- **Don't worry.** Worrying will cause you to lose sleep, lose concentration and lose revision time by leaving it late and then later. When the exam comes, you will have no revision completed and will be tired and confused.
- **Don't cram.** This is the worst revision technique in the universe! You will not remember the majority of the information that you try to stuff into your skull, so why bother?
- **Don't read over old notes with no plan.** Your brain will take nothing in. If you wrote your lecture notes in September and the exam is in May is there any point in trying to decipher your scrawly handwriting now?
- **Don't write model answers and learn by rote.** When it comes to the exam you will simply regurgitate the model answer irrespective of the question – not a brilliant way to impress the examiner!

Tips for exam success

What you should do when it comes to revision

Exams are one form of assessment that students often worry about the most. The key to exam success, as with many other types of assessment, lies in good preparation and self-organisation. One of the most important things is knowing what to expect – this does not necessarily mean knowing what the questions will be on the exam paper, but rather what the structure of the paper is, how many questions you are expected to answer, how long the exam will last and so on.

To pass an exam you need a good grasp of the course material and obvious, as it may seem, to turn up for the exam itself. It is important to remember that you aren't expected to know or remember everything in the course, but you should be able to show your understanding of what you have studied. Remember as well that examiners are interested in what you know, not what you don't know. They try to write exam questions that give you a good chance of passing – not ones to catch you out or trick you in any way. You may want to consider some of these top exam tips:

- Start your revision in plenty of time.
- Make a revision timetable and stick to it.
- Practise jotting down answers and making essay plans.
- Practise writing against the clock using past exam papers.
- Check that you have really answered the question and have not strayed off the point.
- Review a recent past paper and check the marking structure.
- Carefully select the topics you are going to revise.
- Use your lecture/study notes and refine them further, if possible, into lists or diagrams and transfer them onto index cards/Post-it notes. Mind maps are a good way of making links between topics and ideas.
- Practise your handwriting – make sure it's neat and legible.

One to two days before the exam

- Recheck times, dates and venue.
- Actively review your notes and key facts.
- Exercise, eat sensibly, and get a few good nights' sleep.

On the day

- Get a good night's sleep.
- Have a good meal, two to three hours before the start time.
- Arrive in good time.
- Spend a few minutes calming and focusing.

In the exam room

- Keep calm.
- Take a few minutes to read each question carefully. Don't jump to conclusions – think calmly about what each question means and the area it is focused on.
- Start with the question you feel most confident about. This helps your morale.
- By the same token, don't expend all your efforts on that one question – if you are expected to answer three questions then don't just answer two.
- Keep to time and spread your effort evenly on all opportunities to score marks.
- Once you have chosen a question, jot down any salient facts or key points. Then take five minutes to plan your answer – a spider diagram or a few notes may be enough to focus your ideas. Try and think in terms of 'why and how' not just 'facts'.

- You might find it useful to create a visual plan or map before writing your answer to help you to remember to cover everything you need to address.
- Keep reminding yourself of the question and try not to wander off the point.
- Remember that quality of argument is more important than quantity of facts.
- Take 30–60 second breaks whenever you find your focus slipping (typically every 20 minutes).
- Make sure you reference properly – according to your university requirements.
- Watch your spelling and grammar – you could lose marks if you make too many errors.

→ *Revision checklist*

❏ Have you revised the topics highlighted in the revision checklists?
❏ Have you attended revision classes and taken note of and/or followed up on your lecturers' advice about the exams or assessment process at your university?
❏ Can you answer the questions posed in this text satisfactorily? Don't forget to check sample answers on the website too.
❏ Have you read the additional material to make your answer stand out?
❏ Remember to criticise appropriately – based on evidence.

Test your knowledge by using the material presented in this text or on the website: www.pearsoned.co.uk/psychologyexpress

Glossary

acquiescent response set The tendency to agree to a statement regardless of the content of the statement or the person's actual opinion.

aggression Intentional behaviour aimed at doing harm or causing pain to another person.

altruism Acts of helping behaviour, motivated by a desire to benefit another person.

ambivalence The experience of having thoughts and emotions of both positive and negative valence towards someone or something.

belongingness hypothesis The supposition that all people are motivated to seek out and join with other humans and those who are deprived of this contact will experience discomfort and loneliness.

bystander effect People are less likely to help in an emergency when they are with others than when they are alone. The greater the number, the less likely it is that anyone will help.

cognitive dissonance A state of psychological tension or discomfort caused by holding two or more inconsistent cognitions or by performing an action that is discrepant from one's customary, typically positive, self-conception.

cognitive miser A model of social cognition that characterises people as reluctant to expend cognitive resources and looking for opportunities to avoid engaging in efforts of thought.

critical psychology An approach to psychology that takes a critical theory-based perspective. It is aimed at critiquing mainstream psychology and attempts to apply psychology in progressive ways.

cross-sectional research The study of groups of individuals differing on the basis of specified criteria at the same point in time.

de individuation The perception of group membership leading individuals to lose their identity and feelings of responsibility.

descriptive norms Perceptions of what other people commonly do in specific situations.

discrimination Unjustified negative or harmful action towards a member of a group simply because of his or her membership of that group.

discursive psychology A form of discourse analysis that focuses on psychological themes.

dyadic Two individuals or units regarded as a pair.

ecological validity The degree to which the behaviours observed and recorded in a study reflect the behaviours that actually occur in natural settings.

epistemology A branch of philosophy concerned with the nature and limitations of knowledge.

ethnocentrism A term for viewing another society based on the values and beliefs of your own.

explicit measures Measures of constructs such as attitudes and stereotypes that directly ask respondents to think about and report that construct.

false consensus bias The assumption that other people share our attitudes.

hostile aggression Aggression motivated by a perpetrator's desire to vent negative feeling towards the target.

hypothetico-deductive method A proposed description of scientific method based on making a deduction by testing a hypothesis.

ideology A systematically interrelated set of beliefs the primary function of which is explanation. It circumscribes thinking, making it difficult for the holder to escape from its mould.

idiograhic Idiographic approaches seek to highlight the unique elements of the individual phenomenon.

implicit bystander effect The effect of cognitively priming participants to think about the presence of others, inhibiting their helping behaviour.

implicit egotism People gravitate towards people, places and things that resemble themselves. People generally see themselves in a positive manner, so anything reminiscent of themselves could prompt automatic positive associations.

implicit measures Measures of constructs such as attitudes and stereotypes which are derived from the way respondents behave rather than from the content of their answers to explicit questions about these constructs.

implicit prejudice Automatic and unreflexive negative attitudes towards certain people or groups.

injunctive norms Perceptions of what other people approve or disapprove of; what people should do.

instrumental aggression Aggression as a means to some goal other than causing pain.

intergroup processes Processes taking place between groups, especially between social groups.

interpersonal Occurring among or involving several people.

intra-group processes Processes taking place within a group, especially within a social group.

linguistic devices A literary or linguistic technique that produces a specific effect. Disclaimers and extreme case formulations are examples of this.

longitudinal research Research that involves repeated observations of the same items over long periods of time.

mainstream psychology An approach to psychology which adheres to the view of social psychology as a science – similar to the natural sciences.

meta-analysis Statistical procedure that combines data from different studies to measure the overall reliability and strength of different effects.

nomothetic Nomothetic approaches seek to provide general law-like statements about social life.

overlapping selves The more our self concept overlaps with the self concept of our partner, the greater our satisfaction, commitment and investment in the relationship.

phenomenology Detailed accounts of how people experience certain phenomena.

prejudice A hostile or negative attitude towards a person simply because of his or her membership of a certain group.

priming The procedure of recalling accessible categories or schemas that we already have in mind.

projective measurement Personality tests designed to yield information about someone's personality on the basis of his or her unrestricted response to ambiguous objects or situations.

propinquity effect The finding that the more we see and interact with people, the more likely they are to become our friends.

psychodynamic The theory and systematic study of the psychological forces that underlie human behaviour – in particular, the dynamic relationships between conscious and unconscious motivation.

reciprocal altruism The notion that individuals will help each other if they feel the favour will be repaid in the future.

reciprocity The law of 'doing unto others as they do to you'. It can refer to an attempt to gain compliance by first doing someone a favour or to mutual aggression or mutual attraction.

rhetorical devices Strategies used to persuade the audience of a specific viewpoint.

schemas A mental structure or cognitive short cut used to organise knowledge about the social world around subjects or themes, which enables us access to a simplified set of beliefs.

self concept Viewed as a cognitive representation of the self, which seeks to provide coherence and meaning to our experiences.

self-construals The perceptions that individuals have about their thoughts, feelings and actions in relation to those of others.

self-efficacy The belief in one's ability to carry out specific actions that produce desired outcomes.

self-monitors (high and low) The degree to which a person is aware of social demands on and expectations of his or her behaviour and is able to modify it accordingly. High self-monitors often behave in a manner that is highly responsive to social cues and their situational context. People who are low self-monitors are less concerned with how other people perceive them and will be more likely to act consistently across situations.

self schemas Mental structure that people use to organise their knowledge about themselves and influence what they notice, think about and remember about themselves.

similarity–attraction effect The more similar people are, the more attracted they will be to each other.

social cognition Cognitive processes and structures that influence and are influenced by social behaviour.

social comparison Comparing our behaviours and opinions with those of others in order to establish the socially approved ways to think and behave.

social constructionism Sociological theories of knowledge that consider how social phenomena or objects of consciousness develop in social contexts.

social desirability The tendency of respondents to reply in a manner that will be viewed favourably by others. This will generally take the form of overreporting good behaviour or underreporting bad behaviour.

social identity theory Theory of group membership and intergroup relations based on self-categorisation, social comparison and the construction of a shared self-definition in terms of in group-defining properties.

stereotype A generalised belief about a group of people in which certain traits are assigned to all members of the group, regardless of the actual variations within the group.

stress-buffering hypothesis Social resources (supports) will improve the potentially negative effects of stressful events.

tokenism A positive, but maybe 'token', act towards members of a minority group.

traits Enduring patterns of perceiving, relating to and thinking about the environment and oneself that are exhibited in a wide range of social and personal contexts.

weapons effects The mere presence of a weapon, words describing weapons or pictures of weapons may facilitate an increased likelihood of aggression, especially among angered persons.

References

Abrams, D., & Hogg, M. A. (1990). Social identification, self-categorization and social influence. *European Review of Social Psychology, 1,* 195–228.

Abrams, D., Tendayi, V. G., Masser, B., & Bohner, G. (2003). Perceptions of stranger and acquaintance rape: The role of benevolent and hostile sexism in victim blame and rape proclivity. *Journal of Personality and Social Psychology, 84*(1), 111–125.

Adorno, T. W., Frenkel-Brunswik, E., Levinson, D. J., & Sanford, R. N. (1950). *The authoritarian personality.* New York: Norton.

Ainsworth, M. Blehar, M., Waters, E., & Wall, S. (1978). *Patterns of attachment.* Hillsdale, NJ: Erlbaum.

Ajzen, I. (1991). The theory of planned behaviour. *Organisational Behaviour and Human Decision Processes, 50,* 179–211.

Ajzen, I., & Fishbein, M. (2005). The influence of attitudes on behaviour. In D. Albarracin, B. T. Johnson & M. P. Zanna (Eds.), *The handbook of attitudes* (pp. 173–221). Mahwah, NJ: Erlbaum.

Allport, G. W. (1954). *The nature of prejudice.* Garden City, NY: Doubleday.

Altemeyer, R. (1981). *Right-wing authoritarianism.* Winnipeg, Manitoba, Canada: University of Manitoba Press.

Altemeyer, R. (1996). *The authoritarian specter.* Cambridge, MA: Harvard University Press.

Anderson, C. A., & Bushman, B. J. (1997). External validity of 'Trivial' experiments: The case of laboratory aggression. *Review of General Psychology, 1,* 19–41.

Anderson, C. A., & Bushman, B. J. (2002). Human aggression. *Annual Review of Psychology, 53,* 27–51.

Aronson, E., & Mills, J. (1959). The effect of severity of initiation on liking for a group. *Journal of Abnormal and Social Psychology, 59,* 177–181.

Asch, S. E. (1951). Effects of group pressure upon the modification and distortion of judgment. In H. Guetzkow (Ed.), *Groups, leadership and men.* Pittsburgh, PA: Carnegie Press.

Axom, D., & Cooper, J. (1985). Cognitive dissonance and psychotherapy: The role of effort and justification in inducing weight loss. *Journal of Experimental Social Psychology, 21,* 149–160.

Bandura, A. (1998). Personal and collective efficacy in human adaptation and change. In J. G. Adair, D. Belanger, & K. L. Dion (Eds.), *Advances in psychological science* (Vol. 1: Personal, social and cultural aspects, pp. 51–71). Hove, East Sussex: Psychology Press.

Bandura, A., Ross, D., & Ross, S. A. (1961). Transmission of aggression through imitation of aggressive models. *Journal of Abnormal and Social Psychology, 63,* 575–582.

Baron, R. A., Byrne, D., & Branscombe, N. R. (2007). *Mastering social psychology.* Boston, MA: Pearson International Edition.

Baron R. A., & Richardson, D. R. (1994). *Human aggression* (2nd ed.). New York: Plenum.

Baumeister, R. F. (1998). The self. In D. T. Gilbert, S. T. Fiske, & G. Lindzey (Eds.), *The handbook of social psychology* (Vols. 1 & 2, 4th ed., pp. 680–740). New York: McGraw-Hill.

Baumeister, R. F., & Alquist, J. L. (2009). Is there a downside to good self-control? *Self and Identity, 8,* 115–130.

Baumeister, R. F., & Leary, M. R. (1995). The need to belong: Desire for interpersonal attachments as a fundamental human motivation. *Psychological Bulletin, 117,* 497–529.

Berkowitz, L. (1972). Social norms, feelings and other factors affecting helping and altruism. In L. Berkowitz (Ed.), *Advances in experimental social psychology* (Vol. 6). New York: Academic Press.

Berkowitz, L. (1993) *Aggression: Its causes, consequences and control.* Philadelphia, PA: Temple University Press.

Berkowitz, L., & LePage, A. (1967). Weapons as aggression-eliciting stimuli. *Journal of Personality and Social Psychology, 7,* 202–207.

References

Berscheid, E. (2010). Love in the fourth dimension. *Annual Review of Psychology, 61*, 1–25.

Bierhoff, H. W., Klein, R., & Kramp, P. (1991). Evidence for the altruistic personality from data on accident research. *Journal of Personality, 59*, 263–280.

Bierhoff, H. W., & Rohmann, E. (2004). Altruistic personality in the context of the empathy–altruism hypothesis. *European Journal of Personality, 18*, 351–365.

Blackheart, G. C., Nelson, B. C., Knowles, M. L., & Baumeister, R. F. (2009). Rejection elicits emotional reactions but nether causes immediate distress nor lowers self-esteem: A meta-analytical review of 192 studies of social exclusion. *Personality and Social Psychology Review, 13*, 269–309.

Blanchard-Fields, F., Chen, Y., Horhota, M., & Wang, M. (2007). Cultural differences in the relationship between aging and the correspondence bias. *Journal of Gerontology, 62B(6)*, 362–365.

Blanton, H., & Christie, C. (2003). Deviance regulation: A theory of identity and action. *Review of General Psychology, 7(2)*, 115–149.

Bohner, G., & Wanke, M. (2002). *Attitudes and attitude change* (Part II, pp. 69–116). New York: Psychology Press.

Bornstein, R. F. (1989). Exposure and affect: Overview and meta-analysis of research, 1968–1987. *Psychological Bulletin, 106*, 265–289.

Bowlby, J. (1969). *Attachment and loss* (Vol. 1: Attachment). New York: Basic Books.

Buss, D. M. (2003). *The evolution of desire: Strategies of human mating* (rev. ed.). New York: Basic Books.

Buunk, B. P., & Van Yperen, N. W. (1991). Referential comparisons, relationship comparisons, and exchange: Their relation to marital satisfaction. *Personality and Social Psychology Bulletin, 17*, 709–717.

Byrne, D. (1971). *The attraction paradigm*. New York: Academic Press.

Carlson, M., Marcus-Newhall, A., & Miller, N. (1990). Effects of situational aggression cues: A quantitative review. *Journal of Personality and Social Psychology, 58*, 622–633.

Carver, C. S., & Scheier, M. F. (1981). *Attention and self-regulation: A control theory approach to human behaviour*. New York: Springer-Verlag.

Carver, C. S., & Scheier, M. F. (1998). *On the self-regulation of behavior*. New York: Cambridge University Press.

Cate, R. M., Lloyd, S. A., & Long, E. (1988). The role of rewards and fairness in developing premarital relationships. *Journal of Marriage and the Family, 50*, 177–181.

Chiang, S. (2010). 'Well, I'm a lot of things, but I'm sure not a bigot': Positive selfpresentation in confrontational discourse about racism. *Discourse & Society, 21(3)*, 273–294.

Churchill, S., Jessop, D., & Sparks, P. (2008). Impulsive and/or planned behaviour: Can impulsivity contribute to the predictive utility of the theory of planned behaviour. *British Journal of Social Psychology, 47*, 631–646.

Cialdini, R. B., Demaine, L. J., Sagarin, B. J., Barrett, D. W., Rhoads, K., & Winter, P. L. (2006). Managing social norms for persuasive impact. *Social Influence, 1*, 3–15.

Cialdini, R. B., Kallgren, C. A., & Reno, R. R. (1991). A focus theory of normative conduct: A theoretical refinement and re-evaluation of the role of norms in human behaviour. In M. P. Zanna (Ed.), *Advances in experimental social psychology*, (vol. 24, pp. 201–233). San Diego, CA: Academic Press.

Clark, M. S., & Mills, J. (2001). Behaving in such a way as to maintain and enhance relationship satisfaction. In J. H. Harvey & A. E. Wenzel (Eds.), *Relationship maintenance and enhancement* (pp. 13–26). Mahwah, NJ: Erlbaum.

Clarke, V., Burgoyne, C., & Burns, M. (2005). For love or money? Comparing lesbian and gay and heterosexual relationships. *The Psychologist, 18(6)*, 356–358.

Clarke, V., Ellis, S. J., Peel, E., & Riggs, D. W. (2010). *Lesbian, gay, bisexual, trans & queer psychology: An introduction*. Cambridge: Cambridge University Press.

Clary, E. G., Snyder, M., Ridge, R. D., Copeland, J., Stukas, A. A., Hangen, J., & Miene, P. (1998). Understanding and assessing the motivations of volunteers: A functional approach. *Journal of Personality and Social Psychology, 74*, 1516–1530.

Conner, M. T., & Sparks, P. (2005). Theory of planned behaviour and health behaviour. In M. T. Conner & P. Norman (Eds.), *Predicting health behaviour.* Milton Keynes: Open University Press.

Cook, R., & Sheeran, P. (2004). Moderation of cognition–intention and cognition–behaviour relations: A meta-analysis of properties of variables from the theory of planned behaviour. *British Journal of Social Psychology, 43,* 159–186.

Cottrell, C. A., Neuberg, S. L., & Li, N. P. (2007). What do people desire in others?: A sociofunctional perspective on the importance of different valued characteristics. *Journal of Personality and Social Psychology, 92*(2) 208–231.

Crano, W. D., & Chen, X. (1998). The leniency contract and persistence of majority and minority influence. *Journal of Personality and Social Psychology, 74,* 1347–1350.

Crano, W. D., & Prislin, R. (2006). Attitudes and persuasion. *Annual Review of Psychology, 57,* 345–374.

Davis, J. L., & Rusbult, C. E. (2001). Attitude alignment in close relationships. *Journal of Personality and Social Psychology, 81,* 65–84.

Davis, M. H., Luce, C., & Kraus, S. J. (1994). The heritability of characteristics associated with dispositional empathy. *Journal of Personality, 62,* 369–391.

De Dreu, C. K. W., De Vries, N. K., Gordijn, E. H., & Schuurman, M. S. (1999). Convergent and divergent processing of majority and minority arguments: Effects of focal and related attitudes. *European Journal of Social Psychology, 29,* 329–48.

Degner, J., & Wentura, D. (2010). Automatic prejudice in childhood and early adolescence. *Journal of Personality and Social Psychology, 98,* 356–374.

Deutsch, M., & Gerard, H. B. (1955). A study of normative and informational social influences upon individual judgment. *Journal of Personality and Social Psychology, 51,* 629–636.

Devendorf, S. A., & Highhouse, S. (2008). Applicant–employee similarity and attraction to an employer. *Journal of Occupational and Organizational Psychology, 81,* 607–617.

Dick, R., Stellmacher, J., Wagner, U., Lemmer, G., & Tissington, P. (2009). Group membership salience and task performance, *Journal of Managerial Psychology, 24*(7), 609–626.

Dick, R., Tissington, P., & Hertel, G. (2009). Do many hands make light work?: How to overcome social loafing and gain motivation in teams. *European Business Review, 21*(3), 233–245.

Dixon, J. A., Durkheim, K., & Tredoux, C. (2005). Beyond the optimal strategy: A reality check for the contact hypothesis. *American Psychologist, 60,* 697–711.

Dollard, J., Doob, L., Miller, N., Mowrer, O., & Sears, R. (1939). *Frustration and aggression.* New Haven, CT: Yale University Press.

Dovidio, J. F., Gaertner, S., & Kawamaki, K. (2003). Intergroup conflict: The past, present and future. Group Processes and Intergroup Relationships, 6, 5–20.

Duck, S. W. (1982). A topography of relationship disengagement and dissolution. In S. W. Duck (Ed.), *Personal relationships 4: Dissolving personal relationships* (pp. 1–30). London: Academic Press.

Duck, S. (2005). How do you tell someone you're letting go?, *The Psychologist, 18,* 210–213.

Eagly, A. H., & Carli, L. L. (1981). Sex of researchers and sex-typed communications as determinants of sex differences in influenceability: A meta-analysis of social influence studies. *Psychological Bulletin, 90,* 1–20.

Eagly, A. H., & Chaiken, S. (1993). *The psychology of attitudes.* Orlando, FL: Harcourt Brace Jovanovich.

Eisenberg, N., Fabes, R. A., Guthrie, I. K., & Reiser, M. (2000). Dispositional emotionality and regulation: Their role in predicting quality of social functioning. *Journal of Personality and Social Psychology, 78,* 136–157.

Eisenberg, N., Guthrie, I. K., Cumberland, A., Murphy, B. C., Shephard, S. A., Zhou, Q., & Carlo, G. (2002). Prosocial development in early adulthood: A longitudinal study. *Journal of Personality and Social Psychology, 82,* 993–1005.

Esses, V. M., Haddock, G., & Zanna, M. P. (1993). Values, stereotypes, and emotions as determinants of intergroup attitudes. In D. M. Mackie & D. L. Hamilton (Eds.), *Affect, cognition, and stereotyping: Interactive processes in group perception* (pp. 137–166). New York: Academic Press.

Fabrigar, L. R., & Petty, R. E. (1999). The role of affective and cognitive bases of attitudes in susceptibility to affectively and cognitively based persuasion. *Personality and Social Psychology Bulletin, 25*, 363–81.

Fazio, R. H. (1995). Attitudes as object–evaluation associations: Determinants, consequences, and correlates of attitude accessibility. In R. E. Petty & J. A. Krosnick (Eds.), *Attitude strength: Antecedents and consequences* (pp. 247–282). Mahwah, NJ: Erlbaum.

Fazio, R. H. (2007). Attitudes as object–evaluation associations in varying strength. *Social Cognition, 25*, 603–637.

Fazio, R. H. & Towles-Schwen, T. (1999). The MODE model of attitude–behaviour processes. In S. Chaiken & Y. Trope (Eds.), *Dual process theories in social psychology,* (pp. 97–116). New York: Guilford Press.

Festinger, L. (1954). A theory of social comparison processes. *Human Relations, 7*(2), 117–140.

Festinger, L. (1957). *A theory of cognitive dissonance.* Evanston, IL: Row Peterson.

Festinger, L. (1964). *Conflict, decision and dissonance.* Stanford, CA: Palo Alto University Press.

Festinger, L., Schachter, S., & Back, K. (1950). *Social pressure in informal groups: A study of human factors in housing.* Stanford, CA: Stanford University Press.

Finkenauer, C., Kerkhof, P., Righetti, F., & Brange, S. (2009). Living together apart: Perceived concealment as a signal of exclusion in marital relationships. *Personality and Social Psychology Bulletin, 35*(10) 1410–1422.

Fiske, S. T., & Taylor, S. E. (1991). *Social cognition.* New York: McGraw-Hill.

Forsyth, D. (1998). *Group dynamics* (3rd ed.). London: Wadsworth.

Freeman, L., & Greenacre, L. (2010). An examination of socially destructive behaviours in group work. *Journal of Marketing Education, 10*, 1–13.

Fritsche, B. A., Finkelstein, M. A., & Penner, L. A. (2000). To help or not to help: Capturing individuals' decision policies. *Social Behaviour and Personality, 28*, 561–578.

Garcia, S. M., Weaver, K., Moskowitz, G. B., & Darley, J. M. (2002). Crowded minds: The implicit bystander effect. *Journal of Personality and Social Psychology, 83*, 843–853.

Gerber, J., & Wheeler, L. (2009). On being rejected: A meta-analysis of experimental research on rejection. *Perspectives on Psychological Science, 4*(5), 468–488.

Gergen, K. J. (1973). Social psychology as history. *Journal of Personality and Social Psychology, 26*(2), 309–320.

Gergen, K. J. (2008). *An invitation to social construction.* London: Sage.

Gerull, F. C., & Rapee, R. M. (2002). Mother knows best: Effects of maternal modelling on the acquisition of fear and avoidance behaviour in toddlers. *Behaviour Research and Therapy, 40*, 279–287.

Glick, J., & Staley, K. (2007). Inflicted traumatic brain injury: Advances in evaluation and collaborative diagnosis. *Pediatric Neurosurgery, 43*(5), 436–441.

Goncalo, J., & Staw, B. (2006). Individualism–collectivism and group creativity. *Organizational Behavior and Human Decision Processes, 100*(1), 96–109.

Gough, B., & McFadden, M. (2001). *Critical social psychology: An introduction.* Basingstoke: Palgrave Macmillan.

Gouldner, A. W. (1960). The norm of reciprocity: A preliminary statement. *American Sociological Review, 25*, 161–179.

Greenwald, A. G., McGhee, D. E., & Schwartz, J. K. L. (1998). Measuring individual differences in implicit cognition: The implicit association test. *Journal of Personality and Social Psychology, 74*, 1464–1480.

Greenwald, A. G., Nosek, B. A., & Banaji, M. R. (2003). Understanding and using the Implicit Association Test: I: An improved scoring algorithm. *Journal of Personality and Social Psychology, 85*(2), 197–216.

Griffit, W., & Guay, P. (1969). 'Object' evaluation and conditioned effect. *Journal of Experimental Research in Personality, 4*, 1–8.

Haddock, G., & Huskinson, T. L. H. (2004). Individual differences in attitude structure. In G. Haddock & G. R. Maio (Eds.), *Contemporary perspectives on the psychology of attitudes* (pp. 35–56). Hove, East Sussex: Psychology Press.

Harkins, S., & Jackson, J. (1985). The role of evaluation in eliminating social loafing. *Personality and Social Psychology Bulletin, 11,* 457–465.

Harre, N., Brandt, T., & Houkman, C. (2004). An examination of the actor–observer effect in young drivers' attributions for their own and their friends' risky driving. *Journal of Applied Social Psychology, 34*(4), 806–824.

Haslam, A., & Reicher, S. (2006). Debating the psychology of tyranny: Fundamental issues of theory, perspective and science. *British Journal of Social Psychology, 45*(1), 55–63.

Heider, F. (1946). Attitudes and cognitive organization. *Journal of Psychology, 21,* 107–112.

Heider, F. (1958). *The psychology of interpersonal relations.* New York: Wiley.

Heine, S. J., Foster, J., & Spina, R. (2009). Do birds of a feather universally flock together?: Cultural variation in the similarity–attraction effect. *Asian Journal of Social Psychology, 12,* 247–258.

Heine, S. J., Lehman, D. R., Markus, H., & Kitayama, S. (1999). Is there a universal need for positive self-regard? *Psychological Review, 4,* 766–794.

Hendrick, C., & Hendrick, S. S. (1986). A theory and method of love. *Journal of Personality and Social Psychology, 50,* 392–402.

Hendrick, S. S., & Hendrick, C. (1995). Gender differences and similarities in sex and love. *Personal Relationships, 2,* 55–65.

Henriques, J., Hollway, W., Urwin, C., Venn, C., & Walkerdine, V. (1984). *Changing the subject: Psychology, social regulation and subjectivity.* London: Routledge.

Hepburn, A. (2003). *An introduction to critical social psychology.* London: Sage.

Higgins, E. T. (1987). Self-discrepancy: A theory relating self and affect. *Psychological Review, 94,* 319–340.

Higgins, E. T. (1989). Continuities and discontinuities in self-regulatory and self-evaluative processes: A developmental theory relating self and affect. *Journal of Personality, 57,* 407–444.

Higgins, E. T. (1999). Promotion and prevention as motivational duality: Implications for evaluative processes. In S. Chaiken & Y. Trope (Eds.), *Dual-process theories in social psychology.* New York: Guilford Press.

Hodges, B. H., & Geyer, A. L. (2006). A nonconformist account of the Asch experiments: Values, pragmatics, and moral dilemmas. *Personality and Social Psychology Review, 10*(1), 2–19.

Holt, J. (1987). *The social labouring effect: A study of the effect of social identity on group productivity in real and notional groups using Ringelmann's methods.* Unpublished manuscript. Canterbury, Kent: University of Kent.

Holtzworth-Munroe, A., & Jacobson, N. S. (1985). Causal attributions of married couples: When do they search for causes? What do they conclude when they do?. *Journal of Personality and Social Psychology, 48,* 1398–1412.

Hovland, C. I., Janis, I. L., & Kelley, H. H. (1953). *Communication and persuasion.* New Haven, CT: Yale University Press.

Huston, T. L., & Chorost, A. (1994). Behavioural buffers on the effect of negativity on marital satisfaction: a longitudinal study. *Personal Relationships, 1,* 223–239.

Impett, E. A., Kogan, A., Gable, S. L., Gordon, A. M., Oveis, C., & Keltner, D. (2010). Moving toward more perfect unions: Daily and long-term consequences of approach and avoidance goals in romantic relationships. *Journal of Personality and Social Psychology, 99*(6), 948–963.

Jackson, J., & Harkins, S. (1985). Equity in effort: An explanation of the social loafing effect. *Journal of Personality and Social Psychology, 49*(5), 1199–1206.

Janis, I. (1971) Groupthink. *Psychology Today, 5,* 43–46.

Janis, I. (1982). Counteracting the adverse effects of concurrence-seeking in policy planning groups: Theory and research perspectives. In H. Brandstatter, J. H. Davis, & G. Stocker-Kreichgauer (Eds.), *Group decision making.* New York: Academic Press.

References

Jones, E. E., & Davis, K. E. (1965). From acts to dispositions: The attribution process in person perception. In L. Berkowitz (Ed.), *Advances in experimental social psychology* (Vol. 2, pp. 219–266). New York: Academic Press.

Jones, E. E., & Harris, V. A. (1967). The attribution of attitudes. *Journal of Experimental Social Psychology, 3*, 1–24.

Jones, J. T., Pelham, B. W., Carvallo, M., & Mirenberg, M. C. (2004). How do I love thee? Let me count the Js: Implicit egotism and interpersonal attraction. *Journal of Personality and Social Psychology, 87*, 665–683.

Kamau, C., & Harorimana, D. (2008). Does knowledge sharing and withholding of information in organizational committees affect quality of group decision making? *Proceedings of the 9th European conference on knowledge management* (pp. 341–348). Reading: Academic Publishing.

Karau, S. J., & Williams, K. D. (1993). Social loafing: A meta-analytical review and theoretical integration. *Journal of Personality and Social Psychology, 65*, 681–706.

Kaschak, M. P., & Maner, J. K. (2009). Embodiment, evolution, and social cognition: An integrative framework. *European Journal of Social Psychology, 39*, 1236–1244.

Kelley, H. H. (1967). Attribution theory in social psychology. In D. Levine (Ed.), *Nebraska symposium on motivation and emotion* (Vol. 15, pp. 192–238). Lincoln, NE: University of Nebraska Press.

Kelley, H. H. (1972). Attribution in social action. In E. E. Jones, D. E. Kanouse, H. H. Kelley, R. E. Nisbett, S. Valins, & B. Weiner (Eds.), *Attribution: Perceiving the cause of behaviour* (pp. 1–26). Morristown, NJ: General Learning Press.

Kenny, D. A. (1994). *Interpersonal perception: A social relations analysis.* New York: Guilford Press.

Kenworthy, J., Hewstone, M., Levine, J., Martin, R., & Willis, H. (2008). The phenomenology of minority–majority status: Effects on innovation in argument generation. *European Journal of Social Psychology, 38*(4), 624–636.

Kerr, N., & Bruun, S. (1983). Dispensability of member effort and group motivational losses: Free-rider effects. *Journal of Personality and Social Psychology, 44*(1), 78–94.

King, E. B., Hebl, M. R., George, J. M., & Matusik, S. F. (2010). Understanding tokenism: Antecedents and consequences of a psychological climate of gender inequality. *Journal of Management, 36*, 482–510.

Kiviniemi, M. T., Snyder, M., & Johnson, B. C. (2008). Motivated dimension manipulation in the processing of social comparison information. *Self and Identity, 7*, 225–242.

Koenig Kellas, J., Bean, J. D., Cunningham, C., & Yun Cheng, K. (2008). The ex-files: Trajectories, turning points, and adjustment in the development of post-dissolutional relationships. *Journal of Social and Personal Relationships, 25*, 23–50.

Kozak, M. N., Marsh, A. A., & Wegner, D. M. (2006). What do I think you're doing?: Action identification and mind attribution. *Journal of Personality and Social Psychology, 90*, 543–555.

Krahe, B. (2010). *The social psychology of aggression.* Hove, East Sussex: Psychology Press.

Kravitz, D., & Martin, B. (1986). Ringelmann rediscovered: The original article. *Journal of Personality and Social Psychology, 50*(5), 936–941.

Kreindler, S. A. (2005). A dual group processes model of individual differences in prejudice. *Personality and Social Psychology Review, 9*, 90–107.

Krosnick, J. A., Betz, A. L., Jussim, L. J., & Lynn., A. R. (1992). Subliminal conditioning of attitudes. *Personality and Social Psychology Bulletin, 18*, 152–162.

Krosnick, J. A., & Petty, R. E. (1995). Attitude strength: An overview. In R. E. Petty & J. A. Krosnick (Eds.), *Attitude strength: Antecedents and consequences* (pp. 1–24). Mahwah, NJ: Erlbaum.

Langdridge, D., & Butt, T. (2004). The fundamental attribution error: A phenomenological critique. *British Journal of Social Psychology, 43*, 357–369.

LaPiere, R. (1934). Attitudes versus actions. *Social Forces, 13*, 230–237.

Latané, B. (1981). The psychology of social impact. *American Psychologist, 36*, 343–356.

Latané, B., & Bourgeois, M. J. (2001). Successfully stimulating dynamic social impact: Three levels of prediction. In J. P. Forgas & K. D. Williams (Eds.), *Social influence: Direct and indirect processes* (pp. 61–67). New York: Psychology Press.

Latané, B., & Darley, J. M. (1968). Group inhibition of bystander intervention in emergencies. *Journal of Personality and Social Psychology, 10*, 215–221.

Latané, B., Williams, K., & Harkins, S. (1979). Many hands make light the work: The causes and consequences of social loafing. *Journal of Personality and Social Psychology, 37*(6), 822–832.

Le, B., Dove, N. L., Agnew, C. R., Korn., M. S., & Mutso, A. A. (2010). Predicting nonmarital romantic relationship dissolution: A meta-analytic synthesis. *Personal Relationships, 17*, 377–390.

Leary, M. R. (2001). The self we know and the self we show: Self-esteem, self-presentation, and the maintenance of interpersonal relationships. In G. J. O. Fletcher & M. Clark (Eds.), *Blackwell handbook of social psychology: Interpersonal processes* (pp. 457–477). Malden, MA: Blackwell.

Lee, A. Y. (2001). The mere exposure effect: An uncertainty reduction explanation revisited. *Personality and Social Psychology Bulletin, 28*, 129–137.

Lee, J. A. (1988). 'Love styles'. In M. H. Barnes & R. J. Sternberg, *The psychology of love* (pp. 38–67). New Haven, CT: Yale University Press.

Lemos, G. (2005). *The search for tolerance: Challenging and changing racist attitudes amongst young people.* York: Joseph Rowntree Foundation.

Lerner, M. J. (1977). The justice motive: Some hypotheses as to its origins and forms. *Journal of Personality, 45*(1), 1–52.

Lerner, M. J., & Miller, D. T. (1978). Just world research and the attribution process: Looking back and ahead. *Psychological Bulletin, 85*, 1030–1051.

Lewandowski, G. W., & Bizzoco, N. M. (2007). Addition through subtraction: Growth following the dissolution of a low-quality relationship. *Journal of Positive Psychology, 2*, 40–45.

Li, N. P., Halterman, R. A., Cason, M. J., Knight, G. P., & Maner, J. K. (2007). The stress–affiliation paradigm revisited: Do people prefer the kindness of strangers or their attractiveness? *Personality and Individual Differences, 44*, 382–391.

Likert, R. (1932). A technique for the measurement of attitudes. *Archives of Psychology, 140*, 5–53.

Lorenz, K. (1974). *Civilised world's eight deadly sins.* New York: Harcourt Brace Jovanovich.

Luo, S., & Zhang, G. (2009). What leads to romantic attraction: Similarity, reciprocity, security, or beauty?: Evidence from a speed-dating study. *Journal of Personality, 77*(4) 933–964.

Maio, G. R., & Haddock, G. (2009). *The psychology of attitudes and attitude change.* London: Sage.

Malle, B. F. (1999). How people explain behaviour: A new theoretical framework. *Personality and Social Psychology Review, 3*(1), 23–48.

Malle, B. F. (2006). The actor–observer asymmetry in attribution: A (surprising) meta-analysis. *Psychological Bulletin, 132*(6), 895–919.

Malle, B. F., Knobe, J. M., & Nelson, S. E. (2007). Actor–observer asymmetries in explanations of behaviour: New answers to an old question. *Journal of Personality and Social Psychology, 93*(4), 491–514.

Maner, J. K., DeWall, C. N., Baumeister, R. F., & Shaller, M. (2007). Does social exclusion motivate interpersonal reconnection?: Resolving the 'porcupine problem'. *Journal of Personality and Social Psychology, 9*(1) 422–455.

Marcus-Newhall, A., Pederson, W. C., Carlson, M., & Miller, N. (2000). Displaced aggression is alive and well: A meta-analytic review. *Journal of Personality and Social Psychology, 78*, 670–689.

Markus, H. (1977). Self-schemata and processing information about the self. *Journal of Personality and Social Psychology, 35*, 63–78.

Markus, H. R., & Kitayama, S. (1991). Culture and the self: Implications for cognition, emotion, and motivation. *Psychological Review, 98*, 224–253.

Markus, H., & Kitayama, S. (2010). Culture and selves: A cycle of mutual constitution. *Perspectives on Psychological Science, 5*, 420–430.

Markus, H., & Nurius, P. (1986). Possible selves. *American Psychologist, 41*, 954–969.

References

Martin, I., & Levey, A. B. (1994). The evaluative response: Primitive but necessary. *Behaviour, Research and Therapy, 32,* 301–305.

Mason, W. A., Conrey F. R., & Smith, E. R. (2007). Situating social influence processes: Dynamic, multidirectional flows of influence within social networks. *Personality and Social Psychology Review, 11*(3), 279–300.

Matsuba, M. K., Hart, D., & Atkins, R. (2007). Psychological and social–structural influences on commitment to volunteering. *Journal of Research in Personality, 41,* 889–907.

McKenna, K. Y. A., Green, A. S., & Gleason, M. E. J. (2002). Relationship formation on the Internet: What's the big attraction? *Journal of Social Issues, 58,* 9–31.

McNulty, J. K., Neff, L. A., & Karney, B. R. (2008). Beyond initial attraction: Physical attractiveness in newlywed marriage. *Journal of Family Psychology, 22*(1), 135–143.

Milgram, S. (1963). Behavioral study of obedience. *Journal of Abnormal and Social Psychology, 67,* 371–378.

Milgram, S. (1974). *Obedience to authority.* New York: HarperPerennial.

Mondloch, C. J., Lewis, T., Budreau, D. R., Maurer, D., Dannemiller, J. L., Stephens, B. R., & Kleiner-Gathercoal, K. A. (1999). Face perception during early infancy. *Psychological Science, 10*(5), 419–422.

Morgan, M. (2011). Soulmates, compatibility and intimacy: Allied discursive resources in the struggle for relationship satisfaction in the new millennium. *New Ideas in Psychology, 29*(1), 10–23.

Moscovici, S. (1980). Toward a theory of conversion behavior. In L. Berkowitz (Ed.), *Advances in experimental social psychology* (Vol. 13, pp. 209–239). New York: Academic.

Moscovici, S., & Personnaz, B. (1980). Studies in social influence v. minority influence and conversion behavior in a perceptual task. *Journal of Experimental Social Psychology, 16,* 270–282.

Moscovici, S., & Zavalloni, M. (1969). The group as a polarizer of attitudes. *Journal of Personality and Social Psychology, 12*(2), 125–135.

Myers, D., & Bishop, G. (1970). Discussion effects on racial attitudes. *Science, 169*(3947), 778–779.

Neighbours, C., Larimer, M. E., & Lewis, M. A. (2004). Targeting misperceptions of descriptive drinking norms: Efficacy of a computer-delivered personalized normative feedback intervention. *Journal of Consulting and Clinical Psychology, 72,* 434–447.

Nemeth, C. (1986). Differential contributions of majority and minority influence. *Psychological Review, 93*(1), 23–32.

Ng, C–H. (2005). Academic self-schemas and their self-congruent learning patterns: Findings verified with culturally different samples. *Social Psychology of Education, 3,* 303–328.

Ng, K., & Van Dyne, L. (2001). Individualism–collectivism as a boundary condition for effectiveness of minority influence in decision making. *Organizational Behavior and Human Decision Processes, 84*(2), 198–225.

Nisbett, R. E., Caputo, C., Legant, P., & Marecek, J. (1973). Behaviour as seen by the actor and as seen by the observer. *Journal of Personality and Social Psychology, 27,* 154–164.

Oldmeadow, J. A., & Fiske, S. T. (2010). Social status and the pursuit of positive social identity: Systematic domains of intergroup differentiation and discrimination for high- and low-status groups. *Group Processes Intergroup Relations, 13,* 425–444.

Osgood, C. E., Suci, G. J., & Tannenbaum, P. H. (1957). *The measurement of meaning.* Urbana, IL: University of Illinois Press.

Packer, D. J. (2008). On being both with us and against us: A normative conflict model of dissent in social groups. *Personality and Social Psychology Review, 12*(1), 50–72.

Park, C. L., Cohen, L. H., & Murch, R. L. (1996). Assessment and prediction of stress-related growth. *Journal of Personality, 64,* 71–105.

Pederson, W. C., Bushman, B. J., Vasquez, E. A., & Miller, N. (2008). Kicking the (barking) dog effect: The moderating role of target attributes on triggered displaced aggression. *Personality and Social Psychology Bulletin, 34,* 1382–1398.

Penner, L. A., Dovidio, J. F., Piliavin, J. A., & Schroeder, D. A. (2005). Prosocial behavior: Multi-level perspectives. *Annual Review of Psychology, 56,* 365–392.

Peplau, L. A., & Fingerhut, A. W. (2007). The close relationships of lesbians and gay men. *Annual Review of Psychology, 58,* 405–424.

Pessin, J., & Husband, R. (1933). Effects of social stimulation on human maze learning. *Journal of Abnormal and Social Psychology, 28*(2), 148–154.

Pettigrew, T. F., & Tropp, L. R. (2006). A meta-analytic test of intergroup contact theory. *Journal of Personality and Social Psychology, 90,* 751–783.

Pettigrew, T. F., & Tropp, L. R. (2008). How does intergroup contact reduce prejudice?: Meta-analytic tests of three mediators. *European Journal of Social Psychology, 38,* 922–934.

Petty, R. E., & Cacioppo, J. T. (1986). *Communication and persuasion: Central and peripheral routes to attitude change.* New York: Springer-Verlag.

Ployhart, R. E., Ehrhart, K. H., & Hayes, S. C. (2005). Using attributions to understand the effects of explanations on applicant reactions: Are reactions consistent with the covariation principle? *Journal of Applied Social Psychology, 35*(2), 259–296.

Postmes, T., Spears, R., & Cihangir, S., (2001). Quality of decision making and group norms. *Journal of Personality and Social Psychology, 80*(6), 918–930.

Potter, J., & Wetherell, M. (1987). *Discourse and social psychology: Beyond attitudes and behaviour.* London: Sage.

QAA (2010). *Quality Assurance Agency benchmark for psychology.* London: Quality Assurance Agency.

Reicher, S., & Haslam, A. (2006). Rethinking the psychology of tyranny: The BBC prison study. *British Journal of Social Psychology, 45,* 1–40.

Reicher, S., Haslam, A., & Rath, R. (2008). Making a virtue of evil: A five-step social identity model of the development of collective hate. *Social and Personality Psychology Compass, 2/3,* 1313–1344.

Rholes, W. S., Simpson, J. A., & Friedman, M. (2006). Avoidant attachment and the experience of parenting. *Personality and Social Psychology Bulletin, 32,* 275–285.

Riediger, M., & Rauers, A. (2010). The 'I know you' and the 'you know me' of mutual goal knowledge in partnerships: Differential associations with partnership satisfaction and sense of closeness over time. *British Journal of Social Psychology, 49,* 647–656.

Roberts, S. G., Miner, E. J., & Shackelford, T. K. (2010). The future of an applied evolutionary psychology for human partnerships. *Review of General Psychology, 14*(4), 318–329.

Rusbult, C. E. (1983). A longitudinal test of the investment model: The development (and deterioration) of satisfaction and commitment in heterosexual involvements. *Journal of Personality and Social Psychology, 45,* 101–117.

Rusbult, C. E., & Van Lange, P. A. M. (2003). Interdependence, interaction and relationships. *Annual Review of Psychology, 54,* 351–375.

Sabini, J., Siepmann, M., & Stein, J. (2001). The really fundamental attribution error in social psychological research. *Psychological Inquiry, 12*(1), 1–15.

Sanderson, C. A., & Cantor, N. (2001). The association of intimacy goals and marital satisfaction: A test of four mediational hypotheses. *Personality and Social Psychology Bulletin, 27*(12), 1567–1577.

Sandfield, A., & Percy, C. (2003). Accounting for single status: Heterosexism and ageism in heterosexual women's talk about marriage. *Feminism & Psychology, 13,* 475–488.

Schachter, S. (1959). *The psychology of affiliation.* Palo Alto, CA: Stanford University Press.

Scharff, M. (2005). Understanding WorldCom's accounting fraud: Did groupthink play a role? *Journal of Leadership and Organizational Studies, 11*(3), 109–118.

Schnake, M. (1991). Equity in effort: The 'sucker effect' in co-acting groups. *Journal of Management, 17*(1), 41–55.

Schwarz, N. (2007). Attitude construction: Evaluation in context. *Social Cognition, 25,* 638–656.

References

Schwarz, N., & Bohner, G. (2001). The construction of attitudes. In A. Tesser & N. Schwarz (Eds.), *Blackwell handbook of social psychology: Vol 1: Intraindividual processes* (pp. 436–457). Oxford: Blackwell.

Sedikides, C., & Gregg, A. P. (2003). Portraits of the self. In M. A. Hogg & J. Cooper (Eds.), *Sage handbook of social psychology* (pp. 110–138). London: Sage.

Shaw, M. (1976). *Group dynamics* (2nd ed.). New York: McGraw-Hill.

Sherif, M. (1936). *The psychology of social norms.* New York: Harper Collins.

Sherif, M., & Sherif, C. W. (1953). *Groups in harmony and tension.* New York: Harper.

Sherif, M., White, B. J., & Harvey, D. J. (1955). Status in experimentally produced groups. *American Journal of Sociology, 60,* 370–379.

Shiao-Yun, C. (2010) 'Well, I'm a lot of things, but I'm sure not a bigot': Positive self-presentation in confrontational discourse on racism. *Discourse & Society, 21,* 273–294.

Sinaceur, M., Thomas-Hunt, M., Neale, M., O'Neill, O., & Haag, C. (2010). Accuracy and perceived expert status in group decisions: When minority members make majority members more accurate privately. *Personality & Social Psychology Bulletin, 36*(3), 423–437.

Smith, E. R., Coats, S., & Walling, D. (1999). Overlapping mental representations of self, in-group, and partner: Further response time evidence and a connectionist model. *Personality and Social Psychology Bulletin, 25,* 873–882.

Smith, J. R., & Louis, W. (2008). Do as we say and as we do: The interplay of descriptive and injunctive group norms in the attitude–behaviour relationship. *British Journal of Social Psychology, 47,* 647–666.

Smith, J. R., & Terry, D. J. (2003). Attitude–behaviour consistency: The role of group norms, attitude accessibility and mode of behavioural decision-making. *European Journal of Social Psychology, 33,* 591–608.

Son, J., & Wilson, J. (2010). Genetic variation in volunteerism. *The Sociological Quarterly, 51,* 46–64.

Stainton Rogers, W. (2011) *Social psychology.* Maidenhead: Open University Press.

Steiner, I. (1972). *Group process and productivity.* San Diego, CA: Academic Press.

Sternberg, R. J. (1998). *Cupid's arrow: The course of love through time.* New York: Cambridge University Press.

Sternberg, R. J., & Weis, K. (2006). *The new psychology of love.* New Haven, CT: Yale University Press.

Stoner, J. (1961). *A comparison of individual and group decisions involving risk* (unpublished master's thesis, Massachusetts Institute of Technology).

Suleiman, J., & Watson, R. (2008). Social loafing in technology supported teams. *Computer Supported Cooperative Work, 17*(4), 291–309.

Tajfel, H., & Turner, J. C. (1979). An integrative theory of social conflict. In W. G. Austin & S. Worchel (Eds.), *The social psychology of intergroup relations* (pp. 33–47). Monterey, CA: Brooks/Cole.

Tajfel, H., & Turner, J. C. (1986). The social identity theory of inter-group behavior. In S. Worchel and L. W. Austin (Eds.), *Psychology of intergroup relations.* Chicago, IL: Nelson-Hall.

Tashiro, T., & Frazier, P. (2003). 'I'll never be in a relationship like that again': Personal growth following romantic relationship breakups. *Personal Relationships, 10,* 113–128.

Tashiro, T., Frazier, P., & Berman, M. (2006). Stress-related growth following divorce and relationship dissolution. In M. A. Fine & J. H. Harvey (Eds.), *Handbook of divorce and relationship dissolution* (pp. 361–384). Mahwah, NJ: Erlbaum.

Taylor, D., Bury. M., Campling, N., Carter, S., Garfied, S., Newbould, J., & Rennie, T. (2006). *A review of the use of the health belief model (HBM), the theory of reasoned action (TRA), the theory of planned behaviour (TPB) and the trans-theoretical model (TTM) to study and predict health related behaviour change.* London: National Institute for Health and Clinical Excellence.Retrieved from http://www.nice.org.uk/nicemedia/live/11868/44524/44524.pdf

Tenney, E. R., Turkheimer, E., & Oltmanns, T. F. (2009). Being liked is more than having a good personality. *Journal of Research in Personality, 43,* 579–585.

Tesser, A. (1993). On the importance of heritability in psychological research: The case of attitudes. *Psychological Review, 100,* 129–142.

Tesser, A. (1988). Toward a self-evaluation maintenance model of social behavior. In L. Berkowitz (Ed.), *Advances in experimental social psychology* (Vol. 21, pp. 181–227). San Diego, CA: Academic Press.

Tesser, A. (2000). On the confluence of self-esteem maintenance mechanisms. *Personality and Social Psychology Review, 4,* 290–299.

Tetlock, P., Peterson, R., McGuire, C., Chang, S., & Field, P. (1992). Assessing political group dynamics: A test of the groupthink model. *Journal of Personality and Social Psychology, 63,* 403–425.

Thomas, S. P. (2003). Men's anger: A phenomenological exploration of its meaning in a middle-class sample of American men. *Psychology of Men & Masculinity, 4,* 163–175.

Thompson, M., Zanna, M., & Griffin, D. (1995). Let's not be indifferent about (attitudinal) ambivalence. In R. Petty & J. Krosnick (Eds.), *Attitude strength, antecedents and consequences* (pp. 361–386). Hillsdale, NJ: Erlbaum.

Thornberg, R. (2007). A classmate in distress: Schoolchildren as bystanders and their reasons for how they act. *Social Psychology of Education, 10,* 5–28.

Thurstone, L. L. (1928). Attitudes can be measured. *American Journal of Sociology, 33,* 529–554.

Todd, A., Seok, D., Kerr, N., & Messé, L. (2006). Social compensation: Fact or social-comparison artefact. *Group Processes & Intergroup Relations, 9*(3), 431–442.

Triplett, N. (1898), The dynamogenic factors in pacemaking and competition. *The American Journal of Psychology, 9*(4), 507–533.

Tuffin, K. (2005). *Understanding critical social psychology.* London: Sage.

Turner, J. C. (2006). Tyranny, freedom and social structure: Escaping our theoretical prisons. *British Journal of Social Psychology, 45*(1), 41–46.

Turner, J. C., Hogg, M., Oakes, P., Reicher, S., & Wetherell, M. (1987). *Rediscovering the social group: A self-categorization theory.* Oxford: Blackwell.

Turner, R. N., & Crisp, R. J. (2010). Imagining intergroup contact reduces implicit prejudice. *British Journal of Social Psychology, 49*(1), 129–142.

Vangelisti, A. L. (2006). Relationship dissolution: Antecedents, processes, and consequences. In P. Noller & J. A. Feeney, *Close relationships: Functions, forms and processes* (pp. 353–374). Hove, East Sussex: Psychology Press.

Voronov, M., & Singer, J. M. (2002). The myth of individualism–collectivism: A critical review. *The Journal of Social Psychology, 142,* 461–481.

Watts, S., & Stenner, P. (2005). The subjective experience of partnership love: A Q Methodological study. *British Journal of Social Psychology, 44,* 85–107.

Weiner, B. (1995). *Judgements of responsibility: A foundation for a theory of social conduct.* New York: Guilford Press.

White, P. A. (1991). Ambiguity in the internal/external distinction in causal attribution. *Journal of Experimental Social Psychology, 27*(3), 259–270.

Whitty, M., & Carr, A. (2006). *Cyberspace romance: The psychology of online relationships.* Basingstoke: Palgrave Macmillan.

Whyte, G. (1989). Groupthink reconsidered. *Academy of Management Review, 14*(1), 40–56.

Williams, K., & Karau, S. (1991). Social loafing and social compensation: The effects of expectations of co-worker performance. *Journal of Personality and Social Psychology, 61*(4), 570–581.

Williams, T. P., & Sogon, S. (1984). Group composition and conforming behavior in Japanese students. *Japanese Psychological Research, 26,* 231–234.

Wilson, T. D., Lindsey, S., & Schooler, T. Y. (2000). A model of dual attitudes. *Psychological Review, 107,* 101–126.

Wood, W., Lundgren, S., Ouellette, J. A., Busceme, S., & Blackstone, T. (1994). Minority influence: A meta-analytic review of social influence processes. *Psychological Bulletin, 115,* 323–345.

References

Zajonc, R. B. (1965). Social facilitation. *Science, 149*(3681), 269–274.

Zajonc, R. B. (1968). Attitudinal effects of mere exposure. *Journal of Personality and Social Psychology, 9,* 1–27.

Zhang, D., Lowry, P., Zhou, L., & Fu, X. (2007). The impact of individualism–collectivism, social presence and group diversity on group decision making under majority influence. *Journal of Management Information Systems, 23*(4), 53–80.

Zhu, Y., Zhang, L., Fan, J., & Han, S. (2007). Neural basis of cultural influence on self-representation. *NeuroImage, 34,* 1310–1316.

Zimbardo, P. (1989). *Quiet rage: The Stanford prison study.* Palo Alto, CA: Stanford University.

Zimbardo, P. (2006). On rethinking the psychology of tyranny: The BBC prison study. *British Journal of Social Psychology, 45*(1), 47–53.

Zimbardo, P. (2007). *The Lucifer effect: How good people turn evil.* London: Random House.

Index